While the Women Only Wept

While the Women Only Wept

Loyalist Refugee Women in Eastern Ontario

JANICE POTTER-MacKINNON

McGill-Queen's University Press
Montreal & Kingston • London • Ithaca

© McGill-Queen's University Press 1993
ISBN 0-7735-0962-3 (cloth)
ISBN 0-7735-1317-5 (paper)

Legal deposit first quarter 1993
Bibliothèque nationale du Québec

Printed in Canada on acid-free paper
First paperback edition 1995; reprinted 2003

This book was first published with the help of a grant
from the Social Science Federation of Canada, using
funds provided by the Social Sciences and Humanities
Research Council of Canada.

McGill-Queen's University Press is grateful to the Canada
Council for support of its publishing program.

Canadian Cataloguing in Publication Data

Potter-MacKinnon, Janice, 1947–
    While the women only wept: Loyalist refugee women in
    Eastern Ontario
    Includes bibliographical references and index.
    ISBN 0-7735-0962-3 (bnd) –
    ISBN 0-7735-1317-5 (pbk.)
    1. United Empire loyalists – Ontario – History.
    2. Women refugees – Ontario – History. 3. Canada –
    History – 1763–1791. 4. Unites States – History –
    Revolution, 1775–1783. I. Title.
    FC3070.L6P68 1993   971.3'01   C92-090730-X
    F1058.P68 1993

To my sons, Alan and William
my parents, Bill and Linda
and my mentor, George Rawlyk

Contents

Tables

Acknowledgments

Research for this book was facilitated by grants from the Social Sciences and Humanities Research Council and by sabbatical and other leaves granted by the University of Saskatchewan.

Michael Hayden, history professor at the University of Saskatchewan, read the manuscript and offered valuable insights. I am especially grateful to George Rawlyk, history professor at Queen's, who gave me wonderful advice, continuous encouragement, and the support of a true friend.

My family, including my husband, Peter MacKinnon, was very supportive and patient when I spent hours in my study working rather than playing. To them I owe a special thanks.

Preface

History, according to Voltaire, is a bag of tricks we play on the dead.[1] Historians, in other words, reconstruct the past in a way that may or may not be consistent with the truth. Voltaire's comment is especially fitting in a study of Loyalist women, for the Loyalists – as those people who remained loyal to the British crown during the American Revolution have come to be known – were masters at reinterpreting their past to suit their present needs. Moreover, Voltaire's bag of tricks is more likely to be played on women, whose role in history is often ignored or misinterpreted. The fate of Loyalist women in this respect underlines the experience of women in other times and places.

While it is common to lament the fact that women are often denied their rightful place in history, it is only rarely that historians have the opportunity to trace the process by which this occurs. The Loyalist women who left the frontiers of the American colonies in the late 1770s and early 1780s and were resettled in what is now eastern Ontario offer historians such an opportunity. Patriot and British records show the significant role these women played in the American Revolution on the northern frontiers. Other documents, such as the correspondence of British officials and petitions by male and female Loyalists, reveal how women's contributions were minimized and distorted in the 1780s and how this revised view of the past was passed on to later generations of historians and myth-makers.

There are two reasons why the Loyalist women who settled in present-day eastern Ontario were chosen. First, effective monographs focus on an identifiable group of people who share common experiences. The eastern Ontario Loyalists were such a group, and indeed in some ways their experiences were unique. They had to live during and after the Revolution alongside French Canadians, something not experienced by the Maritime Loyalists, and they had to face the disruption of sudden resettlement *en masse*, which was not true of the Loyalists settled in the Niagara area. Secondly, while there are several books about the Maritime Loyalists, eastern Ontario Loyalists have not received the same attention and the women among them have been almost completely overlooked.

The neglect of eastern Ontario Loyalists, and particularly the women in their ranks, is all the more striking when viewed against the background of the considerable literature on various aspects of Loyalism. In American historical writing on the Loyalists, there are excellent biographies, analyses of Loyalist thought, and studies of specific groups – such as those Loyalists who immigrated to Britain.[2] On the Canadian side of the border, there have been studies of the Loyalists who settled in Nova Scotia and New Brunswick, and of black Loyalists.[3] The existing material on Loyalist women includes books about individuals, papers about specific groups, such as the Loyalist women who filed claims for compensation, and some interesting theses.[4] Many Loyalist studies emphasize themes first developed by the Loyalists themselves; these include the motivations of the Loyalists, their loyalty to the British crown, constitution, and empire, their economic status before the Revolution and their property losses during it, the military role of the Loyalist regiments, and the idea that the successful Loyalist settlements in Canada redeemed their defeat in the Revolution.[5]

With regard to the Loyalist women who settled around Cataraqui (present-day Kingston) in the 1780s, there was a certain intellectual cohesion to their experience. They mainly came from the northern frontiers of the American colonies where the economy was based on subsistence farming. Many were members of ethnic communities with a strong sense of communal well-being. Others had paternalistic relationships with powerful father figures which helped to lessen the uncertainty and instability of the Revolutionary era. Many, because of their backgrounds, had been taught to respect authority. There was, then, a social conservatism among these women – and the men too, for that matter – that was rooted in the social relationships between rank-and-file Loyalists and those in authority. This conservatism dovetailed with the political ideas of Loyalist intellectual leaders and British officials.

That said, a word of caution is necessary concerning the place of ideas in the Loyalist experience. For the Loyalist elite, as I argued in *The Liberty We Seek: Loyalist Ideology in Colonial New York and Massachusetts*,[6] ideas were of central importance in shaping their response to the Revolution. The same was not true, however, for rank-and-file Loyalists. Ideas were important to the Loyalists in this study only in helping them *explain* the confusing and troubling events of the 1770s and 1780s. There is no evidence that ideas necessarily motivated them.

Motivation is another problematic concept in that it connotes decision-making: that is, that a conscious decision was made to become a Loyalist or Patriot. In fact, however, many Loyalists were caught in a web of circumstances beyond their control or even understanding. They did not necessarily *decide* to become a Loyalist or Patriot. Rather they decided to follow their leaders, stay with their family, help their neighbours, or marry John Johnson rather than Philip Schuyler. The importance of motivation pales when one considers that between 25 and 30 per cent of the adult eastern Ontario Loyalists were women and for virtually all of them there was no choice to make: they merely lived with the implications of the decisions made by the men in their lives.

Our understanding of Loyalism is also enhanced by broadening our perspective and comparing the experiences of Loyalist refugee women who left the colonies and resettled in other parts of the British empire with the experiences of Patriot women who remained in the United States. Considering what happened to Patriot women helps to highlight the uniqueness of the Loyalist women's lives as refugees. All colonial women, whether Loyalist or Patriot, lived within a patriarchal family which mirrored the hierarchical power structures of colonial political institutions and of the British empire. Studies of Patriot women have shown that the Revolution, although it did not alter women's legal or political rights, dramatically changed their lives. The public recognition of women's role in the Revolution and the anti-patriarchal aspects of the Revolution changed the status of women within the family and the society at the same time as colonial political institutions were altered and the tie with the British empire cut.

Loyalist women's experiences during the Revolution were more disorienting than those of the Patriots. Like their Patriot counterparts, they had to care for their families when their husbands or fathers were gone but many had to do so after their property had been plundered or confiscated. They had to cope as well with the uncertainty and haphazard nature of Patriot decisions about their future. Also, they were forced to leave their homes, extended families, and communities and make their way to British lines. Thus, the Loyalist women's experiences posed challenges far greater than those facing most Patriot women.

There were other differences between the two groups. The lives of Loyalist women did not change for the better after the Revolution; on the contrary, the power structure they lived under was more, not less, authoritarian and patriarchal than that in the former American colonies. Moreover, the Loyalists did not renounce their allegiance to the British empire; on the contrary, devotion to the British constitution and empire became central to their sense of identity. Finally, the Loyalists were masterful at reinterpreting their past to suit changing contemporary situations and they successfully passed on this view of themselves to later generations of popular writers and historians. The results for Loyalist women were significant. Once the Revolution was over and the Loyalists resettled, the women's accomplishments faded as the Loyalists took on a new identity which had no place for women.

The Loyalist women who moved from the frontiers of the American colonies to settle on the very different frontier around Cataraqui can be seen as a case study. While they were different in some respects from other Loyalist women who left the American colonies, they were similar in other ways. Virtually all experienced some form of persecution and shared a common refugee experience. Most also had to live under British-dominated regimes in the short term – at the bases where they sought refuge – and in the longer term since most settled in some other part of the British empire. The conclusions reached in this study, therefore, have broader implications for our understanding of Loyalist refugee women.

The stories of these women are fascinating and largely untold. Difficult as it is to believe, with all of the writing on the American Revolution, there are still aspects of it to be discovered. Nothing has been written, for example, about the refugee camps that were constructed in the late 1770s around Quebec to house the Loyalist women and children. Their stories are filled with drama, intrigue, tragedy, and heroism. For over 200 years historians have overlooked these women and their experiences. My hope is that I can do justice to them. It is long overdue.

The Hungry Year

The war was over. Seven red years of blood
Had scourged the land from mountain-top to sea: ...
Rebellion won at last; and they who loved
The cause that had been lost, and kept their faith
To England's crown, and scorned an alien name,
Passed into exile; leaving all behind
Except their honour and the conscious pride
Of duty done to country and to king.
Broad lands, ancestral homes, the gathered wealth
Of patient toil and self-denying years
Were confiscate and lost; for they had been
The salt and savor of the land; trained up
In honour, loyalty, and fear of God ...
They left their native soil, with sword belts drawn
The tighter; while the women only wept
At thoughts of old firesides no longer theirs;
At household treasures reft, and all the land
Upset, and ruled by rebels to the King.

William Kirby,
Canadian Idylls, 1894

1 Eastern Ontario Loyalist Women

Our Country's in danger, aroun'd at the sound,
See! her standard the sons of the mountain surround;
From the north they advance, like the storm's with'ring breath,
And their words, in angry murmurs, are "Victory ... or Death."[1]

As the British-American crisis intensified in 1775 and 1776 there was no doubt where the Johnsons of Tryon County, New York, stood. Sir John Johnson was a scion of the county's wealthiest and most powerful family, which had close ties to the British and to the Mohawk among the Six Nations Iroquois. Sir John's cousin, Guy, superintendent of Indian affairs, had been drumming up support for the British among the Six Nations and in May 1775 he had fled to Canada with other Tryon County Loyalists and Mohawks. Communication between Canada and Tryon County was maintained by the Indians who carried messages in their tomahawks and hair ornaments and who had marked out an escape route for the Johnsons through the New York wilderness.[2]

Sir John had also publicly declared his loyalty to Britain and secretly planned to raise a regiment of Loyalist soldiers. Seeing him as a rallying point for northern New York Loyalists, the Patriots placed him under house arrest and disarmed his tenants. Within months, it was decided that he had to be removed from Tryon County, but this plan was frustrated in May 1776 when Johnson along with 170 tenants and other Loyalists fled his mansion on the northern New York frontier just before the arrival of a Patriot expedition. His escape would have been a major victory, had it not been for one gnawing fact. Sir John Johnson had been forced to leave without his family. He had reached the safety of British territory but was, in his own words, "exiled from all that was dearest to me in life."[3]

Lady Mary Johnson, who was pregnant, had been left behind with two babies under two years of age and the family of John Butler, another Tryon County Loyalist who had escaped to Canada. Mary, or Polly as she was sometimes called, was a member of the Watts family, prosperous New York City merchants and bankers. She had married Sir John in 1773 at the age of nineteen and moved north to live in Tryon County. When her husband fled, Polly could not accompany him because of her condition, the hastiness of his departure, and the extraordinary rigours of the trip. As Johnson himself knew, reaching Canada necessitated either a journey across one of many lakes "in an open boat" or travel along rugged trails since "there is no road by land to go with a carriage." Pursued by the Patriots, the fleeing party had to move quickly through rugged terrain, often avoiding the best-trodden paths to escape detection. The gruelling trip took Johnson and his followers nineteen days. During this time they almost starved, going nine days without provisions, except "wild Onions, Roots and the leaves of beech trees." When they reached their destination, their shoes were worn through and their clothes in tatters.[4]

The Patriots, disappointed at the escape of Sir John, seized the women and children left at the Johnsons' home, Johnson Hall. Lady Johnson was forced to turn over the keys to "every place"; her husband's private papers were seized, his "books distributed about the country," and their home was plundered and "made a Barrack." Lady Johnson along with the other women and children was sent to Albany, where her baby was born and she was held as a hostage to prevent the Loyalists and Indians from raiding the frontiers. Despite her captivity, she communicated regularly with her husband in Canada through "Indian and white men ... sent through the Woods." Sir John as well as the Watts family pressured the Patriots to allow her to go to New York City, then in British hands. Lady Johnson asked the same favour of General George Washington, to whom she complained of being threatened and treated with "severity." In December she was allowed to go to the provincial congress meeting at Fishkill and make her request to go to New York City; this request was denied.[5]

In January 1777 Lady Johnson, her sister, children, servants, and a nurse disguised themselves as peasants and escaped. They travelled through enemy territory in the cold winter and, after an exhausting journey, finally reached New York City where they were reunited with Sir John. But they did not all live happily ever after. The baby born in

Albany had died and Lady Johnson attributed its death to her harsh treatment during her pregnancy.

The seeds of bitterness had been sown and a pattern set. Within months of Lady Johnson's escape, the war that would rage on the frontier for more than four years began and key participants in this often vicious conflict were the women and children. As their husbands were forced to flee from the Patriots or were captured by them, the women and children were left to face the Patriot's wrath and to play an important military role in the Loyalist-Indian raids on the frontiers. Although Lady Johnson's upper-class background and lifestyle set her apart from the vast majority of Loyalist women, her experiences first as a victim of Patriot persecution and then as a refugee did not.

The experiences of the Johnsons in the 1770s raise intriguing questions. Why, for example, was Polly Johnson left behind on the frontier in May 1776 when her husband fled to safety in Canada? What factors explain the loyalty of rank-and-file colonists such as those who followed the Johnsons to Canada? Why did tenant farmers follow the Johnsons, their landlords? And what is involved in the experience of being a refugee?

In addressing these questions, it must be stressed at the outset that Loyalist women cannot be studied in isolation. They lived in a world in which men made the major decisions. Further, the Revolutionary War was the backdrop for Loyalist women's experiences, and men were the main actors in that conflict. Thus, to understand the women, it is necessary to cast our net widely and examine aspects of the broader society – particularly the relationship between men and women, and the ethnic, religious, and occupational backgrounds of the Loyalists who settled in eastern Ontario.

First, a discussion of the role and status of white colonial women is in order. A rare glimpse into the world of a Revolutionary woman can be found in the diary of Dothe Stone, born in 1756 in Litchfield, Connecticut, and sister of the eastern Ontario Loyalist Joel Stone. A central part of Dothe's diary, which covers the years from 1777 to 1792, is a list of the births of her fifteen siblings and this reflects the importance of marriage and childbirth in women's lives. The major decision in a woman's life was her choice of a mate, especially since a divorce was difficult if not impossible to obtain. Although women by the mid-eighteenth century had some independence to choose a partner, parents still played a significant role in the decision and their consent was required even for the remarriage of a mature widowed daughter. The average woman was married in her early twenties to a man from one to five years older. She could expect to be pregnant within twelve months of marriage and her childbearing years became a cycle of pregnancy, birth, and lactation.

With only about two years between births, she would have from five to seven live children as well as miscarriages, stillbirths, and children who died in infancy.[6]

Gender also determined other aspects of women's lives. As well as caring for children, women were responsible for maintaining the house, which on the frontier would be a small, crudely built log cabin. Cooking, cleaning, washing, and ironing were women's jobs, as were milking cows, taking care of the chickens, planting the garden, and harvesting the orchard. While housekeeping for her brother, Dothe Stone even cut and combed his hair. Food preparation involved salting pork and beef in early winter, preserving fruit and storing vegetables in the fall, and making cider and cheese and drying apples. Soap was made, not bought, and a major chore was making clothing. Dothe wrote of spending days with her sisters at spinning-wheels. On the frontier the rigidity of the sexual division of labour sometimes broke down and women could also be found working in the fields alongside the men.[7]

Colonial women found security in what was familiar to them – their homes, their families, and their circle of community friends and relatives. Dothe wrote fondly about her favourite room, her "once loved chamber," and her diary exudes life and excitement when she describes special social events – such as weddings or gatherings at which a fiddler was fetched and led the party in singing and dancing – or the regular visits from relatives and friends. When living at her father's house, secure in the company of a large family, she was contented. She described a typical evening as follows: "The moon shines pale and pleasant in the south door; Daddy is gone; the children some asleep some awake, Mamma is singing to dear little Polly in the middle of the room; she has a fine soft voice."[8]

Like other colonial women, Dothe was very dependent on the friendship of sisters and other female relatives, and her diary records the hours spent at spinning-wheels in their company. Women also assisted each other with birthing and the care of children. Wherever Dothe lived, at least one of her sisters was usually close by and some of her sweetest recorded memories were not with her husband or children, but with her sisters. One diary entry described a day with sister Hannah. "Sunday afternoon Sister Hannah and I have been walking to the far part of Davis' South lots," she wrote, "being very tyred, I lyed down under a pretty bush, I tied my long pocket handkerchief about my head, and took a stone for a pillow and never did I rest more sweetly, while Sister Hannah set by me making some excellent verses about the gracefullness of my appearance." Home, family, and female companions were what mattered most to Dothe Stone.[9]

Dothe's female relatives and friends were her companions, but it was the men who made the key decisions in her life. The distribution of power within the household, as within the society, was patriarchal. The historian Gerda Lerner describes patriarchy as "the manifestation and institutionalization of male dominance over women and children in the family and the extension of male dominance over women in the society in general." Patriarchy in the eighteenth century meant that within the household there was a hiearchy of power, with men acting as the decision-makers and women and children as the subordinates. This did not mean that the relationship between the household head and his wife and children lacked affection. There was evidence of affection being expressed among family members. Moreover, manliness in the eighteenth century entailed a sense of public spirit and benevolence; it was also the duty of the household head to protect and provide for his subordinates. The relationship might be called paternalistic in that it was the father and husband's role to decide what was in the best interests of the family. In return, wives dutifully obeyed their husbands, and the children were expected to honour and obey their parents, especially their fathers; in sum, there was, in the words of Philip Greven, "dependence and passivity associated with femininity." Basic to the marriage contract was the notion that the man had the power to make the important decisions for the family unit, but he also had the responsibility to ensure its well-being by providing the essentials – food, clothing, and housing.[10]

The subtleties of a mid-eighteenth century husband-wife relationship were reflected in the correspondence between Alexander McDonell, a Loyalist and captain in the Royal Highland Emigrants, who was stationed in Halifax, and his wife, Susannah, who was still at home behind enemy lines in New York. One letter began with "My dear Susannah" and ended tenderly with "I have no time to write more ... Kiss the children for me and believe the one forever to be yours." In another letter to a merchant from whom Alexander was ordering some lingerie for his wife, he even described Susannah as a "lusty" woman. Yet it was also clear that, even in exile, McDonell considered himself the head of the household whose role was to give instructions to his subordinate wife. "Keep the children always clean and well dressed and you must appear in your best colours yourself," he instructed her. Of a fellow soldier, he said, "Keep the old gentleman always at a distance from you and never let him again appear in the House."[11]

Patriarchy was also evident in the Stone family. Whether unmarried and living in her father's or brother's house, or married and in her husband's, Dothe Stone's life was also run by males. Her brother, with whom she lived for nine years, "supported and directed" her and made all of the decisions, including the one to move, without consulting her.

After her brother moved, Dothe returned to her father's house and was gratified, at the age of twenty-seven, that he would take care of her in return for her help in running the house and caring for the young children. The image of the father as patriarch was captured by Dothe when she described "My Dad an old gentleman ... in the other room with a large family of lively children gathering round and looking to him for support."[12]

Dothe, like other white colonial women, appeared to accept her subordinate position within the family. Rather than complaining or contemplating the unfairness of her situation, Dothe knew that her role was to accept her lot in life and do her duty. On being forced to leave her brother's house, she felt not anger but only sorrow and depression and even these feelings were reserved for her diary. "I was obliged and did affect cheerfulness in my behaviour," she wrote. "I answered with a smile when my heart was ready to break." Whatever her inner feelings, Dothe was convinced that she "must submit when it comes to open things."[13] Dothe's comments suggest an interesting dichotomy between her behaviour and feelings. In her behaviour she had to conform to society's expectations of her; however, her inner feelings were sometimes at odds with her role as prescribed by others. Women, because of their subordination, had to suppress their inner feelings and behave in ways consistent with society's view of them.

Femininity in the late eighteenth century was associated with helplessness and inferiority. Women were assumed to be helpless because they were like children who could not provide the basic necessities for themselves, but had to rely on men for food, shelter, and clothing. But they were also helpless, it was thought, because they were inferior. They could not take care of themselves because they were less rational, capable, and competent than men. Not only were women treated as helpless inferiors, they were also expected to speak of themselves in these terms. Another admired female trait was what was called modesty or diffidence, which often turned out to be nothing less than self-abasement. Consider the statement of one strong-minded Patriot, Mary Fish, who saw herself as a widow who was "a poor weak and helpless creature ... [able to] do nothing but lie at the foot of mercy and look for direction." "What," she asked rhetorically, "could a feble woman do?"[14] Mary Fish was conforming perfectly to what society expected of her.

Language, as Joy Parr points out, is "culturally constructed ... [it] can embody rather than illuminate the past we are attempting to explain."[15] In the case of Loyalist women, their use of the language of enfeeblement does not necessarily mean that they believed in their own weakness. It means only that society saw women in this way and expected them to conform in their language to this view of themselves. Yet, whether or not women accepted their own subordinate status, the language they used accurately reflected their position within the household power structure. Whether or not they were weak and dependent, they were assumed to be and they were outwardly treated as such. Morever, the consistent use of language cannot be divorced from self-image. In other words, if women were treated as inferior and if they spoke of themselves as helpless, then how long was it before they came to accept that helplessness was basic to femininity?

The subordination of white women within a patriarchal household was reinforced by their position in society and by the hiearchical nature of authority in colonial institutions. Patriarchy, according to Gerda Lerner, involves male dominance of the household but also "implies that men hold power in all the important institutions of society and that women are deprived of access to such power." What this meant in the eighteenth century was that it was the male head of the household who conducted relations between the family and the broader world. Only males had access to higher education. The male household head ran the family's finances and arranged for credit; if anyone in the family could vote or hold public office it was him, and he represented the family in legal terms. "A married couple," in the words of one historian, "became a legal fiction: like a corporation, the pair was a single person with a single will" – the husband's. The married woman became a *femme covert*, a person whose identity was subsumed in that of her husband's. The subordination of women was believed to be divinely ordained and scripture was called upon to justify the inequality; Dothe Stone told of a man carving meat for dinner picking up a rib and declaring "that was such a thing as woman was made of."[16]

The patriarchal nature of colonial society was also reflected in the almost exclusive male ownership of land, the central foundation of the colonial economy. Title to the family property was in the name of the male household head and this power was a way to ensure that children remained under parental control and lived up to their duty to obey their fathers. Widows were to be taken care of – they had dower rights or were often the responsiblity of the male heir. But widows rarely retained control of land in the long term; if they remarried the property would go to the new husband, and if children came of age a male son would usually acquire control of the land. The same discrimination occurred in inheritance practices. Although there were various inheritance practices, the common theme was that male children inherited the bulk of family property and women's inheritances tended to be in the form of doweries or legacies of personal property, such as household goods. Women's lack of control over land was crucial. As Toby Ditz has put it, "The ability to control the material resources vital to the running of the house-

hold economy is an important foundation of the power to make decisions affecting the fates of all household members. It is a foundation
that women largely lacked."[17]

Patriarchy was rooted in ideas of hierarchy and inequality which were
commonplace in the British-American ideology of the late eighteenth
century. Many colonists in this period still thought in terms of an or-
ganic social order characterized by interdependence and a hierarchy
that distinguished leaders from followers. People saw themselves as
"part of a great chain of being" in which inequality was natural and
even divinely ordained. Just as the father headed the family and had an
obligation to provide for his dependants, political leaders guided the
community but had an obligation to rule in a public-spirited way in the
interests of the whole.[18]

Patriarchal familial ideas also pervaded colonial views of the British
empire. The king, head of the empire and protector of Protestantism,
was seen as a father figure whose duty was to rule in the interests of his
subjects. England, the mother country, was linked to the colonies by the
bonds of heritage, affection, and duty. Like children within the family,
the colonies were to be "obedient, dutiful, grateful and properly subser-
vient."[19]

Although many colonists of all shades of opinion believed in an or-
ganic social order based on inequalities, Loyalists were much more
likely than Patriots to cling to such views. After all, the Loyalists did not
renounce the father-king as did the Patriots. Indeed, the idea that in a
unit such as the British empire there had to be one central authority, the
British parliament, which governed the whole, was central to Loyalist
thought. Moreover, Loyalists tended to accept the virtues of inequalities, a social hierarchy, and the need for a strong government to curb the
excesses of its subjects.[20] Their reasons for doing so, as the case of the
Loyalists of eastern Ontario makes clear, were intertwined with their social background.

In 1784 British officials reported that there were 3,463 Loyalists settled in the townships along the St Lawrence River and the eastern end of
Lake Ontario. This represented the initial group of settlers whose numbers would be quickly swelled as friends and relatives poured into the
colony from the south. As Table 1 indicates, of the 1,992 adults, 586 or
30 per cent were women. Unfortunately, there is no information about
the ages or marital status of these women.

Additional data about the eastern Ontario Loyalists can be derived
from the claims they made for compensation from the British government. In 1783 the British government appointed a commission to in-
quire into the Loyalists' losses and services and to recommend compensation. The commissioners sat in Quebec City, Montreal, and Niagara

Table 1
Familial Composition of Loyalist Settlements in Eastern
Ontario, 1784

Men	Women	Children	Servants	Total
1406	586	1400	71	3463[21]

in 1787 and heard 513 claims from Loyalists settled in eastern Ontario. The claims, it is true, have to be used cautiously. Undoubtedly, when people are seeking compensation they tend to stress and even exaggerate their losses and services and to proclaim the purity of their motives.[22] And it is also true that many of these and other Loyalist petitions for assistance or compensation were quite stylized in their signers' professions of profound attachment to the British empire and disinterested service to His Majesty's cause. Nevertheless, other petitioners were disarmingly frank. Some admitted that they had signed the *Association*, which was established by the First Continental Congress and committed its supporters to boycott British goods and support the Patriot cause. Others admitted that they had mustered with the Patriot militia and one even conceded that his motive for becoming a Loyalist was nothing more glorious than the fact that he had been badly treated by the Patriot army.[23] Thus the claims do provide interesting glimpses of the unfolding drama of the Revolution as it intruded into peoples' lives. Moreover, they contain valuable information regarding matters about which Loyalists had no reason to exaggerate or lie. Information about ethnic or religious origins, place of residence, occupation, or length of residence in the colonies is included in the claims.

While the claims provide some basic factual information, piecing together the history of the women who settled in and around Cataraqui is not an easy task. Information may be obtained from official records, such as military registers or returns of Loyalists and land grants. There is also one diary and a few personal letters; however, most of the women were illiterate. As well, since some fled their homes in haste and many had to carry with them the possessions they took from American to British territory, personal letters would likely have been left behind.

Fortunately for historians, women Loyalists did not escape the scrutiny of Patriot committees. They were hauled before committees charged with such mandates as "detecting and defeating conspiracies" and their stories were documented and published by the Patriots. Then, when they reached British lines, they had to petition for provisions or other aid, with supporting evidence from other witnesses, and their stories appear in the British records. Moreover, once at British bases the women and children had to be provisioned, housed, and otherwise cared for and there is significant material about these experiences as well as about their relocation into the interior. These types of sources, also, do not exist for the period of Loyalist settlement in eastern Ontario. At this point, Loyalist women almost vanish from the historical record, which in part reflects the fact that they had returned to their traditional status within a patriarchal family and society.

There is a further problem with the sources. Although Loyalist women's stories may be pieced together from the kinds of sources indicated above, rarely do the women tell their own stories in their own words. Instead, males reported what women said, did, or even felt. What was being described, then, was what was observable from the behaviour of women and, as Dothe Stone's diary revealed, there was sometimes a dichotomy betweeen outward behaviour and innermost feelings. Also, such information passed through the filter of male attitudes toward women. Even most of the documents signed by women, notably petitions, were cast within a stylized framework which reflected others' expectations of women. The documents do describe what women did and in some cases what they said. What they actually felt or believed must remain a mystery.

"Strange is the collection of people here" was the way that Major John Ross, in charge of the British base at Cataraqui, described the Loyalists who had settled along the St Lawrence and the eastern end of Lake Ontario by 1786. They were an ethnically diverse group that included many recent immigrants. About an equal number of eastern Ontario Loyalists whose birthplace is known were foreign and American-born, with about 45 per cent in each category. Among the American-born were the Stones, an old Connecticut family with sixteen children, born, perhaps fortunately, to two mothers. Joel, the second oldest, settled in eastern Ontario, and continued a lifelong correspondence with his father for whom he displayed a profound respect and even reverence; every letter, for instance, began with the salutation, "Honoured Father." Other American-born Loyalists included Daniel McGuin, who ran a potash and lumber business and signed the *Association*, and James Parrott, another New York Loyalist who had signed the *Association*.[24]

However, many of the American-born were first-generation immigrants who retained their native language and other aspects of their culture. The largest of the ethnic minorities were the Germans, who accounted for about 30 per cent of the total group of eastern Ontario Loyalists. About one-quarter were immigrants and the other three-quarters Americans of German ancestry.[25] An example of the latter was Hans Waltimeyer – known in English as John Walden Meyers. Born near Albany in 1745 to a Prussian German family, he married Mary Cruger in 1765. A prosperous tenant, with about 100 acres of cleared land, an orchard, a brick house, and "quality stock," Meyers was also a hunter and trader who had travelled north as far as Canada, following the old Indian paths used by the Dutch. Despite his American birth, Meyers was fluent in German as well as Dutch; he spoke English with a heavy German accent and he lived in a closely knit community with neighbours who were also his relatives.[26]

The vast majority of German Loyalists were of Palatine origin. Many who were settled in the lower Palatinate by the early eighteenth century were Protestants forced to flee from France, Switzerland, Scandinavia, and the Netherlands for religious reasons. But they did not find peace in the Palatinate. In 1708, after suffering religious persecution, devastation by Louis XIV's armies, and a bitter winter, a small group left for the American colonies and the next year about 12,000 welcomed Queen Anne's offer to seek refuge in England. About one-quarter of the group who migrated to England were sent to America in 1710 as part of an ill-fated government scheme to employ them in producing tar and naval stores. The scheme collapsed; but the Palatines, although embittered by the experience, stayed on. Another quarter of the original émigrés were encouraged to move from England to Ireland to bolster the numbers of Protestant tenants and to work in the linen industry. In the late 1750s many of the Palatines who had settled in Ireland made their way to New York,[27] and later still this same group contributed many of the first Loyalist settlers to put down roots in eastern Ontario.

The importance of religion to the Palatines who migrated from Ireland to the American colonies is illustrated in the life of Barbara Ruckle Heck. Barbara was born in 1734 in Ballingrane, Ireland, where she lived as a member of a closely knit Palatine community. When she was fourteen, she and others in the community were greatly affected by the visit of the Methodist leader John Wesley and they established the Irish Conference of the Methodist church. Barbara introduced Methodism to New York when she immigrated there in 1760 – the same year in which she married Paul Heck – as part of a group of Palatines who planned to establish a linen factory. The scheme failed, but Barbara's religious fervour did not. According to oral tradition, in 1766, when she found friends playing cards, she burned the cards and exhorted her fellow Palatine, Philip Embury, formerly a local preacher, to begin Methodist religious services, which he did. The congregation grew so quickly that the first Methodist church in New York, the Wesley Chapel, was established in 1768. When the Hecks and Emburys moved to Camden Township, near Bennington, Vermont, in 1770, they established another Methodist society at Ashgrove, New York, which later became "a major centre of Methodism in the New York Conference."[28]

One of the old Palatine families divided by the Revolution was the Herkimers, who owed extensive land in Tryon County. One son, Johan Jost, colonel of the militia and friend of Sir John Johnson, signed the *Association*, but was suspected of Loyalism and was kept out of jail only by his brother, Nicholas, an ardent Patriot, who later died fighting for the Revolutionary cause. Suspicions about Johan Jost's loyalty were heightened by the actions of his brothers-in-law. One, Henry Frey, from a family that had been among the first to settle in Tryon County, was justice of the peace, colonel of the militia, and an associate of the Johnsons; he was imprisoned as a Loyalist after his brother fled to Canada with Guy Johnson in 1775. Another brother-in-law, Peter Ten Broeck, was also a Tryon County justice of the peace and Johnson associate. When Johan Jost helped Ten Broeck escape to Canada in 1777, a Loyalist recruiting party persuaded him to flee. Moving north to Canada, he would become a well-known community leader in his new home.[29]

What was remarkable about the rank-and-file Palatines was their cohesiveness and sense of community. Whether in Germany, Ireland, or New York, they lived in communities bound together by the ties of history, language, Protestantism, intermarriage, and even landholding patterns. An example of their sense of history was the portrait of Louis XIV hanging in a Palatine-owned tavern on the New York frontier. Under the portrait, written in German, was the following: "This is the man we all should hate/ Who drove us from our home./ Who burned the old Palatinate/ And sent us forth to roam." One wonders what the average Palatine thought of the Americans' alliance with France in 1778. Besides history and religion, language was a unifying factor; there were even German communities in the 1760s where English was not spoken. Also, land-sharing arrangements of one kind or another were more common among the Palatines than any other group, with fully 30 per cent of the American-born Loyalist Palatines sharing relatives' land.[30] And intermarriage among and within Palatine families was extremely common. Consider the Wiltses. Jeremiah married his first cousin, Mary Cornell, in the early 1740s; one of his sons, Thomas, married his second cousin, Elizabeth Cary, in 1768, and another son, Cornelius, later married his first cousin, Elizabeth Wiltsee. All eventually settled along the St Lawrence.[31]

An excellent example of the cohesiveness of the Palatines was the history of the Hecks, Emburys, Dulmages, Detlers, Switzers, Lawrences, Hoffmans, and Millers, all of whom had been neighbours or relatives in the Palatinate. In 1709 they fled to England as a group, only to leave *en masse* for Ireland. When some of the Irish Palatines left for North America to fight in the Seven Years War, the others soon followed and they settled together again in the Camden valley on the frontier of New York.

For the Palatines, their journey to Canada was their last, not first, pilgramage.

Another group of American-born Loyalists who also retained their culture and sense of community were the Dutch, who had been in New York since the colony of New Netherland was established in the early seventeenth century. Like the Palatines, many of the Dutch had been refugees from religious persecution in other parts of Europe. A strong sense of community loyalty, the survival of the Dutch Reformed Church, and the use of the Dutch lanaguage, especially in religious services, meant that the Dutch culture flourished in parts of New York over a century after the Brtitish takeover.[32] Although the Dutch were found on both sides during the Revolution, it has been suggested that they "seem to have inclined towards supporting the Revolution where they were already anglicized but not where they had kept their language and separate outlook."[33] The Dutch Loyalists, who represented about 5 per cent of those who came to eastern Ontario, were concentrated in New York communities such as Rensselaerwyck, Livingston Manor, and Kinderhook.

An interesting case of Dutch Loyalism was Kinderhook, where the Dutch represented about 36 per cent of the total population but about 78 per cent of the Loyalists. Isolation was the key to the political complexion of this community. Kinderhook residents, mostly small landowners and rivermen, did not engage in foreign trade; being on the east side of the Hudson River below Albany, Kinderhook was "very well sheltered from invasion" and was characterized by a "certain cultural isolation"; for example, it was not until 1765 that the first local boy went away to school. Typical perhaps of Kinderhook Loyalists were Peter Van Alstine and his wife, Alida Van Allen. Their two families could trace their roots back to the Dutch regime in New York, and as early as 1702 they were associated with each other, initially in signing a petition to the New York Council and later, in 1732, by the ties of marriage. Alida Van Allen came from a well-to-do patrician Dutch family and in 1768 she married Peter Van Alstine, a blacksmith and farmer. The Van Alstines had three children before the Revolution – Alexander in 1770, Alida in 1772, and Cornelius in 1774 – and had prospered to the extent that they lived in a comfortable, new brick house.[34]

Dutch Loyalists were also concentrated in the stronghold of New Jersey Loyalism, Bergen County, which was just across the Hudson River from New York City, the main market for local produce and fish. One such Loyalist who migrated to the area around Cataraqui was Lawrence Van Horn, a reasonably comfortable farmer and miller. Other Bergen County Loyalists were also farmers, artisans, or even small merchants, many of whom retained their language, religion, and strong family ties.

Loyalist-Patriot divisions in the county mirrored divisions within the Dutch Reformed Church. The Loyalists tended to be families belonging to the *conferentie*, committed to retaining the traditionalism of the Dutch Reformed Church and opposed to the revivalism of the Great Awakening in the 1740s and to what they saw as the Americanization of their church. The Hackensack River valley, where most of the New Jersey Dutch lived, spilled over into Tappan, or Orangetown, the county seat of Orange County, New York, as did the religious dispute within the Dutch Reformed Church. Gilbert Bogart was only one of several Tappan farmers who later settled near Cataraqui.[35]

The largest of the immigrant groups was the Scots, which is interesting in light of their numbers relative to other immigrants from Great Britain. Between 1760 and 1775 there were 125,000 immigrants from Great Britain; 44 per cent of these were Irish, 32 per cent Scottish, and 24 per cent English. Among the eastern Ontario Loyalists who were British immigrants, however, only 23 per cent were Irish, only 12 per cent English, and an amazing 65 per cent Scottish.[36] In other words, the Loyalists were underrepresented among Irish immigrants and especially among the English, and greatly overrepresented among the Scots, as Table 2 shows.

Table 2
Ethnic Composition of Eastern Ontario Loyalists

Nationality	% of immigrants from Great Britain	% of Cataraqui Loyalist immigrants from Great Britain
Irish	44	23
Scottish	32	65
English	24	12

What distinguished the Scots from the Irish and English? The Scots were accustomed to a hierarchical social order and had strong communal relationships which, in the case of the Lowlanders, "bore a striking resemblance to patterns normally associated with Scottish clans." In comparison with the English, the Scots were more likely to cross the Atlantic not as individuals but as families or in larger groups, such as whole neighbourhoods. An excellent example of this would be the 300 Scots who settled in Tryon County in 1773; the core of the group was the Macdonell clan, three brothers and a first cousin, while the rest were from the neighbouring glens. On their arrival in New York the Scots gravitated to communities where relatives or friends lived. Evidence of their clannishness was the fact that about 70 per cent of the Scottish

Loyalists who later settled in the Cataraqui area were settlers on the Johnson lands. Even the Lowlanders preserved and indeed enhanced their sense of group distinctiveness in North America as they identified with their Scottish ethnic and Presbyterian religious heritage and set themselves apart from the English.[37]

Many of the Scots were Highlanders distinguished by their recent arrival and the strength and vibrancy of their culture. Nancy Jean Cameron was an American-born Scot whose grandparents had "sought this new land after the risings of Prince Charlie" and who still, two generations later, communicated with relatives in Scotland. But she was the exception; over 90 per cent of the Scots Loyalists were immigrants and of these about 70 per cent arrived within three years of the Revolution. The Highlanders were Catholics and Jacobites who reluctantly left their homeland because of poverty and declining opportunities. The rocky, barren soil of the Highlands limited agricultural potential and aggravated overpopulation problems at the best of times. By the late 1760s the situation was worsened by rising rents and the enclosure of land by landlords.

When they reached North America, the Highlanders tended to live in their own closely integrated communities in which they continued to speak Gaelic and practise their Roman Catholic religion. Described as being "as much a race apart as the Germans," the Highland Scots were "less amenable to assimilation" than other ethnic groups. The Highlanders were also used to a quasi-feudal social structure based on the clan and a deeply ingrained respect for authority. They were people who would look to their leaders for guidance in a time of crisis.[38]

Another group of Loyalists with a distinctive culture were the Mohawk Indians. Because of their strategic location in northern New York, wedged between the American colonies and Quebec, their allegiance was crucial to the defence of Canada and they played a central military role in the Revolution. The Mohawk were, in the words of the governor of Quebec, "the only obstacle to the Americans marching directly up to our posts." Fears of the Indians were believed to be important in the success of Loyalist-Indian raids on the frontiers and in dissuading Americans from joining the rebels.[39] Both the British and Americans courted the Mohawk, who paid dearly for choosing the British side.

The Mohawk lived in a cultural half-way house, combining the traditional occupations of hunting and fishing with sedentary farming. They still retained traditional aspects of their lifestyle, such as the sharing of accommodation in the longhouse, and kinship ties remained important in the government of the clans and of the Six Nations Confederacy. At the same time, they had become dependent on white trade goods, had established strong trade and personal ties with the Johnson family, had allied themselves with the British against the French, and had come to depend on the British to protect them from the land-hungry New York landlords and speculators.

The distinctiveness of Mohawk culture was graphically illustrated in the elevated status of women in their society. Mohawk society was ma-trilineal; the children belonged to the mother's rather than the father's clan and women chose and deposed the chiefs. Women were also influ-ential in war councils and in determining the fate of captives. Since women prepared the food and clothing for the warriors, they could ef-fectively veto a declaration of war by withholding these supplies. The local economy of the predominantly agrarian Mohawk was also con-trolled by the women. While hunting and fishing were regarded as mas-culine occupations, agriculture was considered women's work. The men assisted in clearing the land, but the planting, harvesting, and distribu-tion of the crops were done by the women. The status and influence of Mohawk women such as Molly Brant distinguished them from white women and was reflected in their differing roles in the American Revolution.[40]

Molly Brant, Konwatsi'tsiaienni, meaning someone lends her a flower, was vital in ensuring that the Mohawk continued to support the British during the Revolutionary War. Descended from a high ranking Mohawk family, an Indian matron (or clan mother) who had a great deal of influence in the matrilineal Iroquois society and was sister of the famous Mohawk chief Joseph Brant, Molly "was a woman of great prestige in her nation and throughout the Confederacy." As early as 1754–55 she accompanied twelve principal men of the confederacy on a diplomatic expedition to Philadelphia. Her power and influence were further heightened after 1759 when she became the consort of Sir William Johnson, who described her as his housekeeper. Together they had eight children. Equally at home in the Indian village and the war council, as the charming and gracious hostess at Johnson Hall or as the person responsible for running Johnson's massive estate during his fre-quent absences, Brant was a remarkable woman. She fostered the ties of loyalty, self-interest, and history which underpinned the Mohawk sup-port of the British during the Revolution. Symbolic of her stature was her pension from the British – it was the largest given to any Indian.[41]

Molly Brant was aided by other colourful personalities in her task of maintaining the loyalty of the Mohawk. One was John Deserontyon, a Mohawk who accompanied Guy Johnson to Canada in 1775. Another was the Reverend John Stuart, missionary to the Mohawk, whose stat-ure of six feet two inches led to his nickname, the "little gentleman." In 1710 some Mohawk chiefs visited Queen Anne, who gave them four bibles, a prayer book, and a custom-designed communion plate for their chapel. When the Mohawk pledged their loyalty to the crown and requested missionaries, the practice began of sending Anglican ministers to the Mohawk to convert them, provide schooling for their children, and cement their ties to the British government. In 1770 Sir William Johnson brought thirty-year-old John Stuart to the Mohawk valley to be their teacher, minister, and spiritual guide. With a BA, an MA *honoris causa*, and a love of the classics, Stuart was one of the most learned of the Loyalists who settled in eastern Ontario. Born into a staunch Presbyterian family, he was converted to Anglicanism while studying under Provost William Smith at the College of Philadelphia. Stuart displayed his sense of subordination to his patriarchal father when, in the hope of gaining the latter's approval for one of the most important decisions of his life, he waited seven years to convert formally to Anglicanism. In 1775 Stuart brought his bride, Jane Okill, daughter of the warden of Christ Church in Philadelphia, to his parsonage at Fort Hunter.[42]

Another person influential among the Mohawk was Sarah Kast McGinnis, an American-born Palatine German, who, as a child in the northern New York community of German Flats, lived with the Mohawk, was adopted by them, and learned their language. In the 1740s Sarah married an Irishman, Timothy McGinnis, who became involved with Sir William Johnson in the fur trade and as a captain in the Indian Department. After her husband was killed in the Seven Years War, the widow McGinnis carried on his trading business. During the Revolution, both sides courted Sarah because of her ties to the Mohawk. However, she supported the British, a decision that had painful consequences for both her and her family.

The ethnicity and culture of many Loyalists who later settled around Cataraqui isolated them from the mainstream of mid-eighteenth-century colonial society, and this fact helps to explain why they remained loyal and why a patriarchal family structure was more likely to persist. In an increasingly liberal, individualistic society, many Loyalist groups retained values and lifestyles that were more conservative and communal. The German Palatines and the Scots, who comprised over 50 per cent of the eastern Ontario Loyalists, had a strong sense of communal bonds and migrated and lived as groups rather than as individual family units. Communal loyalities were also important to the Dutch and the Mohawk.

There was also a greater tendency among these people to respect authority generally and to look specifically to the British government for protection. The Scots were accustomed to a hierarchical social order. The Palatines, for their part, were only one group that had found in Britain a refuge from religious persecution; some eastern Ontario Loyalists, such as the Ruttans, were Huguenots, who had fled France for

Britain to escape persecution as Protestants. Consequently, while some Patriots could claim that their ancestors, the Puritans, had fled to America to escape religious persecution in England, German Palatines and French Huguenots, conscious of their own religious history, might respect George III as the upholder of Protestantism in the world. Even the New York Patriot John Jay, whose ancestry was part Huguenot, felt chagrined at having to turn his back on his mother country. He wrote: "The destruction of Old England would hurt me. I wish it well ... It afforded my ancestors an asylum from persecution."[43] The Indians also looked to the British government for protection. Although the Mohawk considered themselves an independent people, they spoke of the king as a paternalistic father figure and, in a more substantive sense, looked to the British government to protect them from the rapaciousness of the powerful New York landlords who had spent much of the eighteenth century defrauding the Indians of their land.

There were other ways in which these Loyalists were different from the Patriots. According to the historian William H. Nelson, "Among almost all cultural minorities, the proportion of Tories seems to have been clearly higher than among the population at large."[44] Relative to the Patriots, the Loyalists tended to include more recent immigrants or members of ethnic minorities which had retained their distinctive culture and traditions. Being part of an emerging American consensus and sharing a common set of colonial or American beliefs and values would have been less meaningful to these people than retaining the language, culture, and religion of their own particular ethnic community.

The recency of their immigration also meant that many were not Americanized. Some 45 per cent were immigrants and of these over 50 per cent had come to the colonies during the troubled period of the 1760s and 1770s and another 18 per cent during the Seven Years War, in many cases to fight for the British. There had been insufficient time for them to be totally assimilated into colonial society, and during the crucial period of the 1760s and 1770s they were more likely to be adjusting to a new environment and establishing themselves than being caught up in the colonial protest.

An examination of the geographical origins and occupations of the Loyalists in eastern Ontario lends further support to this argument. In terms of residence, about 80 per cent came from New York and the vast majority, over 70 per cent of the whole, from the northern counties of Tryon, Charlotte, and Albany. About 6 per cent came from New Jersey, Connecticut, and Pennsylvania, and many of the Pennsylvanians were from the frontier settlements along the Susquehanna River. Those coming from other colonies represented only about 1 per cent of the total, and the residence of about 12 per cent is unknown. The Loyalists who ended up in the vicinity of Cataraqui, then, were mainly frontier people from northern New York.[45]

Many Loyalists who eventually came to what is now eastern Ontario had in the 1760s and 1770s been part of one of the great mass migrations in North American history. With the end of the Seven Years War and the French-Indian raids on the northern and western frontiers, tens of thousands of settlers surged northward and westward in search of land and new beginnings. Many were Americans facing land shortages in their own communities, and over 200,000 were immigrants for whom the colonies were "a magnet and a refuge for the threatened, the discontented, the impoverished and the ambitious of the western world." In family or community groups they covered mile after mile, "pulling loaded carts and sledges and driving wagons along Indian paths across the foothills and through the gaps in the first mountain barriers to the west, poling rafts loaded with farm equipment, animals, and household goods, and paddling canoes into the interior." Between 1760 and 1780 the population of New York increased by 68 per cent as settlers took up fertile land in all directions from the juncture of the Mohawk and Hudson rivers. To the north, settlements reached as far as lakes George and Champlain; to the east, they melded with the expanding New Hampshire frontier in present-day Vermont; to the west, they stopped where the Six Nations Indian land began; and to the south, they spilled over into the Susquehanna River system in Pennsylvania.[46]

Land was what the scramble to the frontiers was all about and this was reflected in the Loyalists' occupations. Of those whose occupations are known, about 5 per cent were artisans: blacksmiths, carpenters, weavers, tanners, shoemakers, a saddler, a potash-worker, a whip-sayer, a tailor, and a king's ferryman. About 3 per cent were engaged in commerce as merchants, mill or tavern owners, tradesmen, or clerks. Another 3 per cent were professional men – military officers, surgeons, teachers, and a vendue master. And about 1 per cent were officeholders, such as Jonathan Jones of Albany, who was a justice of the peace, and Richard Cartwright Sr, the former deputy postmaster in Albany. The remainder, about 75 per cent of the total, called themselves farmers. But even this statistic understates the importance of land because on the frontier occupations overlapped. Farmers, unable to find or afford skilled craftsmen, had to be their own blacksmiths or carpenters and women had to be tailors, weavers, barbers, and bakers. Similarly, the majority of artisans or professionals held and worked some land if for no other reason than to provide their own food.[47]

Land may have been the quest of all, but there was diversity in the ways in which the quest was undertaken and in the degree of success. There were vast disparities in the amount of land held. Sir John Johnson inherited around 200,000 acres of land, while the Jessup brothers, Edward and Ebenezer – married to sisters Abigail and Elizabeth Dibble – took the gift of their father, of about 100 acres of land each, and built it up into holdings in excess of 100,000 acres by 1777. But these were definitely the exceptions. Only about 1 per cent of the Loyalists held more than 500 acres of land, about 50 per cent held less than 200 acres, and approximately 35 per cent less than 100 acres. Further, even these figures exaggerate the affluence of the farmers since many holding 100 or even 200 acre farms would have cleared less than twenty acres. Over 40 per cent of Loyalist claimants, for example, stated that they had cleared less than ten acres of land.[48] The majority of Loyalists, then, lived on the frontier and engaged in non-commercial, family-based farming.

The fact that so many Loyalists who later settled around Cataraqui lived and worked within the framework of a family farm meant that the patriarchal power structure within the family was reinforced. Most came to the frontiers not as individuals but as families who settled in communities with other friends and relatives. In Bennington, Vermont, for example, the first settlers "were not strangers; most knew each other before they moved and very few arrived in town who could not point to some connection to those already settled." The same could be said of the Germans or Scots who settled in New York. In addition, the household was the basic social and economic unit. It is significant that the average farm – from eight to ten cleared acres – was just the acreage which could be seeded and harvested by the average family. The household was not only the centre of production and consumption, it was also the place where the children were raised, given a rudimentary education, trained for their future occupations, and given religious and moral guidance. The primacy of its role meant that the dominance of the father as head of the household was especially strong. Women had no sphere – not even the household itself – which was their own domain beyond the reach of the male household head.[49] Patriarchy was a deeply rooted and pervasive reality for many eastern Ontario Loyalist families.

Patriarchy was also reflected in the way in which land was held or acquired. Admittedly, there were instances in which Loyalist women acquired land. The fathers of Sarah McGinnis and Eva MacNutt left land to them and Sir William Johnson, probably because of his many close ties with the more matriarchal Mohawk, left land to his daughters as well as sons. Moreover, at least one Loyalist woman was given ten acres of land for devoted service to Guy Johnson. But again, these were the exceptions. The norm was that male Loyalists passed their land on to their male sons. Some, such as William Orser, a tenant on the Philipse Manor, left everything to his eldest son; others, such as John Hogal, had his estate divided among five sons. There were also extensive land grants from the crown for past services. James Rogers was one of several Loyalists who had fought during the Seven Years war, perhaps serving for a while in Canada, and was given generous land grants for his military service.[50]

Another important factor in understanding the Loyalists who settled in the Cataraqui area is the tenure by which land was held: only about 20 per cent owned their own land or held it in freehold, and of this total not all had clear title. Ownership to some lands was hotly disputed. Several Pennsylvania Loyalists had lived along the Susquehanna River as squatters with no clear title to their land. Most controversial, however, was the battle between New York and New Hampshire over the highly prized lands of Vermont. After the Seven Years War both colonies granted huge tracts of land in the disputed territory. In the 1770s, after the British government awarded the land to New York, violence erupted. Under the leadership of Ethan Allen and the Green Mountain Boys, Yankee speculators – those whose grants came from New Hampshire – turned their anger against New York, or Yorker, landlords.[51]

Loyalists who ended up in the Cataraqui area were on both sides of the dispute in Vermont. Loyalist supporters of Ethan Allen included Jeremiah French and Justus Sherwood. The Sherwoods, like the Frenches, were an old Connecticut family which joined in the rush to the frontiers by taking up cheap land in Vermont, where Justus married Sarah Bottum of Welsh ancestry. Justus was more than merely a farmer. He was also a land speculator – his claim for over 2,000 acres of land, much of it wild, seems proof of this – and he was involved in the timber business, driving timber rafts down Lake Champlain and the Richelieu River to Sorel. The Lake Champlain region of Vermont was geographically more naturally part of Quebec and Justus was only one of several Loyalists previously acquainted with Canada. But in 1772 his main concern was protecting the fragile title to his lands, which had been granted by New Hampshire officials, and this resulted in a confrontation with another future Loyalist, John Munro.[52]

Originally from Scotland, Munro had immigrated to northern New York in 1756. He fought in the Seven Years War, married Mary Brower, joined the Presbyterian Church, and prospered. By 1776 he owned grist and saw mills, pot- and pearl-ash works, a "substantial Dwelling House 80 feet in length with piazzas round the Front," and some 10,000 acres of land, some of it improved with gardens and orchards. Virtually all of this vast estate was in Vermont and had been granted by New York officials.[53] In 1767 he had been appointed justice of the peace for Albany County, and given the impossible task of imposing law and order on Ethan Allen and his supporters. Another Loyalist in a similar situation was John Peters, a Yale graduate from an old New England family, who took up land under New York title in 1770 and became a prominent local officeholder: he was at once colonel of the militia, justice of the peace, judge of probates, registrar of the county, clerk of the court, and judge of the court of common pleas.[54] As those holding New Hampshire titles flaunted the law, harassed New Yorkers and destroyed their property, officials such as Munro despaired of ever making them "good and faithful subjects." He wrote: "If you was to bestow all your lands upon them without any fee or reward they will never be faithful to this Government for they are all possessed of a spirit of contradiction ... They talk so smooth and hensom yet the devil lies at the bottom."[55] In March 1772, as Munro tried to arrest one of the Green Mountain Boys, Remember Baker, and take him to Albany, a band of men caught up with Munro and freed Baker. Involved in this challenge to Munro's authority was Justus Sherwood, destined to be a neighbour of Munro's along the St Lawrence.

As well as disputed land, there were other landholding arrangements; over 10 per cent of the Loyalists who settled around Cataraqui had either held land with relatives or been partners in some other mixed-ownership arrangement. Thomas Sherwood, brother of Justus, held half of his brother's land and land-sharing arrangements were common among the Jessup brothers and members of the Munro family. Israel, Richard, and Farrington Ferguson worked three different farms on the frontier in partnership. John Coon farmed his father's land along with his brother but had a separate house. There is even evidence of some sharecropping; Israel Tompkins from the frontier community of Saratoga "had the land on shares" with John Aurie. Tompkins was allowed to keep a cow and a calf on the land and was to receive a share of the corn and flax crop; unfortunately, he was forced to leave before harvest. And there were some imaginative arrangements regarding payment for land; for example, the one dollar per acre that Alexander Nicholson owed for his wild land was to be paid for "part in work – part in money."[56]

However, by far the largest group, comprising about 50 per cent of the farmers, were tenants. In New York, as well as small family farms, there were manors owned by prominent New York families such as the Livingstons, Van Cortlandts, Van Rensselaers, and Philipses. Tens and even hundreds of thousands of acres in extent, the manors, which were farmed by tenants, dwarfed the southern plantations. Originating in the Dutch regime, the manors were extended by the British in the 1680s to encourage settlement and foster a conservative, landed élite that would act as a counterweight to the Assembly. Although originally endowed with feudal powers, such as lordship – administrative and judicial autonomy and immunity from county jurisdiction – by the 1730s these powers were no longer being exercised. Other powers retained by the landlord that could be a burden to tenants included the alienation fee – the right of the landlord to a certain percentage of the sale price of the tenant's farm – the landlord's right to first refusal of crops sold by tenants, and the stipulation that tenants use only their landlord's mill.[57] And there were land riots at Livingston Manor in the 1750s and on other manors in the 1760s, although land squabbles between New York and Massachusetts and specific grievances largely explain these troubles.

Landlord and tenant also needed each other. Several of the manorial titles were suspect, having been acquired from the Indians by dubious means, some were being challenged, and all landlords were being pressured by the British government to settle their estates in the 1760s. All in all, the landlords needed tenants and were willing to make significant concessions to attract them.

For colonial Americans looking for new land and especially for immigrants, freehold ownership was the ideal but tenancy was an acceptable, if temporary, alternative. Landlords, anxious to attract tenants, often gave upwards of five years free rent and in some cases provided dwellings, livestock, and tools. An aspiring farmer, with little or no capital, could become a tenant, work hard to clear the land, plant gardens and orchards, build a frame house and a barn, and then sell the improvements to another farmer starting out and use the cash to buy freehold land. There were thus advantages to tenancy; by 1775 there were between 6,000 and 7,000 tenant families in New York and it was becoming more and more lucrative to be a landlord.[58]

Unrest among Loyalist tenants occurred during the Revolution. At Rensselaerwyck, where the landlord was a Patriot, 400 tenants were in arms in 1776. On Livingston Manor, as elsewhere, tenants rallied in 1776 and 1777 in expectation of a British expedition south from Canada. Yet there is also evidence that, when it came to actions beyond protesting or sporadic violence, Loyalist tenants rarely acted on their own initiative but tended instead to follow their landlords or other prominent leaders in their community. A Loyalist *Association* circulated on Cortlandt's Manor, for example, declared its signers' "loyalty ... to the best of Kings ... [which was] the grand magnetic point that will infallibly fix us on a solid basis"; however, the sophistication of the ideas suggests that, although tenants may have signed it, others wrote the *Association*. Similarly, over one hundred tenants in Westchester County protested the holding of an "illegal" meeting and declared their loyalty; but again they were led by a prominent member of the New York Assembly, Isaac Wilkins.[59]

Several factors help to explain the Loyalism of those tenants who later settled around Cataraqui, one being their isolation from the American mainstream and the Revolution. As the Patriot leader John Adams, said, "The real American Revolution" occurred in the decade before independence, and involved the "radical change in the principles, opinions, sentiments and affections of the people." In the 1760s and 1770s, as the British government tried to tighten its rein on the colonies, a process of disaffection occurred. Many Americans became convinced through pamphlets, broadsides, newspaper articles, protests, and hangings in effigy or other Patriot rituals that there was a British plot to enslave the colonies, and they determined to seek independence even if this meant fighting to achieve it. However, the majority of Loyalists who migrated to the Cataraqui area were geographically isolated from the centres of colonial protest, living as they did on the frontier. At the very time that colonial attitudes toward Britain were being altered dramatically, they were preoccupied with carving a future out of the wilderness – clearing the land, planting crops, building rudimentary shelters for themselves and their cattle. In some ways these people were like the Nova Scotia Yankees, who moved from New England to the remote colony of Nova Scotia in the 1760s and remained remarkably untouched by these contemporary currents of opinion that were radically changing the Thirteen Colonies' view of the relationship with Britain.[60]

There was another sense in which the Loyalists who settled around Cataraqui were socially and culturally isolated in the Thirteen Colonies. What mattered most to tenants on the great estates were their lands and local attachments. A tenant farmer, Finlay Ross, described having 100 acres of land, with ten cleared, a house, a barn, and a stable; but he also described in minute detail the tools and implements on his farm – "broad and narrow chisels, one churn, four water and milk pails, two washing tubs for the cleaning of Graim, one mounting pistol and one grinding stone"[61] – which suggests both his humble circumstances and his detailed knowledge about and concern for every aspect of his homestead's operation. Though plain folk such as Ross were not necessarily unaware of the larger world around them, this world was distant and of secondary importance to them.

Another factor that helps to explain the Loyalism of tenants was the relationship they had with their landlords. Some tenants were more likely than others to follow Loyalist landlords. Some landlords – in tune with the growing liberal individualism of late-eighteenth-century colonial society – ran their estates primarily as money-making business ventures, whereas others, retaining a vestige of the medieval manorial sense of community, treated their tenants more paternalistically. Tenants of the latter kind of landlord were much more likely to follow their landlord's leadership.[62] A prime example of such a landlord was the Johnson family of Tryon County.

Sir William Johnson, the founder of the short-lived dynasty and one of the most fascinating figures in colonial history, is a central figure in the history of Loyalism on the New York frontier. Johnson came to America from Ireland in 1738 at the age of twenty-three to manage the large northern New York estate of his uncle, Vice-Admiral Sir Peter Warren, who had married into the prosperous and prominent Delancey family. By 1775 Johnson had acquired an estate of about 200,000 acres, eclipsing some of the longer-established landed families to become the largest landowner in northern New York. He had developed a profitable trading relationship with the Mohawk, outdoing traditional Albany traders such as the Schuylers, and equally important he had won the Indians' trust. He participated in their hunts, defended their land rights, became skilled in their diplomacy, and took Molly Brant as his consort. The British government, recognizing the strategic importance of the Iroquois and Johnson's influence among them, made him commander of one of the main military operations during the Seven Years War, a baronet in 1755, and superintendant of Indian affairs the following year.[63]

Sir William Johnson was an upstart who became the great patron of the Mohawk valley. By the 1770s his patronage was immense and his following considerable. The significant expenditures of the Indian Department and the British army in the north were at his disposal and, when Tryon county was created in 1772, Johnson chose all but one of its many officials. Moreover, he had business dealings with many future local Loyalists, such as the Jessups and Cartwrights. And much of the power and influence remained within the Johnson clan: Sir William's nephew and son-in-law, Guy, was elected to the Assembly and was involved in Indian affairs, as was another son-in-law, Daniel Claus, a German immigrant.[64]

With Sir William's untimely death – after delivering an impassioned two-hour oration to the Indians in the hot sun of July 1774 – the leadership mantle in Tryon County passed to his son, Sir John. Raised quite differently from his father, Sir John had been educated at the Philadelphia Academy, sent to England on a grand tour, and made a baronet when he turned twenty-one. Perhaps the difference between father and son was revealed in the women with whom they lived. While Sir William had his first three children, including John, by Catherine Weisenberg, a Palatine-German indentured servant, his son was forced to give up his mistress, Clarissa Putman, a local farmer's daughter with whom he had two children, and marry a young woman whose parents both came from wealthy and distinguished New York families. Life at Johnson Hall was a study in contrasts; inside the solid stone structure was the finest china, furniture, and mahogany wood, while outside was the crude rusticity of the frontier.[65]

About 20 per cent of Tryon County's population were tenants of the Johnsons, who displayed a paternalistic concern for them and a desire to create a thriving and progressive community. After coming to New York in 1738, Sir William worked hard to attract tenants from Ireland, Scotland, England, and the colonies to his land. Attractive terms, such as five years free rent as well as some financial assistance in getting started, were part of what he offered. By 1776 tenants owed the Johnsons in excess of £2,000, and when some tenants found themselves in financial difficulty Sir William threw their debtor notes into the fire. There is also the example of Richard Mandevell, a "Breeches Maker" who later settled in eastern Ontario. Johnson financed Mandevell in establishing his trade and sent him to a county settlement with the following note to its residents: "As He [Mandevell] is but a Beginner here, I doubt not but you will be as favourable to him as you can." As well as giving tenents financial aid, Johnson built roads, schools, and mills, and introduced sheep and new crops, efforts that contributed to his election to the American Philosophical Society in 1769. At Johnstown, the county seat, he began a county fair, encouraged the settlement of artisans, and built and owned the county jail, court-house, and Anglican church.[66]

The paternalistic relationship between Johnson and his tenants was a recurring theme in the history of eastern Ontario Loyalists. "Interference with people's liberty for their own good" is a commonly accepted definition of paternalism, although the slightly different notion that one person decides what is in the best interests of another might be more appropriate when considering the Johnsons and their tenants.[67] Paternalism in the eighteenth century involved a personal relationship between two unequal parties in which the subordinate paid deference to the superior and in return expected some tangible benefit. The dominant party benefitted by using his patronage to build a following whose loyalty was firmly rooted in self-interest. Tenants and followers of the Johnsons who benefitted from their patronage looked up to the Johnsons as their patrons. They followed the Johnsons' leadership but they expected the Johnsons to advance and protect their interests, by, for example, granting them land on favourable terms, forgiving their debts, or giving them a patronage appointment.

While some rank-and-file colonists might have become Patriots in the hope that the Revolution would bring dramatic social changes which would improve their lot, others, who became Loyalists, may have preferred to look to established, powerful leaders, with land or patronage at their disposal, to provide some measure of security and stability in the turbulent decades of the 1760s and 1770s. Such a relationship need not be harsh and can be described as "co-operative." The relationship, like the patriarchal relations within the family, may be a close and caring one in which the dependent party feels the need to be guided and is willing to exchange some independence of action for security, but the reality is that the power remains firmly in the hands of the dominant party.[68]

Like patriarchal familial relations, paternalistic social relationships thrived in more remote communities where the economy was non-commercial and the labour market personal rather than impersonal.[69] In communities such as colonial Tryon County, where there were no powerful state or other agencies of social welfare, and where face-to-face economic relationships still prevailed, a powerful personality such as Sir William Johnson, armed with the ownership of thousands of acres of land and the support of the Mohawk, could dominate a whole community and bend it to his will, just as a strong patriarch would do within a colonial family.

Paternalism, like patriarchy, was a concept consistent with the élitist, hierarchical, and authoritarian political ideas of Loyalist leaders, a fact that is highlighted when one considers the assumptions upon which it is based. In a paternalistic relationship, as in a patriarchal family, there is a hierarchy or at the very least inequality – there are superiors and subordinates, leaders and followers. Paternalism, in the words of Bryan Palmer, "rationalized inequality and provided for a hierarchical order ... " Secondly, the relationship is deferential. The dominant party feels an obligation to protect the interests of the subordinate, or is pressed to recognize such interests, in return for loyalty and deference – letters to Sir John Johnson, for example, often began with "May it Please your Lordship."[70] Finally, the relationship is more communal than individualistic or class-oriented. Members of a paternalistic society do not think of themselves as individuals or parts of an oppressed class; instead they identify with the interests of the larger whole and of their leaders. In sum, a social counterpart to the Loyalists' conservative ideology was the paternalistic relationships between people such as the Johnsons and their tenants.

The background and experiences of the Loyalists who settled around Cataraqui not only helps to explain their allegiance during the Revolution, but also underlines why the war was such a shock to them – and especially to the women. Coming as many did from isolated communities with strong communal bonds and hierarchical social structures, these rank-and-file Loyalists were more likely to follow established Loyalist leaders, such as the Johnsons, first into battle and then into exile. The dislocation they experienced was considerable, and no one suffered more than the women. Attached to familiar surroundings and accustomed to obeying the head of the household, Loyalist women found the

Revolution especially disrupting as they struggled with the new reality of life as refugees.

Considering what it means to be a refugee further illuminates the experience of Loyalist women. One possible definition of a refugee is a person who seeks sanctuary, having been driven out by centrifugal forces beyond his ability to control; the refugee is therefore an outcast who has been banished. Loyalist women, by becoming refugees, experienced a dislocation uncommon to most Patriot women. All eastern Ontario Loyalist women, whatever their status and backgrounds, became refugees, forced to leave one set of familiar surroundings and venture into the unknown.

Once the safety of British lines was reached, the Loyalist women became exiles. Relative to other groups of exiles, those who settled in present-day eastern Ontario were fortunate in that they enjoyed linguistic and cultural compatability with their new masters – the British officials in Quebec or New York City – and they could look to the British to protect and resettle them. But this protection came at a cost. Like other exiles, they faced the overcrowding, lack of privacy, and uncertainty associated with life in "camps," or temporary asylums. They also experienced the dependency and powerlessness characteristic of exiles as well as the mental anguish of such displaced people.

En route to becoming refugees, Loyalist women participated in fighting the Revolutionary war and were targets for Patriot harassment. In confronting these dangers they were forced to step outside the confines of their previous experiences and to undertake new roles and responsibilities generally presumed to be the preserve of males. The next two chapters deal with the actual experiences of the Loyalist women in the American colonies during the Revolution and their contribution to the war effort and to the survival of their families.

2 Fighting the War and Facing Harassment

The late Triall of this County drove Numbers of hidden Enemies into the Woods, severall have joined the Enemy, a considerable Number is absconding yet in the Woods, supplied by their Families ... The Women of those Enemies is still living among us, some behave very rudely at present, and have proved very active to support and spirit up the opposite Cause.

Tryon County Committee of Safety, 25 August 1777[1]

When Sir John Johnson returned to the Mohawk valley that he had been forced to leave in May 1776, he did so as a soldier intent upon devastation. His expedition of June 1780 was typical. Accompanied by a party of 528 that included Indians and Loyalist refugees, he made his way from Quebec through the wilderness to within five miles of his former home, Johnson Hall. Although he was nominally in command, he was unable to persuade his Indian allies to follow his battle plan, so he had to adopt theirs. The raiders marched through the countryside "burning and laying waste to everything before them." "Vast quantities of flour, bread, Indian Corn and other provisions were burnt ... a great number of Arms, Cash etc [were taken], many Cattle were killed ... about Seventy Horses brought off," and about 120 houses, barns, and mills were put to the torch, as property was plundered and the terrified inhabitants fled desperately to hastily constructed fortifications. Some twenty-seven prisoners, to be exchanged later for Loyalists being held by the Patriots, were taken, although over half were allowed to return home "being either too old or too young to march" and, according to

Johnson, eleven men were killed by the Indians. As the raiders hastily retreated, with the Patriot militia on their heels, they took with them over 100 Loyalists, many of whom would be recruits for the Loyalist regiments.[2] After marching and fighting for two days with no sleep, the men could congratulate themselves on their endurance and on their accomplishments. Yet many must have been saddened as they retreated to the safety of Quebec knowing, in the words of one of Johnson's foot soldiers, that he was "leaving behind his Wife and Family together with the Remains of his Property to the fury of an enraged and merciless Multitude."[3]

Raids such as this on the New York frontier and elsewhere were part of the vicious Revolutionary war between Patriots, on the one side, and Loyalist regiments and Indian allies on the other. As early as January 1776, Johnson, alarmed by the "devastated and convulsed state that this unhappy Country is now worked up to" and aware of the "many obligations that our family are under to the best of Sovereigns," had planned to organize a Loyalist battalion to take on the Patriot forces. He had even "named all the officers, most of whom have a good deal of interest in their respective neighbourhoods." What Johnson and other aspiring Loyalist military leaders needed for their regiments was British authorization, which Johnson received a few months later, and recruits to fill their battalions. The latter were provided by the refugees who flooded to British bases in the late 1770s and early 1780s.[4]

An Albany County Loyalist, Alexander Campbell, used language typical of other Loyalists when he explained his loyalty and flight to Canada. "Frequently at the risk of his Life and Fortune," he wrote in 1778, he had "manifested his Zeal for the Cause in which the British Arms are now exerted against America" and as a result had been subjected to "a series of oppressions." Finally, "being reduced" to the "sad dilemma" of taking a Patriot oath "replete with Treason to his Sovereign" or "quitting the country," he chose the latter. "Loyalty prevailed over every other consideration."[5]

Campbell's testimonial was typical in its declaration that he was motivated by loyalty to the British empire and constitution. Beneath this rhetoric, however, there was an important reality. It was "circumstances," not ideas or sentiments, which forced the flight of Loyalists such as Campbell. The Loyalists' unwillingness to go along with some aspect of the Revolution – in Campbell's case, the signing of an oath of allegiance – marked them as dissidents and eventually forced them to leave and seek asylum elsewhere. The crux of the matter, then, was that Campbell was a dissenter whose behaviour put him at odds with the prevailing regime and made him a refugee.

Understanding Loyalists such as Campbell is made easier by comparing refugees to immigrants. An immigrant leaves one place willingly to move to another, whereas a refugee leaves under duress and is, therefore, sometimes forced to do things that would never otherwise be contemplated. An important criterion distinguishing refugees from immigrants is the relative weight of what have been called "push" and "pull" factors in the decision to leave the homeland. For immigrants, there may often be important "push" factors – reasons for wanting to leave – such as economic hardship. However, there are also "pull" factors for immigrants – positive reasons for believing that their lives would be better in their adopted country. For refugees, however, the "push" factors far outweigh the "pull" ones. What they are fleeing from is much more important than what they are going to, because the need to escape is paramount and the assumption usually is that they are seeking not a permanent home but only a temporary refuge.[6]

"Push" factors are especially important when considering groups such as the Loyalists, who would be categorized by certain experts on the refugee experience as participants in an "acute refugee movement" which results from "great political changes." Unable to conform in their behaviour to the changes, refugees in these circumstances flee "in bursts of individual or group escapes" with the goal of reaching safety in a neighbouring country which will grant them asylum. Most Loyalists, despite the diversity of their backgrounds and case histories, were definitely part of an "acute refugee movement." As the Patriots defined more stringently what loyalty to the Revolution meant, the Loyalists did not conform in various ways to what was expected of them. They came to the attention of the Patriots, suffered harassment, and were eventually compelled to leave.[7] Once in Canada, the men had to join the various Loyalist regiments which cooperated with the Indians to launch punishing raids on the American frontier. For the British, the raids had military purposes: to harass the enemy and destroy food supplies. For many Loyalist soldiers, the raids were an opportunity to seek revenge on their foes in the colonies, to find new recruits, to make contact with their families, and occasionally to bring the families back to Canada.

The process that forced Loyalist men to flee and join military units began in the mid-1770s as a host of Patriot committees established standards of acceptable behaviour and compelled people to either conform or be punished. The committees, established as early as 1775, were called Committees of Correspondence, Committees of Safety, or Commissions for Detecting and Defeating Conspiracies, and had broad powers to enforce Patriot edicts and to ensure that dissidents were weeded out and brought to heel. Some committees acted as local governments and exercised significant power. In July 1776, for example, the Committee of Safety for Westminister County in Vermont heard the complaint of Abigail Fuller, single woman, against Gardner Simonds, yeoman, whom she alleged "had Carnal Knowledge of your Complainants Body ... several times ... and got yr. complainant with a Bastard Child"; the committee ordered Simonds to support the expected child.[8]

The Patriot committees and their extensive powers were the bane of Loyalists. Pamphleteers such as the Reverend Samuel Seabury, an Anglican minister from Westchester, New York, railed against the committees, which he saw as illegal and unconstitutional entities that presumed to regulate the actions of free-born Britons. Taking upon themselves powers unknown to the British constitution, such as the power of one body to pass laws, try offenders of them, and prescribe punishments, the committees, along with their unofficial allies the mob, were seen as agents of oppression. Seabury lashed out at his fellow Americans for allowing committee members to search homes for goods prohibited under non-importation and non-consumption regulations:

Do as you please: If you like it better, choose your Committee, or suffer it to be chosen by half a dozen Fools in your neighbourhood – open your doors to them – let them examine your tea-cannisters, and molasses-jugs, and your wives and daughters pettycoats – bow and cringe, and tremble and quake – fall down and worship our sovereign Lord the Mob ... And shall my house be entered into and my mode of living enquired into, by a domineering Committee-man? Before *I* submit I will die: live *you* and be slaves.[9]

The Patriot committees angered Loyalists such as Seabury in part because they were so effective in pressuring colonists to conform.

There were many ways in which a colonist could fall afoul of a local committee. By 1775, committee members were going from house to house requesting signatures on *Associations*. Many Loyalists refused to sign and had to appear before the local committee which meted out the appropriate punishment, varying from a stiff fine to cutting off all trade and other relations with the offenders, to imprisonment. Speaking ill of the Continental Congress or praising the king was another kind of offence and citizens were sometimes paid for informing on others guilty of these infractions. George Ramsey of Schenectady earned the odious but often-used label "inimical to American Liberty" for "calling those in favour of America, Rebels and Traitors," and he was disarmed and forced to provide a bond for his future good behaviour.[10] William Johnson, son of Sir William and Molly Brant, came to the attention of the local committee for his boast that he had "kill'd and scalp'd and kicked the arses" of the Patriots and for his promise to do so again.[11] Other evidence of hostility to the Patriot cause included refusing to take continental currency, selling proscribed goods, charging exorbitant prices, or ignoring other local edicts.[12] The most serious offences were going to, or aiding, the enemy and they were punished by hard labour, imprisonment, whippings, banishment, or even death.[13]

A common offence was unwillingness to serve with the Patriot militia. To cite one example, when trouble broke out on Livingston Manor in February 1776 and the militia from neighbouring communities had to be summoned, the visible sign of dissent was the unwillingness of the tenants to muster with the militia.[14] The New York Provincial Congress had already dealt with the problem in August 1775, when it established fines for failing to exercise with the militia and provided that any person defaulting "three times successively, or refus[ing] to enlist and do such duty ... shall be advertised and held up as an enemy to his country," to be punished with a fine and arrest.[15] Able-bodied males drafted to serve with the militia could avoid military service either by paying a fine or finding a replacement; however, these ways of avoiding military service could not be an excuse for the "disaffected"; "suspected persons had to march in person" or face imprisonment. Johan Jost Herkimer, for example, had signed the *Association* but was still suspected of Loyalist leanings. As a result, the local committee expected him to serve personally in the militia and reportedly planned to put him at the front of the unit. Unwilling to do this, Herkimer hid and eventually fled.[16]

Colonists could easily be labelled as Loyalists without ever doing anything as dramatic as refusing military service. In Bergen County, a bastion of New Jersey Loyalism, many residents continued to supply New York City with fish and agricultural produce after the city had fallen to the British in 1776. Being paid with "British gold" rather than "worthless provincial and continental currency" would have been a powerful inducement to supply the British in New York. Yet trading with the enemy was considered to be a serious crime and offenders were assumed to be Loyalists.[17]

It was easy, therefore, to be suspected of Loyalist sympathies. As well as what might be called "sins of commission" – words or deeds that were at odds with Patriot positions – there were also "sins of omission" – the failure to sign an oath or show up for militia duty. In either case the suspect was hauled before a committee, pressured to recant, and usually pardoned if an oath of allegiance was taken. Just as it was easy to fall afoul of the committees and be suspected of Loyalism, it was also easy to satisfy committees by conforming in one's behaviour.

The combination of Patriot pressure to conform and the ease with which recantations and oaths were accepted by the committees meant that many Loyalists' paths to exile took remarkable twists and turns. Several Loyalists who would later settle along the St Lawrence and the eastern end of Lake Ontario had shown some visible sign of support for the Patriots. Over 500 filed claims for compensation from the British government and it has been established that each claimant represented 2.5 people.[18] Of 240 such Loyalist claimants, representing some 600 people, who discussed their record of loyalty, 16 or 6 per cent admitted signing a Patriot oath or mustering with the militia, while only 66 or 36 per cent explicity denied ever siding with the Patriots.

Some signs of supporting the Patriots, notably signing the *Association*, were not necessarily at odds with later becoming a Loyalist, as the case of James Parrot shows. In February 1776, as a member of the local Committee of Correspondence, Parrot signed the *Association*, an action that suggested Patriot leanings. There were, however, parts of the *Association* not incompatible with Loyalist views. The need to avoid "Anarchy and Confusion, which attend a Dissolution of the Powers of Government" was mentioned and the signers were committed to seeking "a Reconciliation between Great Britain and America on Constitutional Principles (which we most ardently desire) ... " Within weeks of signing the *Association*, Parrot was re-elected to the local committee, but he refused to serve and shortly thereafter joined the British at Crown Point and had his property confiscated. A similar path was followed by Daniel McGuin, who signed the *Association* but then joined the British, raised men for them, and was twice imprisoned and sentenced to death for his activities.[19]

To many colonial Americans an oath was a sacred contract in which God was "the guarantor" of a person's "integrity."[20] Yet there are also examples of Loyalists – such as the Empys – who did sign Patriot oaths. The Empys, although they had signed the *Association*, were accused of plotting "to run off to our Foes in Canada," of denying the right of Congress to raise taxes, and of claiming that the oath they had taken was "forced." After being hauled before the local committee in April 1777 and fined, the Empys took a more comprehensive oath: they swore that their former "oath of association" was not "forced" but "voluntary," denied any involvement in a plot to go to British lines, and pledged "never to desert this country, nor run away to our Enemies at any time ... but stay and defend the Country."[21] Within two years, however, they were in Canada and at least seven of them were fighting in the Loyalist regiments. For Loyalists such as the Empys, surviving meant complying in word if not deed with Patriot demands until escape was possible.

The shifts in people's behaviour during the Revolution were also reflected in the frequency of desertion from the Loyalist regiments. Some Loyalist soldiers, concerned about the welfare of their families, drifted home, only to be pressured to join the Patriot militia. There were also planned desertions. When one Loyalist regiment was on a scouting expedition, for example, and the men stopped for breakfast, six of them grabbed their weapons at the prearranged call "Men to Arms" and announced their intention to desert, promising death to any trying to stop them. The incidence of desertion was related as well to the quality of recruits. Competition for recruits was so intense that anyone, including "Vagabonds, Deserters from the Continental Army" or boys of ten, were recruited and many, of course, stayed only briefly. Also, zealous recruiters often raised unrealistically high expectations and disappointed soldiers consequently deserted.[22]

But desertion was common to both sides, with men moving back and forth as the tide of war or their own personal circumstances changed. Joshua Bergen of Connecticut did not want to serve in the Patriot militia and paid for others to do his service until "his money ran out" and he had to join; when an "officer treated him ill" he deserted, but after a brief stint in the British service he deserted that camp as well. Another colonist, James Jones, had come to Canada with the invading Patriot army in 1775 but had been left behind because of illness. After working in the colony for four years, he was willing in 1779 to take an oath of allegiance and join Sir John Johnson's regiment, although it was admitted that he was an "indifferent character as to loyalty."[23] Some, it seems, took the idea of allegiance and the swearing of oaths cavalierly indeed.

It is difficult, through all of this maze of seemingly contradictory or ambivalent behaviour, to accept at face value the testimonials of Loyalists such as Alexander Campbell who proclaimed that they were motivated by undying devotion to the British cause. Significantly, such declarations were made not to the Patriots but to British officials after Loyalists had been forced to flee.

Coercion and fear of punishment were also important in explaining the behaviour of some Loyalists. Sir John Johnson claimed that at least two-thirds of the colonists who signed the *Association* were coerced into doing so. There is evidence to support his point, if not his numbers. In devising an additional oath declaring that previous oaths were voluntary rather than forced, the Patriots themselves were conceding that some oaths were signed under pressure. John Peters was only one of several Loyalists who served with the Patriots, participating in the invasion of Canada, so that he could desert when he reached a British base; others joined the Patriot militia to get out of jail. Also, it was common for Loyalist soldiers to take prisoners into their regiments, in part because they needed the recruits but also because Loyalist soldiers often found that their prisoners were former Loyalist friends or neighbours who had been forced into Patriot service.[24]

The threat of imprisonment might also deter a principled Loyalist. Of 265 eastern Ontario Loyalist claimants who described their experiences during the Revolution, 72 or 27 per cent had been imprisoned because of their behaviour and for many it was a traumatic experience. Because of the number of new offences and offenders, the jails were over-crowded, and this problem combined with poor sanitation led to frequent illnesses. Innovative arrangements also had to be made. In Tryon County, for example, the "goaler" was given a salary, two rooms, and the right "of keeping Tavern in the Goal ... and of supporting the prisoners with Necessaries of Life."[25] As these terms show, prisoners often had to pay for their own keep and conditions varied greatly since many were kept in private homes or make-shift jails.

A shortage of facilities along with the difficulties of keeping prisoners on the frontiers meant that many captives were sent to New England jails, a prospect that horrified Loyalists such as Justus Sherwood, condemned to the infamous Simsbury Mines. The prison, dubbed the "Catacomb of Connecticut," was in former copper mines, forty yards below the surface. Prisoners, in the words of a former inmate, were "let down on a windlass into this dismal cavern, through a hole which answers the triple purpose of conveying them food, air and – I was going to say – light, but that scarcely reaches them." Cooped up in crowded, dark, and damp quarters full of foul air, "in a few months the prisoners are released by death and the colony rejoices in her great humanity and the mildness of her laws [because the men were not hanged]." Imprisonment broke the physical or mental health of several Loyalists and the threat of spending time in Simsbury or other prisons might well have convinced Loyalists to sign an oath or flee.[26] As one Loyalist put it, "Thro their Severity they [the committees] have made a Great Many Tories for it is natural when a man is hurt to Kick."

Consider the case of Peter Van Alstine, a reasonably prosperous farmer and blacksmith in the Dutch community of Kinderhook, who was a lieutenant in the local militia, a magistrate, and a member of the local Committee of Correspondence. Although a Patriot supporter, by 1776 he had reservations. Concerned about increasing evidence of lawlessness – past memories of boundary disputes with Massachusetts were rekindled when armed men from that colony invaded and abused local people suspected of Loyalism – Van Alstine was reluctant to sign the *Association*. But neutrality was not acceptable to the Patriot committees, which ordered in militia from neighbouring districts to disarm and arrest Van Alstine and sixteen others. Detained for seventeen days and denied basic rights, such as *habeaus corpus*, Van Alstine and his associates were later freed but forced to pay the costs of their captivity. The group, fearing for their safety, did not return home, instead becoming a band of "renegade Loyalists" who lived in the woods in caves or hollow trees and harassed the Patriots by burning buildings or stealing horses and cattle. Finally in 1777, with a price on their heads, they were forced to join the British.[27]

There were thus strong "push" factors forcing the Loyalists out of the colonies: a failure to conform in their behaviour to the standards set by the Patriots drove many into exile. Contrary to their own claims, however, consistent loyalty to the British crown, empire, and constitution was not the guiding light for most Loyalists. The shifting behaviour of some suggests that they groped to come to grips with unfolding events and succumbed at various times to different pressures. Nevertheless, once committed to the path that led to exile, Loyalists such as Alexander Campbell had to explain their behaviour to British officials who questioned their motives and to themselves. Defining themselves as Loyalists committed to the British cause was easy since this was how the Patriots had categorized them and justified their harassment and punishment. Also, this explanation gave the Loyalists a sense of identity and obliged the British to reward their efforts and provide aid.

As well as the "push" factors forcing Loyalists out of the colonies, there were "pull" factors enticing some to join other Loyalist recruits. Bounties were offered to prospective recruits; however, more important was the promise of freehold land.[28] As early as 1775 recruiters for the Royal Highland Emigrants, a corps of Scots Highlanders, promised 200 acres of land to prospective soldiers. In March 1777 the governor of Quebec promised Loyalists who "shall continue to serve His Majesty until the rebellion is suppressed and peace restored ... His Majesty's bounty of 200 acres of land." In May 1781, when recruiting was more difficult, recruits were promised the same land after only three years of service and were given six guineas for enlisting. Recruiters in Bergen County, New Jersey, were even more generous, promising 200 acres of land for each adult male, 100 acres for his wife, and fifty acres for each child. Promises of land were also made by Loyalist officers. Ebenezer Jessup, lieutenant-colonel of the King's Loyal Americans and a large landowner, pledged 24,000 acres of his land to those who "would serve faithfully during the War ... and 20,0000 more to such of my officers as shuld merit the same by their good conduct."[29]

Jessup's offer reflects a basic Loyalist assumption about the promises of land – it would be freehold land in the American colonies. Loyalists assumed that the British would win the war, the Patriots would be punished as rebels, and the Loyalists would be rewarded for their services. A Loyalist soldier denounced the idea of a general amnesty for Patriots in 1777 and expressed the belief that the Patriots, guilty of treason, would forfeit their land to the faithful Loyalists: "How are we to be rewarded for our Attachment & Loyaltie forsaking & leaving to the mercy of a Brutall Savage enemie our wieves Chielderen House lands & every thing that was Dear to us if those Villains who had been the promoters of this unnatural rebellion are restored to their Estates which ought to be the Reward of our Phidellity & they Drove to the Woods, to cultivate new lands."[30] Loyalist recruiters boasted in 1778 that, when the British regained control of the region, neutrals would be spared, Patriots destroyed, and Loyalists given $40 and forty acres of land. Few Loyalists could have imagined that they would collect their reward of land not in the colonies but in Canada and not in freehold but in seigneurial tenure.

The dream of having clear title to land would have been close to the hearts of many Loyalists who would later settle around Cataraqui. Most lived on the frontiers and had either emigrated from Great Britain or left overcrowded coastal colonies in search of land, and, although the vast majority were farmers, only about 20 per cent owned their own land. It has been argued that some tenants whose landlords were Patriots became Loyalists in the hope of acquiring freehold title to their land after the Revolution when their landlords would forfeit their estates.[31] By the same token, tenants who joined Loyalist regiments were promised that at war's end the long-sought title to land would be their reward.

Equally important, however, in attracting able-bodied males to the Loyalist regiments were traditional ethnic and community ties. Becoming a Loyalist and seeking refuge at a British base was a group experience. Loyalists such as Joel Stone of Connecticut who went to British lines by themselves were very much the exception; most Loyalists arriving at British bases came in groups. Leaving the colonies undetected was not easy and groups of Loyalists conspired for some time to make their escape. Caches of food and other supplies for the long and difficult expedition to Canada had to be collected and hidden in the woods and the escape had to be timed so that those fleeing would not be quickly missed. Also, it was often necessary to have Indian guides show Loyalists the route to Canada. Many rank-and-file Loyalists worked together for months to plot their flight. Groups of blacks in New York met regularly to plan their escape and were sometimes assisted by other Loyalist leaders. The Loyalist sheriff of Tryon County promised to "protect and defend all slaves and negroes that would resort to him and put themselves under his protection," and the Patriots imposed curfews on blacks and servants to prevent such activities.[32] Tenants on the large New York estates formed groups in 1777 and schemed to join Major-General John Burgoyne's expedition from Canada. Whole parishes joined together to engineer their flight to British lines; Father John Mac-

Kenna, a Catholic priest in the Mohawk valley, boasted that not one of his parishioners joined the Patriots.[33]

Alongside ethnic and community bonds in drawing men to Loyalist regiments were family ties. Of 274 Loyalist claimants who later settled in the area of Cataraqui and who discussed military service, ninety-three or 36 per cent stated that they had other family members also serving the British. In Bergen County, New Jersey, "of 59 Tories for whom family data could be found, 46 had one or more relatives who also supported the Loyalist cause" and it was common in a community for a whole family to be known for its Loyalist sympathies. In a return of thirty-four officers of Jessups Loyal Rangers, fifteen or 44 per cent had the same name as others serving in the corps; and a return of thirty-three officers in Johnson's regiment, in which family ties were specifically mentioned, showed that eighteen or 54 per cent of the officers had family members serving in Johnson's or other regiments. Moreover, when it came to leaving for British lines, it was common for one member of a family to flee and be followed later by others.[34]

Kinship ties and longstanding relationships were also important in the Mohawk response to the Revolution. The Mohawk, like the other Six Nations, initially leaned toward neutrality in what was seen as a white man's quarrel. Their eventual alliance with the British resulted from practical considerations, notably their belief that the British would do more than the Americans to protect their lands from the encroachments of whites, and from family and tribal bonds. The Mohawk's close ties to the Johnson family were important in determining their actions, as was the decision by the established and respected Mohawk leaders, Joseph and Molly Brant, to support the British. The Mohawk responded as a group to the Revolution and white Indian agents used paternalistic imagery to appeal to them to support the British father-king in battle.[35]

Many rank-and-file Scots, in following their traditional leaders into war on behalf of the Loyalist cause, demonstrated their attachment to the hierarchical and clan social structure with which they were familiar. Captain Alexander McDonell of the Royal Highland Emigrants wrote of going to the Mohawk valley "where there was two hundred Men of my own Name ... [and] the Leading Men of whom most chearfully agreed to be ready at a Call." A major in Johnson's regiment also commented on the Highlanders' desire to follow their traditional ethnic leaders. Forty-five Highlanders wanted to serve during the war, he observed, but only under their formers chiefs since they were "so attached to their chiefs that they can't think of parting with them."[36]

Recruiting itself was structured in a hierarchical way. British officials gave commissions to prominent local leaders such as the Johnsons and

Jessups, who in turn appointed men of some means and stature as officers. Supposedly, these local leaders would be respected in their communities and able to attract recruits to fill their corps. The leaders, besides promising bounties, land, and pay to soldiers, had to use their own money to equip their followers: Sir John Johnson spent close to £400 arming and equipping the 170 men who followed him to Canada and Ebenezer Jessup spent £700 in four months for equipment. Many of the eighty men following Jessup to Canada were tenants from the patroon of Rensselaerwyck, where the landlord was a Patriot, and included Henry Young, a forty-year-old American born farmer who had served in the Seven Years War in which Jessup had been an officer.[37]

As indicated earlier, the paternalistic relationship between the Johnson family and their tenants helps to explain what happened in Tryon County during the Revolution. It was the Tryon County grand jury, comprised of the Johnsons and their appointees, which set out the Loyalist case for opposing the Revolution in March 1775. The signers of the widely distributed document declared that they "abhorred and still do abhor all measures tending, through partial representation, to alienate the affections of the subjects from the Crown." As was true of other Loyalist leaders, those in Tryon County saw the Patriots as posing a far greater threat to freedom than the British. The British constitution, they asserted, "does appear to be in more danger from the intemperate warmth and dangerous politicks of ignorant men, or crafty Republicans than from any Measures which it appears to be either the aim or interest of Government to enforce." The declaration concluded with a pledge to "exert themselves in the support of Government" and the monarchy.[38] This intellectual rationale for Loyalism, devised by the Johnsons and their large circle of followers, was adopted by rank-and-file Loyalists to explain their actions.

The Johnsons also provided more concrete leadership. They disrupted Patriot activities by going armed to meetings and intimidating potential Patriot supporters; they stopped and interrogated people travelling through the county, thereby disrupting communication among the various Patriot bodies; and they armed the militia to prevent the Patriots from harassing local Loyalists. Their loyal following included the 150 to 200 "highlanders (Roman Catholicks) armed and ready to march" and the Mohawks. Little Abraham, a Mohawk chief, told a Patriot committee in May 1775 of his alarm at reports that Patriots from New England were coming to "take away by Violence our Superintendant [Guy Johnson] and extinguish our Council Fire." Although hoping to remain neutral, the Mohawk, he said, "shall support and defend our Superintendant and not see our Council Fire extinguished." "But should our Superintendant be taken from us, we dread the Consequences," he concluded, for "the innocent might fall with the guilty."[39] In 1775, when the Patriots sent an expedition into the county to disarm Johnson's tenants and take hostages for the good behaviour of the rest, as has already been pointed out, Guy Johnson fled to Canada taking many of his followers with him.

Accompanying Johnson to Canada was John Freel, a tenant who had emigrated from Ireland in the 1760s and had a farm of which ten to twenty acres were cleared. After reaching Montreal, Freel returned home to be with his family and he was seized and interrogated by the Tryon County Committee of Safety. Freel claimed that he knew nothing about Johnson's plan to go to Montreal and that he only accompanied Johnson north to do some "Taylors work." He testified that he protested going further than Oswego, but Johnson "stopped" him "by force" and threatened to "Flock anyone, that would insist upon returning back from Oswego." When in Montreal, he claimed that he resisted strong pressure "to engage him in the King's service ... and did work upon his Taylor's trade." He concluded with an oath supporting "the American liberty's Cause."[40]

Although Freel's testimony has, of course, to be viewed skeptically, especially since within two years he was back in Canada fighting with Johnson's regiment, there might be some truth to his account. The larger issues at stake in the Revolution might well have eluded Freel; for him, the only issue was whether or not to follow Johnson's orders. Freel decided to follow the Johnsons and explained, perhaps candidly, why: he was a "Man, who must live by his Trade, and in particular who has earned a great Deal of that Family." Freel had a paternalistic relationship with his landlord, the Johnsons providing him with his livelihood in return for loyalty and obedience. Following his landlord into battle and later exile was merely the logical outcome of this relationship.[41]

Many other rank-and-file Loyalists followed traditional leaders or joined relatives, friends, or kinsmen into the Loyalist regiments. On one of their raids to their former homeland, Johnson's men appealed to friends and relatives as follows:

The Officers & Soldiers of Sir John Johnson's Regiment present their affectionate and loving wishes to their Friends & Relations on the Mohawk River & earnestly entreat them to assemble themselves and come into Canada or the upper Posts, where under that Gallant leader, they may assist their Countrymen to quell and put an end to the present unnatural Rebellion, in hopes soon to return to their native homes, there to enjoy the happiness they were formerly blessed with under the best of Kings who is willing to do every thing for his subjects.[42]

The appeal centred around kinship ties, service under an established leader, the hope for peace, and the desire to return home, rather than on common loyalty to the British crown, empire, and constitution.

In returning to their former homes to recruit, the Loyalist soldiers were establishing a pattern. As families and friends welcomed or aided the raiders, more Loyalists within the colonies were incriminated in the eyes of the Patriots, harassed, and forced to leave, becoming in turn recruits and then recruiters themselves. Large numbers of women and children, however, remained to fight the war behind enemy lines and became targets for the wrath of outraged Patriots.

Many colonial women, whether Loyalist or Patriot, were forced during the Revolution to act in ways inconsistent with their subordinate status within patriarchal households and to take their first tentative steps into the traditionally male-dominated worlds of politics and warfare. Patriot women joined in rituals and protests. They circulated petitions, wrote pamphlets and other literature in defence of the Revolution, formed colony-wide associations, and raised money. The success of the boycott on tea and other British goods depended to some extent on the willingness of women to forego purchasing these goods. And wearing homespun became a sign of patriotism, elevating the importance of the feminine task of spinning.[43]

Loyalist women were also active participants in the Revolution. They took their first steps into the political realm by petitioning and writing pamphlets. In one such piece of literature, *A Dialogue Between a Southern Delegate and His Spouse*, a Loyalist woman berated her husband, a delegate to the First Continental Congress, and warned of the dire consequences of the Congress's actions:

To your mighty Congress, your members were sent
To lay our complaints before Parliament,
Usurpation reared its head from that fatal Hour
You resolved, you enacted like a Sovereign Power.
Your non-imports, and Exports are full fraught with
Ruin,
Of thousands and thousands the utter undoing,
If Philadelphia or New York proposed some wise Plan
From that moment on you branded the man ...
Instead of imploring their Justice or Pity,
You treat Parliament like a Pack of Banditti.
Instead of Addresses fram'd on Truth or on Reason,
You breathe nothing but insult, rebellion and Treason.
In all the Records of the most slavish Nation,
You'll not find an instance of such usurpation,
If spirits infernal for dire vengeance design'd,

Had been named Delegates to afflict humankind,
And in Grand Continental Congress had resolved,
Let the bonds of social bliss be henceforth dissolved.
Oh! My Country! Remember that a woman unknown
Cry'd aloud like Cassandra in Oracular Tone,
Repent! or you are forever, forever undone.[44]

Loyalist women even played a military role in the Revolution. Ann Novil, a Pennsylvania Loyalist, acted as a guide during the 1777 Burgoyne expedition from Canada. Another woman, Frances Child, helped British and Loyalist prisoners being held in southern New York escape, while Hannah Tomlinson "aided and assisted upwards of 100 Prisoners of War in making their escape into the British lines." Other women spied for the British and passed on intelligence.[45]

Women on both sides during the Revolutionary War were camp followers who accompanied the troops on their expeditions. An infamous camp follower was Elizabeth Loring, mistress of General William Howe, the commander of British troops. Howe's inaction during the war was attributed to his preoccupation with Mrs Loring, who loved drinking and gambling and became a legendary figure in "The Battle of the Kegs": "Sir William, he, snug as a flea, / Lay all the time a-snoring; / Nor dreamed of harm, as he lay warm / In bed with Mrs. L———g."[46] Other officers, such as General Friedrich Adolphus von Riedesel, the commander of the Hessian troops who fought for the British, brought their families to North America. Madame general, Baroness Friederike Charlotte Louise Riedesel, and three children under five accompanied the troops on the Burgoyne expedition; in the entourage were two maids, a calesh, and other amenities. One child was born and another conceived during the campaign and they were aptly named Canada and America.[47]

More common camp followers were the wives or girl-friends of the foot soldiers and homeless or runaway women of every description. In November 1777 a Patriot woman described the women accompanying the recently defeated Burgoyne expedition:

I never had the least Idea that the Creation produced such a sordid set of creatures in human Figure – poor, dirty, emaciated men, great numbers of women, who seemed to be the beasts of burthen, having a bushel basket on their back, by which they were bent double, the contents seemed to be Pots and Kettles, various sorts of Furniture, children peeping thro' gridirons and other utensils, some very young Infants who were born on the road, the women bare feet, cloathed in dirty rags, such effluvia filld the air while they were passing, had they not been smoaking all the time, I should have been apprehensive of being contaminated by them.[48]

Women camp followers could be tough customers, as the story of Mary Driskill shows. After her husband was killed in action, Mary was confined in one prison from which she escaped only to be recaptured and imprisoned again with men from Burgoyne's army. After escaping again she was retaken and imprisoned for a third time and escaped again, this time with two other women and the twins to whom she had given birth while in jail. With her two babies, Mary travelled by canoe along the Susquehanna River, "lying in the woods with her two twins" at night, an experience that caused her to lose her hearing. After a long and exhausting journey through the back country of New York and Pennsylvania, she finally reached the British base in New York City, with two healthy babies.[49]

Commanding officers, foreshadowing a later view of the Loyalist women who arrived at British bases, saw women camp followers as nuisances and tried in vain to regulate their numbers and activities. For them, the camp followers were mouths to be fed and they insisted on work – most frequently washing clothes for the army – in return for provisions. Officers also disliked the women because they slowed down the army, encumbered as they usually were with children or by pregnancy. Yet, at the same time, the women made important contributions to the war effort. They performed such services as cooking, washing, ironing, or mending clothes. They also provided badly needed medical services. Army medical and hospital services were crude, with surgeons mates, who were in short supply, being responsible for administering medicine and supervising the wounded or ill. Because there was always a shortage of nurses, women camp followers cared for and fed the patients as well as ensuring that there was a minimal level of cleanliness in the surroundings.[50]

At least one Loyalist who later settled in the Cataraqui area became a camp follower during the Burgoyne expedition. Barbara Heck, who lived on the New York frontier, loaded her five children and a grandfather clock into a wagon and made her way to the British-Loyalist army where she served as a "nurse."[51]

Most Loyalist women, however, stayed within their communities behind enemy lines, where they were a valuable military asset of the British and a thorn in the side of the Patriots. Women often made better spies than men since their actions were less carefully scrutinized. Because they did not have to serve in the militia or sign oaths, women found it easier to escape being branded as dissidents. Also, it was easier for them to travel from British- to American-held territory and, if questioned, to avoid being searched. George Washington and other Patriot military leaders were convinced that property and information were being conveyed by Loyalist women. Similarly, a Patriot official in Tryon County complained that "women are permitted to go out & into New York without Interruption." A mulatto woman was suspected of travelling in 1777 from New York City to the frontiers, bringing information about friends and relatives to frontier Loyalists and then proceeding with the rest of her intelligence to Burgoyne's army.[52] Women coming to Canada brought intelligence with them and many Loyalist women in the colonies passed information on to British or Loyalist officials.[53]

Women also were involved in other military or para-military activities. Three women were implicated in a plot to kidnap the mayor of Albany and one, an Indian, confessed to having lured the mayor to the woods by reporting that she had found a dead body there. Another woman was arrested and jailed along with twenty men for "having assisted in the destruction of Currey Town." Women were arrested and some imprisoned for their roles in robberies or in protecting robbers and possessing stolen goods.[54]

Women were also accused of inciting others to treason by encouraging them not to take Patriot oaths or join the militia. Two women in Albany were imprisoned and exiled for urging others to refuse to fight with the Patriots. Another woman was charged with protecting "Negroes" and soldiers, "in whose minds she instills nothing but disaffection," and inciting them to "Steal" and rob "the Soldiers of their Ammunition & Blankets." The future eastern Ontario Loyalist Mrs Jeremiah French, whose husband had joined the British and suffered the loss of all of his property and cattle, defiantly refused to recognize Patriot authority. Known for her "bitter tongue," Mrs French was described by the Patriots as "very turbulent & Troublesome" and unwilling "to obey orders." The Patriot committee became so exasperated with her that they ordered her to be taken to "the East side of Lake Champlain when she can go to the enemy in order to git to her husband."[55]

At the beginning of the Revolution, Patriot oaths were compulsory for men since they were deemed capable of making political choices, but not for women, who were seen as subordinates within a patriarchal family in which the male household head made all of the political choices. This changed, however, as the threat Loyalist women posed to American security become clear. Soon Patriot statutes defining treason referred to "persons" or "he or she," which meant that women were deemed to be capable of actions that threatened the well-being of the state.[56]

Of special concern to the Patriots were the Loyalist women on the northern colonial frontiers. Geography dictated that they would be especially important to the British military strategy of raiding the frontiers of the American colonies. Located between the Patriots to the south and the British to the north, the women were caught in a region that would be a major theatre of war and whether they liked it or not many would become combatants. In Vermont, the Council stated that Loyalist women were "dangerous persons to Society and instruments of Great Mischief to this and the United States of America" for such activities as "Riding post, carrying Intelligence to the Enemies Camp and Scouts." In Tryon County, the chairman of the Committee of Safety complained, "The Women of those Enemies is still living among us, some behave very rudely at present, and have proved very active to support and spirit up the opposite cause." A Patriot within the county, Isaac Paris, was more specific. When "the Roman Catholic Scotch Inhabitants" of Johnstown and "the disaffected Germans" of Johnson's Bush and Butlersbury fled to Canada, they left behind about 400 "wives and children, which dwell in the back settlement of Johnson's Bush," and "it is supposed that they will, or at least can constantly succor our enemies with provisions, and give them intelligence of our situation and proceedings."[57] And it was true that when the men raided the frontiers from Canada, their families and friends in the colonies fed, sheltered, and supplied them. Just as family, ethnic, or community ties were important in explaining why males joined the Loyalist regiments and fled to Canada, they also help to explain why the Loyalist families left behind in the colonies became participants in the Revolution.

Some Loyalist women who would later settle in the Cataraqui area participated in the war by either shielding their husbands or acting on their behalf. In October 1776, as the Tryon County militia was mustering, Johan Jost Herkimer disappeared. When committee members appeared at his home, Mary, his wife, assured them that her husband had gone to another town to look for a shoemaker. They remained unconvinced and asked to search the house, but she "utterly refused." After forcing their way into the house, the Patriots discovered Mary's husband hiding in the cellar.[58]

In March 1777 a tenant of Sir John's, Helen McDonell – whose husband, Collachie, had been taken by the Patriots along with five other McDonell clansmen as hostages for Johnson's good behaviour – wrote a blunt letter to the local Patriot committee. She began by emphatically denying that the Scots had been involved in any treasonous activity before 1775; as she put it, "There was no such thing then in agitation as you was pleased to observe in your letter to me." Speaking on behalf of her people, she informed the Patriots that they would not "goe in to sign

and swear [Patriot oaths] ... being already prisoners to Genll Schuyler."
She reminded the Patriots of their promise that the tenants should "return to there farms and they should be no more troubled nor molested during the war to this they agreed and have not since doen anything against the contry nor never intends to doe if let alon." A stiff warning ended the letter: "They [her kinsmen] will loze their lives befor taken prisoners again ... " Helen McDonell was obviously an eloquent and courageous voice for her kinsmen.[59]

Mary Munro, who had been "brought up in a Genteel sphere of Life," took over from her husband, John, after his arrest by the Patriots. John had been suspected of recruiting for the British in Vermont but had managed to spirit his officers and men off to the woods, along with his cattle to feed them, before he left for New York City to request money from Governor William Tryon. After returning home through Patriot-held territory with £100 for his men, Munro was resting peacefully when his home was surrounded by two hundred Patriots. When Mary saw the Patriots coming, she quickly took the money and hid it. After her husband was taken to jail, she immediately contacted his followers to give them the money and tell them that "it was necessary to endeavour by every means to make off for Canada and join General Carleton with the Troops under his command on Lake Champlain." She also brought with her "provisions and every necessary in her power" to speed them on their way.[60]

Mohawk women played an especially significant role in the Revolutionary War. In the matrilineal Mohawk society women had significant influence on the conduct of war; the matrons were highly regarded and their views on military matters taken seriously. Moreover, Indian women, armed with guns or tomahawks, sometimes fought side by side with their husbands and during the raids on the colonial frontiers Indian women with tomahawks lurked at the rear of the armies waiting to pillage.[61]

As noted in the previous chapter, two women – one Indian and one white – were instrumental in maintaining the British-Mohawk alliance. The Indian was Molly Brant. Molly shared the traditional loyalty to the British typical of her Mohawk ancestors and of her mate, Sir William Johnson. But she also had her own reasons for hating the Patriots, particularly Philip Schuyler, the prominent Albany trader and military leader, who had forced her family to flee the Mohawk valley and deprived her children of their rightful heritage in their ancestral homeland.[62]

Molly Brant made a tremendous and varied contribution to the war effort. She helped white Loyalists fleeing from the Patriots make their way to Canada. One group of Tryon County Loyalists was advised to escape from Patriot persecution by contacting Molly Brant. Molly "conducted them to a secure hiding place in the woods, and there took them food each morning and evening during a week" while the Patriots searched for the dissidents. After the Patriot search had ended, she prepared them for the trip to Canada. Each was given "a sack of provisions, weighting them with steelyards" and an Indian guide to take them through the woods.[63] This was only one of many groups of Loyalists who made their way to Canada because of the help of Molly Brant.

Molly also encouraged other Indians to support the British. One of her feats was wooing Mary Aaron, the Mohawk mistress of Philip Schuyler, to the British side. Schuyler had used his relationship with Mary Aaron as a way to spread rumours among the Mohawk and try to influence their decisions. However, Molly Brant persuaded Mary to leave Schuyler and live with her at Niagara and to use her considerable influence on behalf of the British. In November 1780 Daniel Claus, the Indian agent, reported intelligence received from Mary Aaron.[64]

Molly could also be very straighforward and sharp-tongued in her criticism of the British. To cite one example, in April 1781 she discovered that her brother, Joseph, had almost been killed accidentally by Loyalist Indian agents at Niagara. She wrote angrily to the governor complaining that Joseph had "just returned from a dangerous expedition to rebel country" and to be "thus treated by king's people who always stay quietly at home in the Fort, while my Brother continually exposes his life in going against the Enemy" was intolerable. She demanded that the governor act, in part because of her personal feelings; "it is hard," she explained, "to have an only Brother whom I dearly love to see him thus treated." But her other concern was how the incident might "affect the King's Indian interest" since the other Iroquois saw the "abuse of Brant" and "remember Schuyler saying Indians would be ill treated by the King's people."[65] Molly's blunt criticism shows that, as well as being influential with the Mohawk, she was a woman of stature in the eyes of the British.

The white woman who played an important role in upholding the Mohawk-British alliance was the already mentioned Sarah Kast Mc-Ginnis, who had grown up with the Mohawk, learned their language, and maintained close trading ties with them. When the war broke out, the Patriots offered her twelve shillings York currency per day and a guard of fifteen men if she would try to influence the Mohawk on their behalf. However, like the Mohawk, Sarah and her family were supporters of the British and the Johnsons in northern New York. Sarah's family contributed to the war by "sending every intelligence ... by Indians to Niagara," by "receiv[ing], supply[ing] & forward[ing] Loyalists" en route to Canada, and by working to sustain the Mohawk's alliance with the British.

In 1777, as news spread of Burgoyne's expedition from Canada, Sarah's son-in-law was arrested and her property plundered and then seized by the Patriots. Sarah, her daughter, and her granddaughter watched as the Patriots sold all of their possessions, "except what would scantily support them in victuals and clothes," at public auction. After this, the women were imprisoned in a local fort and so badly treated that Sarah's granddaughter later died. When the British appeared to have the upper hand in the region, the Patriots, fearing British retaliation, released the women. Within eight days, however, the Patriots had regained the momentum and they tried to recapture Sarah and her family who had "escaped at night with only what they could carry on their backs." They had left with the British troops for Canada, although Sarah was forced to leave behind a son "who was out of his senses and bound in chains ... and who some time afterward was burnt alive."[66] Soon after her arrival in Canada, Sarah was asked by the British to return to Indian country to steady the Indians in their attachment to the British cause. Sarah agreed to winter with the Indians even though she was sixty-four years old at the time.

The most common way in which future eastern Ontario Loyalist women contributed to the Revolution was by harbouring and helping Loyalist-Indian raiding parties and by giving them information about the local Patriots' activities. When the raiding parties descended on the frontiers of the colonies, it was only natural that they would seek out their families and it was equally natural for the women to feed, clothe, and protect their husbands, fathers, or brothers and to pass on information to them. Yet, in doing so, Loyalist women were puting themselves at serious risk; in the eyes of the Patriots they were guilty of protecting traitors and carrying on a treasonous correspondence with the enemy.

The Fergusons, who owned a farm "in partnership" near Fort Edward and settled west of Cataraqui on the Bay of Quinte after the Revolution, illustrated how all members of a family were involved in fighting the war. In 1777 the eldest son, Israel, joined the Burgoyne expedition at Skenesborough. A year later the second son, Richard, joined, to be followed the next year by Farrington, who was still very young. Rachel, the mother, and her daughters remained at home behind enemy lines where they supplied and hid raiding parties. In 1779 they were imprisoned "for harbouring & entertaining a Number of Tories who come down from Canada with an inte[n]tion of Murdering the Defenceless Inhabitants on the Western Frontiers ... " When the women were released on bail, they followed the men to Canada.[67]

There are other examples of women assisting the Loyalist-Indian raiding parties. Wounded soldiers in one of Sir John's raids were taken care of by a woman who kept the Loyalist men in her house dressed in women's clothing until they were well enough to escape to Canada. Isabel Parker and her family "aided and succoured his Majesty's Scouts on secret service by procuring them provisions and Intelligence and encouraging sundry persons to Join His Majesty's service at her great expense Peril and risk." In Tryon County, the local committee ordered in 1777 that ten wives of Loyalists who had joined the British be confined under guard in a house. On another part of the frontier, the Tunacliffe family fell afoul of the local committee for aiding Joseph Brant on his raids.[68] The women's support for the raiding parties was crucial to the success of the military operations and the Patriots knew it.

For the Patriots, the Loyalist women left behind by men fleeing to the British were like a viper living in their midst. Many were punished for their behaviour. The Vermont Council declared in September 1777: "Several Women, wives to those Merciless & unprovoked Murderers have aided & assisted in Bringing about Such their designs by harbouring, secreting, feeding & Giving private Intelligence to such Immesaries of Great Britain ... " For their efforts the women were to be removed to British lines. Other Patriot committees interrogated Loyalist women for "carrying on an Intercourse with the Enemy and harbouring British officers who were passing through the Country as Expresses," "harbouring and supplying parties from the Enemy with provisions," "keeping up a dangerous correspondence with the enemy," or "hiding Tories."[69]

But the women were also incriminated by the actions of the men in their lives. By joining the enemy and participating in the often vicious raids on frontier communities, the men had tainted not only themselves but also their families. The Patriots felt justified in striking back and punishing those raiding their frontiers and participating in treason. The men, however, were in Canada, beyond the Patriots' reach. It was the women and their families who bore the brunt of the Patriots' rage.

As the Loyalist men fled to the safety of British lines, some at least hoped that their families, left behind in the colonies, would be spared; as one husband and father put it, "Surely the people [the Patriots] has not got so barberously mad as to Mollest or hurt a poor innocent woman and still more Innocent poor Children."[70] There was a theoretical rationale for treating women and children as innocent bystanders. Women were *femmes coverts*, mere appendages of their husbands, with no independent wills or political roles of their own. They, therefore, could not, and the vast majority did not, *decide* to become Loyalists. Some colonial governments recognized this fact by confiscating the male Loyalists' property while allowing their wives to claim dower rights.

More often, however, Patriot committees and colonial governments assumed, unless there was evidence to the contrary, that the families of Loyalists shared in the guilt of one member. And such treatment had a rationale, too: since women could not act independently of the men in their lives, the political decisions of the men also incriminated the women.

The case of the Cartwright family shows how the actions of some members, in this case the children, incriminated all members of the family as far as the Patriots were concerned. Richard Sr, landowner, deputy postmaster of Albany, and keeper of an inn at which the local Patriots met regularly, had visibly supported the Revolution in 1775 when he gave money to the Patriot expedition against Ticonderoga. However, his daughter, Elizabeth, had married a British soldier and moved to Niagara, leaving behind a granddaughter, Hannah. Then, in February 1777, a letter from his son, Richard Jr, to Elizabeth in Niagara was intercepted by the Albany County Committee of Correspondence and Richard Jr had to "enter into security for his future good behaviour." In October, Richard Jr and his young niece, Hannah, were granted permission to leave and travelled through the wilderness of northern New York to Canada. But the parents, tainted by the Loyalism of their children and unwilling to take a Patriot oath, were harassed. One mob "destroyed and plundered" the Cartwrights' property and a second, numbering hundreds of people, damaged more property and "beat and abused" the Cartwrights. In early July 1778, the Cartwrights were hauled before the Committee for Detecting and Defeating Conspiracies and ordered to leave; shortly after, they were "conveyed away by a Guard to Crown Point" and the parents reluctantly joined the children in Canada.[71]

More frequently it was the male family head who incriminated the wives and children. On one occasion, a Patriot committee denied the request of a Loyalist woman to join her husband by pointing to his actions not hers. As the committee members explained, "no permit or Indulgence" could be given "to any part of a Family whereof the Husband or Master" had been involved in raiding the frontiers and had thereby "so far deviated from humane principles as to associate with Barbarians & assisting in Imbruing his Hands in the Blood of Women and Children and peaceable Inhabitants."[72] The whole family was assumed to share in the guilt of the family head and accordingly all family members were possible targets for Patriot harassment.

Women who had either participated in the war themselves or were married to men who had were subjected to various forms of punishment, the most common and devastating being the confiscation of their property. In 1776 the Continental Congress decided that those who had fled to the British were guilty of treason and their property should be confiscated. By 1777 committees within each colony were formed to oversee the seizure and sale at vendue, or public auction, of Loyalist property. Again the concept of familial guilt generally prevailed. Unless there was evidence to the contrary, it was assumed that, if the male family head had joined the enemy and was no longer entitled to his property, then his family shared in his guilt. Seizing the property of families whose heads had fled to the British warned others of the dire consequences of being a Loyalist and it enhanced the power of the committees, which then had property to sell and distribute.

The story of Abigail Lindsey was typical. Her husband, John, a "native of America," was tried and fined three times for not supporting the Revolution. Finally in 1780 he was recruited into Jessup's regiment and went to Canada, leaving his wife and two children in charge of the farm and "1 Horse, 2 Cows, 10 sheep." Soon after her husband's departure, "The Rebels came & took them from her, because her Husband was gone to the Brit." and they also took "all her furniture." Abigail eventually followed her husband to Canada, but shortly after arriving her husband died and she was left a widow.[73]

Many other Loyalist women who would later settle in and around Cataraqui were deprived of their property and even forced to watch as it was auctioned off. Alida Van Alstine was left in Kinderhook amidst her family and in-laws when her husband, Peter, was forced to flee to the British in 1777. Shortly after his departure she gave birth to her fourth child, who died within the year, and then she lost her property. Although Van Alstine had been a reasonably prosperous farmer and blacksmith, Alida's assets in the 1779 tax list were valued at a mere $6 while those of her brother-in-law, who had taken over most of the property, were worth $750.[74] Ann Peters had her property "seized [and] confiscated" after her husband, John, showed his Loyalist colours by deserting the Patriot army invading Canada. Mary Herkimer suffered the same fate in New York, when her husband was banished and all the family property and personal effects, with the exception of "one sheep allowed for each child," were sold for over £2,000. When Garnet Dingman, a squatter on land along the Susquehanna River, joined the British in 1781, he left his cattle, utensils, and furniture to his wife and friends; however, shortly after his departure, the rebels, in the words of an observer, "stript [his wife] of every thing." And Mary Waldec, wife of a tenant in Tryon County who had fled to Canada with Sir John Johnson in 1776, found that the "rebels ... took most" of her "things ... and sold them at Vendue."[75]

Mobs were as active as Patriot committees in seizing and plundering Loyalist property. Colonial political culture legitimized the use of the mob – a group of citizens expressing the general will of the community

– in the interests of the public good.[76] Since Loyalists were considered enemies of American liberty, confiscating or destroying their property could be justified. Local committees might proclaim that they alone had the power to seize property, but enforcing such edicts was another matter.[77]

The disorder of the Revolutionary War years also made it easier for roving bands of colonists to plunder people guilty or suspected of Loyalist leanings. Robberies were a problem, especially on the Manor of Rensselaerwyck, and women who were either widowed or left alone by their husbands were easy targets and common victims. "A Number of Persons," as one woman victim described her anonymous assailants, used the "excuse" that she was "disaffected" to tear down her house and destroy her belongings.[78]

Looting and property destruction often occurred at the hands of troops, whether British, Loyalist, Indian, or Patriot. Loyalist and Indian raiding parties sometimes looted, destroyed property, and took prisoners without asking whether their victims were Loyalists or Patriots. In a petition to the governor of Quebec, inhabitants of the New York and Pennsylvania frontiers complained that despite promises that those not assisting the Patriots would not be molested, bands of Indians raided their communities, destroyed property, and took innocent people as prisoners. There are many tales of women and children being spared during Indian raids on the colonial frontier by the intervention of the Mohawk chief Joseph Brant. During an attack on Minisink on the New York frontier, for example, the Indians tomahawked a local schoolteacher and were about to turn their attention to his young pupils when Brant intervened to place his mark of adoption on the aprons and dresses of the little girls, who in turn protected the boys by sitting beside them and spreading their dresses over them. All of the children were spared. Other people were not as fortunate. British troops made more enemies than friends among the colonial population by looting property, seizing supplies without compensation, and engaging in violence.[79]

The Patriot troops were not much better. In Vermont, the Council of Safety in January 1777 received "reports to the prejudice of the Rangers" to the effect that "great injustice have been done to the Inhabitants by them, they having plundered them contrary to the Express orders and designs of this Council." In Tryon County, the local committee warned soldiers that future misbehaviour would be merit a jail term. An Albany resident complained that the Patriot Company of Rangers "had taken from him two Gammons, two Sides of Pork and forty odd Fowls, and that they had drove and made his Wife cook it for them, some of them paid what they pleased for it, and others not."[80]

The Patriots on the New York frontier avenged themselves against Molly Brant and the Mohawk for their support of the British by looting and seizing their property. The chairman of the Committee of Safety returned several times to fill his wagons with Indian possessions. From Molly Brant, the Patriots took "Sixty half Johannesses [Portuguese gold coins], two Quarts full of silver, several Gold Rings, Eight pair silver Buckels; a large Quantity of Silver Broaches, Together with several silk Gowns." Children of the Patriot leaders paraded around in Molly's silk gowns, while their parents helped themselves to her belongings and moved into her home.[81]

Elizabeth Cary Wilstee, a resident of the New Hampshire grants whose family had been victimized by the Green Mountain boys in the 1760s, watched helplessly as a Patriot band ransacked her home in 1776. In the middle of winter, the "outlaws" broke into her home and ordered her and her children to leave for her father's place. Although it was snowy and cold, she had no choice. "Looking back while on her way," she saw the "outlaws moving her furniture and provisions from the house and loading them into a wagon." Next she witnessed them "open her feather beds and shake the feathers from the ticks out of the windows and put the ticks and bed clothes into the wagon." Finally, she watched them "pry the logs of the sides of the house out at the corners until the roof fell in." Having finished with the Wiltsee home, the band moved on to the homes of other tenants in the neighbourhood.[82]

The havoc wreaked by some Patriots occasionally disillusioned even their own supporters, as an October 1775 letter to the Albany Committee of Correspondence shows. When local Patriot troops broke into the house of a resident of Albany, they "beat his Wife and Daughter, the latter of whom in so severe a manner as would be shocking to humanity to repeat & destroyed some of his property." The same night the troops "behaved extreamly disorderly in the City to the great disturbance and disquiet of it its Inhabitants." The authors concluded poignantly: "It gives us sensible Concern that Soldiers whom we were induced to believe were raised for the defence of our Liberty and property, should give us so early an Instance of their Inclinations to deprive us of both."[83]

Whether they were Patriot troops exceeding their orders or "mobs" inflicting popular justice, many victimized future eastern Ontario Loyalist families by destroying the property upon which they depended for their livelihoods. Helena McLeod, a Scots Highlander whose husband had fled to Canada with Guy Johnson in 1775, reported that "the rebels have destroyed a considerable property" because her husband had "joined the King's troops." Her countrymen the MacDonnels were too old to aid the British militarily, the husband being seventy-four and the wife sixty-seven, but they had nine sons in the "king's service" and this provoked the "rebels" to steal their cattle and burn their home, which was rebuilt and "again plundered of everything ... [they] had in the world." After Mary DeForest's husband was imprisoned by the "rebels," she and her seven children were "greatly distress'd by being Plundered of all their Effects," and Rachel Macintosh had her house burned "on acct of her Husb. joing ye Brit. Army." The wife and eight children of Valentine Detlor, a farmer in Albany County, "were stript by the Rebels of every individual thing belonging to them ... being destitute of Money, Cloathing and every other Necessary of Life except a poor pittance."[84]

The experiences of the Hare family, American-born tenants of the Johnsons, can be reconstructed in graphic detail. The husband, John, was a captain in the Indian Department and his family was obviously marked by his service. In early 1776, when General Schuyler came to Johnstown to disarm the Johnsons, his troops plundered the Hare's house, taking farm equipment, cattle, household goods, and a silver watch. Shortly after, John Hare returned from Canada on a scouting expedition and took more grain and livestock for his comrades. Then came Colonel Dayton, sent to arrest Sir John Johnson and take over Johnson Hall; he and his men again plundered the Hares, even taking timber and boards from their home to build a blockhouse and chopping up their fence for firewood. All of this destruction occurred, leaving Margaret Hare in dire need, even though there was no "official" committee edict depriving Mrs Hare and her children of their property.[85]

The account of the losses of Richard Cartwright Sr depicts the various ways in which Loyalists lost their property and possessions. Some $60 worth of "Apparel of myself & Wife [were] stole by provincial (loyalist) soldiers." Another $156 was spent to "provision poor Loyalists," $63 was advanced "to Prisoners escaped from Prison," and $195 went to "Maintaining Sheriff White & several others near two years." Thus, almost $500 was spent assisting Loyalists. The Patriots took another $1000 worth of possessions from the Cartwrights. "Liquor, China & Glass [were] destroyed by the Mob"; "Damages" amounting to $95 were inflicted by the "Mob" on "the King's birthday"; some $56 worth of furniture was "lost & destroyed at Vendue"; and Cartwright paid $45 in "Fines for non Attendance on Militia Service." In addition to all of these losses, the Cartwrights had their property seized by the Patriots.[86]

Loyalist women experienced other trials. A Vermont woman who had been jailed asked the Cumberland County committee that she either be tried for a crime or released since she wanted "to go home to my poor Children, as you must be Sencible it must be hard for a poor Woman to be in Confinement from her family that is Inossent."[87] Some women even suffered physical abuse. When Patriot parties sent to seize male family members were frustrated by their flight, the pursuing Patriots often turned to violence – usually against property but sometimes against people.

The case of the Empy family was especially tragic. Philip, the husband and father of eleven children, was subjected to "many insults and abuses from rebels," perhaps because a son had joined Sir John Johnson in Canada, and in 1777 he was imprisoned for not swearing allegiance to the Congress. After taking a Patriot oath he was released, only to be imprisoned again, along with three of his sons, when Burgoyne's expedition reached the frontiers. When Philip and his three sons escaped from prison, the local Patriots turned their eyes to his wife and seven other children. Mrs Empy and her children were imprisoned in Johnstown jail and all of their real and personal property was confiscated. After the Patriots suffered a setback at Fort Stanwix, Mrs Empy and her family were released. But when she returned to her home, she was "beat and abused" by "4 men" who left her on the road. Although she was rescued by friends and taken to Schenectady, she later died.[88]

Mrs Empy's story underlines the differences in the experiences of Patriot and Loyalist women. Most Patriot women did not experience the loss of their land, removal from their homes, and confiscation of their possessions. As well as the monetary loss, there was also a psychological dimension. Land was what the women and their families had moved to the frontier to acquire. The Patriots, by stripping the Loyalists of their land and the improvements on it, were taking away from them the most visible sign of their success and achievement as pioneers. Also, when they lost their homes, their furnishings, and some of their personal belongings, Loyalist women were deprived of the familiar pillars that lent stability to their lives on the frontiers. The result was dislocation, instability, and often acute anxiety.

Literature on the stress commonly felt by refugees deepens our understanding of the Loyalists' experiences. Refugees' experiences have been compared to the "ultimate trauma" of being born in that they involve "an emergence from what was supposed to be a safe, warm hospitable environment to a cold, hostile one ... [it is like] a cutting of the umbilical cord tying oneself to a secure past." The change from being citizens to becoming refugees involves, in the words of another expert, "a transition from relative security and prosperity to uncertainty and poverty." Refugees lose the security associated with familiar surroundings and relationships and the stability that comes from a predictable lifestyle, and this in turn exposes them "to extreme forms of stress which affect their mental health." Feelings of abandonment and betrayal are common to refugees and the eastern Ontario Loyalist women were no exceptions.[89]

Among many of these women, there is evidence of stress produced by instability, uncertainty, and separation from the men in their lives. One soldier claimed that his wife had "miscarried after Six Months gone with Child through Mere heart break discontent and villains round about her threatening to do this and that." John Munro described how the wives and children of Loyalist men being executed for treason watched in agony as their husbands and fathers were "dragged from their cells ... denied even cold Water when fainting with the heat of the Weather." He also told of the Patriots' cruelty in using the separation of him from his family to "terrify his Family" by spreading rumours that he had been executed, and in telling him that "his Family was burnt and destroyed by the Indians."[90]

Men experienced similar emotional crises. Catherine Cryderman testified that her husband, Valentine, a tenant farmer who was too old to serve in the Loyalist regiments himself but sent his three sons instead, was arrested in 1776 after refusing to take a Patriot oath and became so ill "in Consequence of his Sufferings, that he never recovered – he lost his Senses" and died after being bedridden for four years. Elizabeth Schermerhorn testified that her husband, William, a prosperous tenant on Rensselaerwyck, was "almost out of his mind from his Distresses" and his own letter to Sir John Johnson at the end of the war revealed a profoundly bitter man.[91]

Some of the innermost feelings and anxieties of at least one family can be gleaned from the copious correspondence between Joel Stone and his family. The Stones, whose roots in Connecticut dated back to the 1630s, were a large and close family. The patriarch, Stephen, who was a farmer, had nine children with his first wife, Joel being the second oldest, and when tragedy struck the family in the 1760s – a son, a daughter, and his wife all died – he quickly (within six months of his first wife's death) remarried and fathered seven more children. The family lived initially in Guilford and then moved in the 1750s to Litchfield in western Connecticut. As the children grew up they left, although most stayed close to home, and they continued to gravitate back to their father's house and to keep in touch with each other. The Stones were extremely supportive of each other and especially of Joel, the only family member forced to leave because of his Loyalism. Joel's family helped him document his claims for compensation, they cared for his wife, they raised his children, and, as his sister Rene once wrote, they regularly sent "what you are ever sure of, their love and good wishes."[92]

Joel's route to exile was a difficult one. When he left home in 1771 at twenty-one, he became a merchant and he prospered until he and his partners came to the attention of the Patriots for supplying the British army. This alone does not explain his Loyalism, however, since his partner managed to switch sides and make money by supplying the Patriots. Joel's father was regularly harassed by the Patriots for his outright Loyalism, and Joel himself, while initially trying to remain neutral, also became an object of rebel fury when he helped Loyalist prisoners – such as David Mathews, a former mayor of New York accused of plotting to assassinate General George Washington – escape from a Connecticut jail. When in 1776 the Patriots demanded that Joel serve in the militia or provide a replacement, he refused. The Patriots came to arrest him and, though he eluded his captors, his sister Rene was left to meet the "resentment" of the "tumultuous mob which attended the party." The mob verbally abused her, and then proceeded to "actual violence breaking open every lock in the house and seizing all the property ... [which they] confiscated" and sold. Joel escaped to New York and was recruiting for the British in 1778 when he was captured while asleep and returned to Connecticut.[93] His request to be considered a prisoner of war was denied and he was charged with high treason.

Joel's sisters Dothe and Hannah, after spending three days just trying to find where their brother was being held, finally found him in a Fairfield jail awaiting execution. They watched him "walking, pensive and thoughtful backwards and forwards" in the yard before they announced themselves. When he saw his sisters he exclaimed, "My dear sisters ... [and] could hardly speak." After spending the day chatting, "Night came on [and] he said he must go up stairs and be locked in prison." With Joel gone, the façade of conviviality was over and Dothe scribbled in her diary "Oh that dear brother" and described how she and Hannah "cried ourselves to sleep."[94]

Within days of this visit, Joel escaped from prison. His trials continued, however, as did the anguish of his sister Dothe. For fifteen years, even after she was a married woman with her own family, Dothe confided to her diary her private thoughts and in entry after entry she worried about and lamented her separation from her brother. For instance, in 1784 when her other brother, Leman, was also gone from home, she wrote, "Oh, how we scattered. Oh, my brother." "I don't hear a word from my absent brothers," she continued, "they are gone. Alas they are, they are gone. I forbear this is too much for me to forbear." She worried when she did not hear from Joel when he was in New York, in England, and in "Canady ... that distant wilderness." And when Joel returned in 1792 to visit his children, who were being raised by one of his sisters, Dothe wrote with anguish: "So good a man so unfortunate: O my brother." Even Nancy, her young daughter, knew that "Mamma would cry when Uncle went home." In one of her moments of anguish at the scattering of her family as a result of the Revolution, Dothe communed with her first and dearest female companion, her long dead mother, "buried in my fathers field." "Oh could that dear parent see her children mourning round her grave, could she see or know the many misfortunes that attend the family she once loved and left," she wrote. "Could she know what we bear? What we feel? It would be too oh too much for a tender parent's feeling heart." She concluded, "She is gone. I hope it is well for her."[95]

In conclusion, Loyalist women who were left behind when the men in their lives fled had to bear various kinds of burdens. Many lost their property – the main reason why most had come to the frontier. They also had to contend with the seizure or theft of valued personal belongings and the violence of mobs and other unofficial bodies. These realities alone could produce stress, but anxiety was also increased because of the instability and unpredictability in their lives. The men who had been their emotional companions and had headed their households were gone or no longer in control. Instead, the fate of the women and their children rested with Patriot committees or with mobs whose behaviour was even more unpredictable.

Living on the frontiers of a major theatre of war, Loyalist women faced difficulties and challenges far more serious than those confronting most Patriot women. Yet they also had more scope to make a valuable contribution to the war. The idea that women lived as subordinates within a male directed household was undermined by the reality of the Revolutionary War on the New York frontier. With the men in their lives gone, the women had to make decisions and act on their own. Their location on the frontiers meant that they were drawn into the war effort. By passing on intelligence, housing, feeding, or supplying raiding parties, or by taking over the Loyalist activities of their escaped husbands, these women were active and invaluable participants in the Revolutionary War. A measure of their military value was the attention they attracted from the Patriots.

The Patriot committees punished Loyalist women in part because of their husband's treasonous behaviour but also because they posed a threat in their own right. Patriot committees carefully watched Loyalist families' activities and sometimes removed them from areas within easy reach of raiding expeditions from the north. In 1776, after Sir John Johnson and his followers had fled to Canada, the Patriots considered the "Removal" of the "female old and infirm" left behind, a scheme that was abandoned only because of the "Unnecessary Expence." The next year, however, the wives of two well-known Loyalists were removed from their homes on the frontier, where they would have been in a position to communicate with their husbands, to "some interior part of the colonies"; the women had to pay the costs of removing their families and were allowed to take only clothing and basic necessities with

them. In 1778, when a group of Tryon County Loyalists, probably trying to escape the surveillance of the local Patriots, moved to the Manor
of Rensselaerwyck, the local Patriot committee found out about their
arrival and gave them ten days to leave. Another group of Loyalist families living on the frontier on Jessups Patent was ordered in 1781 to "re-
move from thence with all their Effects down into the Interior parts of
the Country, without delay" and "all Males of 16 years old and upwards" were ordered to appear before the Commission for Detecting
and Defeating Conspiracies. And when a group of Loyalist women
moved to the outlying settlement of Saratoga, the same committee ordered that the women "be all brought down below Saratoga and ordered there to Remain as they will answer the Contrary at their peril."[96]

But Patriot harassment accomplished little. Loyalist women continued to threaten the security of the colonies, and some of them, deprived
of their source of income, became public charges. There was really only
one solution to the problems posed by the Loyalist women – they would
have to leave, not just their homes and their communities, but also their
country. The Loyalist women would be forced to follow the men in their
lives. Fighting the war and enduring harassment was the first stage in
their experience as refugees. Leaving home was the second.

3 Leaving Home

For heavens sake, my dear Mr. Munro, send me some relief by the first safe hand. Is there no possibility of your sending for us? If there is no method fallen upon we shall perish, for you can have no idea of our sufferings here; Let me once more intreat you to try every method to save your family; my heart is so full it is ready to break; adieu my Dearest John, may God Almighty bless preserve and protect you, that we may live to see each other is the constant prayer of your affectionate tho' afflicted wife ... P.S. The Childer's kind love to you.

Mary Munro to John Munro[1]

The Burgoyne expedition assembled in Quebec in June 1777 to invade the American colonies was described as "a spectacular pageant, brilliant in its color, light and motion, thrilling in its purpose and intention." The flotilla of boats that made its way up the Richelieu River stretched for more than a mile and included birchbark Indian canoes, gunboats, the batteaux transporting the troops, and the frigate *Royal George*, carrying General John Burgoyne, his staff, and probably his mistress. Among the 9,000 people were the brightly painted Indians, some Canadians, Loyalists, and British redcoats as well as Highlanders in their kilts, German mercenaries in their deep blue uniforms, and a motley crew of women, children, and other camp followers. Adding to the pageantry was the music: the Scots playing their bagpipes, the Germans their brass instruments, and the English and Loyalists their fifes and drums.[2]

As the expedition moved south with the aim of dividing the colonies and breaking the back of the revolt, Loyalists and Patriots made their preparations. To the Patriots, the troops were invaders and they prepared by summoning the militia, removing civilians from the frontiers, and imprisoning those whose loyalty was suspect. To the Loyalists, the troops were liberators and some rushed to join or help Burgoyne while others waited in their homes. All had high hopes about what a Burgoyne victory would mean – an end to the committees that harassed Loyalists, imprisoned them, or confiscated their property. It would also mean that Loyalists could once again live in their homes in peace under stable and familiar institutions and leaders.

Loyalist women were involved in various aspects of the expedition and for many their lives were changed dramatically by the events. Lady Johnson and her children accompanied Sir John Johnson as he marched under General Barry St Leger through Oswego to Fort Stanwix, close to the Johnson's former home. As the contingent laid siege to the rebel-held fort, Patriot militiamen were marching to relieve it. Molly Brant, who was at Canajoharie, discovered the Patriot plans. She responded by sending Indian runners to warn St Leger. As a result of Molly's efforts, the Patriots were ambushed at nearby Oriskany, an exchange that left over 400 dead, many of them Indians. Among the victims was John Hare, a lieutenant in the Indian Department, whose wife and children had already suffered harassment and property losses because of his military service. Although the Patriots were defeated at Oriskany, St Leger was forced to retreat. The dream of Lady Johnson and others of returning home was shattered and women such as Margaret Hare were left widowed.

The tragic fate of another woman also helped turn the tide against the ill-fated main expedition under Burgoyne as it moved south from Lake Champlain to the Hudson River. Jane McCrea, a seventeen-year-old from a staunchly Patriot frontier family, was engaged to David Jones, a Loyalist soldier accompanying Burgoyne. Jane and David planned to rendezvous at Fort Edward as the army travelled south along the Hudson. The plan was that she would be taken to the army by friendly Indians and she and David would be reunited and married. The plan went tragically awry when the Indians began to fight about whose captive she was. Jane was killed, scalped, and mutilated by Indians accompanying Burgoyne. The brutal killing of an innocent young woman lent substance to the Patriot claim that Burgoyne was not a liberator but an invader and rekindled colonial fears of savage Indian raids on the frontiers.[3]

The murder of Jane McCrea was followed by major military defeats. After capturing Ticonderoga, Burgoyne became bogged down in building a road to the Hudson River rather than using Lake George, which meant that the Patriots had more time to organize their forces and supply shortages became a problem. The seizure of supplies from the local population again added substance to the idea that Burgoyne was an invader, and indeed it was this very kind of activity that led to the British defeat at Bennington, Vermont – a key engagement of the campaign.

The battle at Bennington began when a British contingent sent to the town to seize supplies ran into a Patriot force. It pitted friends and relatives against each other since many of the Loyalist soldiers involved came from the area. During the heat of the battle, the commander of the Queen's Rangers, John Peters, was attacked by an assailant who cried, "Peters you damned Tory, I have got you." As Peters later wrote, the foe "rushed on me with his bayonet, which entered just below my left breast, but was turned by the bones." Peters recognized the man as Jeremiah Post, "an old schoolmate and play fellow and a cousin of my wife." "Though his bayonet was in my body," Peters wrote sadly, "I felt regret at being obliged to destroy him."[4] The rout at Bennington in August foreshadowed the ultimate defeat and surrender of Burgoyne's army two months later at Saratoga. The mighty army of liberation had failed in its mission and this profoundly affected the lives of many future eastern Ontario Loyalists.

The Burgoyne expedition was a turning-point in these people's lives because it led to the exile of so many of them. In 1777 large numbers of Loyalists declared their colours and for most there was no going back. Hundreds of Mohawk and other Indians fought alongside Burgoyne and St Leger, exposing themselves and their families to savage Patriot counterattacks on their settlements. Of 264 Loyalist claimants who specified when they joined the British-Loyalist side, 140 or over 50 per cent stated that it was in 1777 and most specifically mentioned the Burgoyne expedition. Some fought with the army; many others helped by acting as guides or pilots or by providing supplies. Still others were rounded up by the Patriots to prevent them from assisting Burgoyne. With Burgoyne's defeat these people were marked, and it was only a matter of time before they had to flee.

The women, left behind in the colonies after the men fled to British lines, had to take a much more active role in running the farm and in making decisions for the family. During the war traditional relationships and lines of authority were disrupted; as Mary Beth Norton puts it, "The line between male and female behaviour ... became less defined ... [and] traditional sex roles did not provide adequate guidelines for conduct under all circumstances."[5] Women could and did do things that they might never have dreamed of doing earlier and their actions were considered socially acceptable, if for no other reason than that the boundaries of socially acceptable behaviour are more flexible in wartime than in peacetime.

The effects of Burgoyne's failure were especially evident in the case of the Indians. During the expedition, Indians had aligned themselves with the British in large numbers. Over 500 Western and St Lawrence-area Indians accompanied Burgoyne and the Mohawk were among the 600 to 800 Indians with St Leger.

Tensions in the alliance between the British and Indians were reflected during the expedition and after. From the British point of view, the Indians were unreliable, disappearing for key battles and preferring pillaging to fighting. One British officer wrote: "It is mortifying to reflect that the immense Treasure lavished upon these people should have so little effect."[6] As well, some British officers were concerned about the atrocities committed by the Indians, such as the murder of Jane Mc-Crea, and their helplessness to stop or punish the Indians for their actions. British officials such as Haldimand also complained that the Indians demanded expensive luxuries, such as "Tinsel, Lace ... Gold and Silver"; the Mohawk, he claimed, were "not so fond of gawdy colours, as of good and substantial things," being "passionately fond of silver ornaments and neat arms." Another officer complained that, when they were drunk, Indians ruined their blankets or gave them away. A 1777 ordinance prohibited the selling of strong liquors to Indians in Quebec and the buying of their arms or clothing.[7] The Indians could have pointed out that the enormous expenses of the Indian Department were mainly caused by the corruption of the whites in charge; even Superintendent Guy Johnson was involved in a scandal over fraud. Moreover, the effectiveness of the department was undermined by jealousies and squabbling among the white Indian agents.

As if all this were not enough, the British desire to control the Indians clashed with the latter's belief that they were, in the words of Sir John Johnson, "free and independent people, liable to no Subjection or Subordination to any power." The Mohawk leadership rallied their tribesmen to fight with the British, but they saw themselves as allies rather than as subordinates subject to British military discipline. One example of the Mohawk's independent spirit was their wish to continue the custom of adopting prisoners into their tribes. The British insisted, however, that all prisoners be turned over to them and the governor of Quebec used paternalistic language when he explained that "all the king's undutiful Children [the Patriots] who are taken in it [the war] ... must be delivered up to be corrected by their Father as he shall think fit."[8] The Mohawk also were upset that their counsel often went unheeded. After Burgoyne's defeat the Mohawk pressured the British to garrison Fort Ontario on the Oswego River to help protect Indian villages and provide a refuge for Indian women and children in the event of a Patriot attack. The British ignored this advice, with devastating consequences for the Indians.[9]

The Indians who sided with the British in 1777 suffered greatly. The Patriots in the Mohawk valley, smarting over their defeat at Oriskany, took their anger out on the nearby Mohawk Indians. Indian property was looted, their livestock carried off, their crops destroyed, and their agricultural equipment stolen. Often more prosperous than the white inhabitants, the Mohawk saw their corn, vegetables, farm implements, wagons, sleighs, and window-glass stolen. Captain John Deserontyon, a Fort Hunter Mohawk, catalogued his losses as follows:

82 acres of rich flat Land commonly called the Mohawk Flatts:
   @ 100% New York Curry   410.00.0
Grain of difft. kinds left in the Barn & Barracks   51.15.00
House & Barn   125.00.00
a 4 Wheel Waggon   22.00.00
Plough & Harrow   11.00.00
Pleasure & Wood Sled   18.00.00
3 Horses   37.00.00
2 Cows   10.00.00
5 fatning Hogs   12.00.00
10 Beaver Traps   10.00.00
several Suits of Cloaths broad Cloth &c   38.00.00
4 Scarlet Blankets wth. Silverwork & Ribbns   14.00.00
6 blue Stroud Blankts do do   10.00.00
6 Kettles   12.00.00
5,000 Wampum in Bolts &c   25.00.00
Bed, Bedstead & Curtains   27.00.00
pewter Basens & plates   4.06.00
Total   836.11.00[10]

Molly Brant was a favourite target because of her role in warning the Loyalist-Indian expedition of the approach of the Patriot militia at Oriskany. She was insulted, her home was ravaged, and her possessions seized or destroyed. Molly and her children eventually had to flee to Cayuga, where they were welcomed by Indian relatives, and they then moved to Niagara.[11]

After the defeat of the Burgoyne expedition, the Mohawk wavered in their support of the British. Situated as they were between the British in Canada and the Americans, the Mohawk were bound to continue to suffer heavy losses if they remained aligned with the British. Moreover, not all of the Six Nations supported the British; some, such as the Oneida, fought for the Patriots, while the allegiance of others fluctuated. When the Americans sent peace overtures to the Indians, neutrality loomed as a very real possibility.

At this point, the intervention of Molly Brant and Sarah McGinnis was decisive. Molly remained among her people in the Indian villages in 1777 and she rebuked the Indian leaders who wanted to sue for peace. As Indian agent Daniel Claus, a son-in-law of Sir William Johnson, reported, Molly went to Cayuga and "fixed herself and her family at the principal chief's house." At the Council with the Seneca, she reminded the Indians of their former "great Friendship & Attachment" to Sir William Johnson, whom "she never mentions but with Tears in her Eyes which affects the Indians greatly." The Indians promised "to remain true to their tie with Sir William & support the British vigorously & steadily" and "to steadily avenge her Wrongs & Injuries for she is in every Respect Considered & esteemed by them as Sir William's Relict and One word from her goes farther with them [the Six Nations] than a thousand from any white Man without Exception who in general must purchase their Interest at a high rate."[12]

Sarah McGinnis had fled to Canada in 1777 after she and her family were harassed and imprisoned by the Patriots, but she was persuaded to return to Indian country in the winter of 1777 to help counter the negative effects of Burgoyne's defeat. On her arrival in one of the central villages of the Six Nations, the Indians "flocked to her from the remotest villages and thanked her for coming ... to direct and advise them in that critical time." Soon after her arrival, the Patriots sent messages to the Iroquois "with a most exagerrated account of General Burgoyne's disaster" and "belts" inviting them to join the Patriots along with "threats" in case the Indians refused. In response to the Patriot overtures, the Indians "consulted with" Sarah and sought her "opinion and advice ... then after that with an Authority and privilege allowed to women of Consequence only among Indians, [she] seized upon and cancelled the [Patriot] Belts, telling them such bad news came from an evil Spirit and must endanger their peace and union as long as it was in their sight and therefore must be buried underground ..."[13] The crisis passed. Largely because of Molly Brant and Sarah McGinnis, the Mohawk maintained their alliance with the British.

The Mohawk paid the full price for their decision in 1779 when the Patriots launched a punitive expedition against them. Over forty villages were levelled and more than 160,000 bushels of corn and other crops destroyed. The Mohawk were crushed; during the winter of 1779–80 some froze to death and others starved. They were also angry at the British for not joining the fight against the Patriot expedition and, as noted above, for not garrisoning the fort on the Oswego River as they had requested. Once again Molly Brant and Sarah McGinnis were called into action. Molly realized that her place was with her people; she wrote, "Her staying away at this critical time may prove very injurious to her character thereafter, being at the head of a Society of Six Nations Matrons who have a great deal to say among the young men in particular in time of war." Colonel Guy Johnson agreed that "she will be of great use to the King's service at this time." Another Indian agent, Daniel Claus, persuaded Sarah to return with the Indians because, as he explained, "her presence ... would be very consequential on the present crisis on acct. of the great esteem she was always held in by those people for a number of years past and she was of great service among them in 1777 and 1778."[14] Molly and Sarah once again acted as vital linchpins in the British-Mohawk alliance.

Ironically, the devastation of the Indian villages did not realize Patriot hopes of demoralizing the Indians and making the frontiers safe; in fact, the destruction did the opposite. The events of 1779 only stiffened the resolve of Indian warriors to gain vengeance by launching raids on the American frontier. As for Indian families, with their homes destroyed and their crops decimated, they became dependent on the British for survival. Like other Loyalist women and children, the Indians were forced to flee to Canada and by September 1777 there were over 5,000 at Niagara looking to the British for housing, clothing, and food.[15]

Necessity caused many white women and children Loyalists to flee to British bases for refuge. Some, such as Samuel Perry's wife and seven children, accompanied their husbands or fathers to Canada. However, the journey through the wilderness was long and difficult and posed dangers for women and children. Mary Johnson, a daughter of the late Sir William Johnson, was pregnant in 1775 when she accompanied her husband, Guy, to Canada. Mary, however, did not survive the trip; she died in childbirth before reaching her destination. When Mrs Buel and her nine children accompanied her husband, Timothy, to Canada after Burgoyne's defeat, she suffered many trials. The family hid in the woods for fifteen days, travelling at night and hiding by day, "always in Danger of being taken and hanged by ... worse than Savage Countrymen or Scalpt by the Savages"; by the time they reached Canada, many of the family were ill from the rigours of the trip.

Loyalist women were sometimes left behind in the hope of saving the family's property, a strategy that usually failed as Patriots assumed that wives shared in their husband's guilt. Many others stayed behind when the men had to flee with little or no warning and it was uncertain as to whether their families could be housed and cared for at the British bases. Patrick McNiff explained that he left his family behind because he was "unable for want of clothes and money to bring them with him in[to] a strange country without any money or friends."[16]

Notwithstanding the hazards, most Loyalist women remained in the colonies to run the family farm or business and care for their families. Although many Patriot women also had to take more responsibility for the farm and family, there was one crucial difference between Patriot and Loyalist families. While Patriot men were away from home either fighting the war or helping the cause in other ways, most could return home without fearing for their lives. Many Loyalist women, however, were left behind enemy lines. It was, therefore, difficult and dangerous for their husbands to come home and risk being charged with treason, mobbed, or even killed. Thus, in practice, Loyalist women were even more likely than their Patriot counterparts to have to make decisions on their own, even though in theory males remained the heads of the household.

The gap between theory and practice was illustrated nicely in the correspondence between Alexander McDonell, stationed in Halifax, and Susannah, his wife stranded behind enemy lines in New York. While stationed in Halifax, Alexander tried to continue in his role as family head by sending detailed instructions to Susannah about running the property and household. But the many changes of the Revolutionary years and his prolonged absence meant that Alexander was out of touch with the realities of his family's life in New York. He instructed Susannah to "endeavour to get hard cash" for debts. Obviously unaware of the way in which Loyalist families were being treated, he added, "The people surely about you will not be such Enemys to themselves as to offer you any Violence because they may depend on being severely Checked for it, in the End." He expressed regret, in 1777, that a relative had been "idle enough to take Congress Money for the Mortgage," oblivious to the fact that the Patriots were forcing people to accept "Congress Money" and punishing those who refused.[17]

He also advised Susannah to "keep the house and Garden and Lett the rest of the farm on shares to some honest Clever fellow ... Reserving to yourself, one, two, or three Milch Cows, grazing." He later instructed her to give the house up to the British if they needed it, advising her of the appropriate rent. While Alexander was telling Susannah in minute detail what to do with the property and how to run the farm, the Patriots had possession of both and were quartering their troops in his house.[18]

As well as having to take on added decision-making responsibilities because they were behind enemy lines, Loyalist women faced other burdens not shared by their Patriot counterparts. The Revolutionary years brought hardship to both Loyalist and Patriot women who had to contend with food shortages, rationing, inflation, and cash shortages. At the same time, armies on both sides often left in their wake destruction, disease, and death. But many Loyalist women also lost the very foundations of their livelihood when they had their property confiscated or their buildings destroyed. Others lost their belongings or were jailed. All were eventually wrenched from the familiar and comforting surroundings of their world – their homes, their extended families, their neighbours, and their communities. Arrangements had to be made for their departure and finally there was the exhausting and dangerous trip to British bases in New York City or Canada.

Loyalist women, coping with the reality or the threat that Patriots would confiscate their property, struggled to provide for their families in the turbulence of the Revolution. Many turned first to their families for support. In a society lacking other institutions to provide social assistance, mutual support among family members was essential. Individuals naturally looked to extended family members when in trouble. However, as already noted, family ties were especially important to eastern Ontario Loyalists, many of whom were members of cohesive ethnic communities or of groups who had migrated to the frontier together.

For some Loyalist women, such as Sarah Bottum Sherwood, the family-support system worked well to shelter them somewhat from the trauma of the Revolution. In 1774, at the age of twenty, Sarah left her parents home in Shaftsbury, Vermont, to join her new husband, Justus, seven years her senior, at their recently built cabin at New Haven on the frontier of Charlotte County. Within a year, a son was born and Justus was elected town clerk. But Justus's unwillingness to sign a Patriot oath and the allegation that he was providing intelligence to the British made the Sherwoods a target for harassment. In August 1776 an armed band of Patriots charged into their cabin, ransacked their home, broke into chests, and scattered their private papers. Soon after the first band left, another came and kept the Sherwoods prisoners in their own home for a month, forcing them to feed and care for their captors. Then Justus was hauled before the local Patriot committee and sentenced to life in prison in the greatly feared Simsbury Mines in Connecticut. Fortunately, he escaped his captors and made his way along with forty followers to the British base at Crown Point. Sarah was left behind in their cabin on the frontier with a toddler and an infant.[19]

Soon after Justus's flight, Sarah went to live with her parents and then later they moved to her cabin to help her with the farm and children. Title to the land was transferred to her brother to prevent the Patriots from confiscating it. Justus managed to steal back to visit his wife in April 1777 and she became pregnant during his stay, an embarrassing situation for a wife supposedly living separate from her husband. In October 1777 Sarah learned that Justus had been wounded and she decided she had to join him. With the help of her family, she went to the

Vermont Council of Safety and asked permission to leave, a request that was granted. Sarah Bottum Sherwood had escaped some of the worst horrors of the Revolution because of support from her family and probably because her husband had been a supporter of the Green Mountain Boys, the dominant faction in Vermont in the 1770s.

Many other Loyalist women who would later settle around Cataraqui were not so fortunate. Maria Young, of Dutch ancestry, was living with her husband, Henry, and their seven children as tenants on the Patroon of Rensselaerwyck in New York when the Revolution broke out. Henry fled to Canada with the Jessups in 1776, leaving behind his family, although his oldest son, Daniel, later ran away from his grandparents' home and made his way through the wilderness to join his father in Canada. The family home was raided by a Patriot band and stripped of everything; because even the Bible was stolen, some of the children were never sure of their exact ages. In September 1780 Maria and her young children were ordered to leave the colony and, when an appeal of the decision by her and another female relative failed, she turned to her father for protection. Although her parents took in her oldest son, there is no evidence that they helped Maria. On the contrary, there is evidence that she was struggling. In September 1780 she borrowed £6 10s on a promissory note and the next day she wrote to "Mr. Henry Young Liuftent in Capt. Peak's Company ... You bee pleast to lete the Bearer have five gineys wich i have boreed from Elisabuth Router," another Loyalist women whose husband had fled. Maria's mark ended the letter.[20]

Some Loyalist women who asked their families for support were rejected and even betrayed by them. Mary Meyers, also of Dutch ancestry, lived on Cooney's Patent, New York, with her German husband, Hans Waltimeyer (or John Walden Meyers). His family split during the Revolution, with only Hans and his brother-in-law supporting the Loyalists. Despite her Patriot sympathies, Hans's mother warned him in 1777 of his danger and he escaped from his home leaving Mary with seven children, the oldest being eleven and the youngest one week old. Mary eked out an existence by herself for about a year until her cousin, who had been entrusted with taking care of the farm, arrived and announced his intention to take over the land for himself. Mary had no choice but to leave with her young family. She worked with another Loyalist woman left alone on the frontier to get permission from the Patriot committee to go to the British base at New York City.[21]

Mary Munro, another eastern Ontario Loyalist, was similarly betrayed by her family when she needed them most. In 1760 young Mary, whose maiden name was Brower, married a recent Scots Presbyterian immigrant, John Munro. The decision was wise, for the twenty-nine-year-old Munro could provide a comfortable living for his wife. He received land for his military service during the Seven Years War, he and Mary's family joined together in 1765 to apply for even more land, and John became a local justice of the peace. By 1775 Mary and John had eight children, a comfortable home in Shaftsbury, Vermont, a barn, stables, and saw and grist mills as well as thousands of acres of undeveloped land.

But then the Revolution intruded into their lives. In 1775 John was enlisting soldiers for the British when one of his recruits was captured and forced to confess. The Albany Committee of Correspondence sent men to the Munro home to arrest John; they also ransacked his house. John was released but he was soon retaken and imprisoned, often in chains, in Connecticut and Albany. In 1777, with a death sentence hanging over his head, Munro escaped and joined Burgoyne.

Mary Munro was left to provide for her eight children when her husband was taken from their home in 1776. Because her husband had been unpopular with the Green Mountain Boys, the dominant faction in Vermont, her property "became the prey of every person around" and soon she was in "great distress, having been plundered of most of ... [her] effects." In August 1777, in the wake of the Burgoyne expedition, the Vermont Council of Safety ordered that all of John Munro's property and "moveable effects" were to be seized, except "Two Cows & such other effects as are wanted for the Support of said Munro's Family," which were to be left with the "Woman, Taking a proper account of them." An earlier order by the same body had allowed her to keep her "cattle sheep and swine" and to go to Bennington if she wanted to retrieve her riding horses. Another edict in early 1778 allowed her to continue in her home until further orders.[22]

Mary Munro was obviously leading a haphazard and stressful existence, uncertain as to what the local Patriots planned for her in the future. She was running the farm and caring for her children by herself. She had no source of income and the Patriots threatened to "retaliate" against her if her husband appeared in a raiding party from Canada. It was under these circumstances that she turned to her family in Schenectady for help, "in hopes of meeting Consolation and parental Affection." Instead she found "reproaches and bitter invectives." Her family not only refused to help her but took advantage of her husband's absence to take title to much of the Munro property. Spurned by her own family, Mary had to fend for herself. She had had the foresight to bury some valuable "plate" as the Patriots were seizing the rest of her possessions and she dug this up and sold it to provide for her family. When that money ran out, she began appealing to friends of the family and was finally helped by the family of a soldier serving with her husband.

In a heart-rending letter to John, who was in Canada, she wrote of the betrayal by her own family:

My dear John
I hope when you receive these few lines they may find you in good health. Your Dear Children are all well. As for myself, I am in a poor state of health and very much distresst. I must leave my house in a very short time and God knows where I shall get a place to put my head in, for my own relations are my greatest enemies, the mills they have had a long time in their possession – likewise all their tenants' houses and lands. They have distresst me beyond expression. I have scarcely a mouthful of bread for myself or children.[23]

As well as struggling to survive the turmoil of the Revolution, Loyalist women such as Mary Munro had to accept what in the eighteenth century was a very bitter fate – they had been abandoned by their own families.

Faced with the loss of their property and the absence of their husbands, Loyalist women had to devise strategies to provide for their families and, if all else failed, make arrangements to leave for British lines. In 1772 Margaret Swartz married Michael Grass, a Palatine immigrant saddle-maker who had moved from Pennsylvania to the Mohawk valley in the early 1770s. Five years after their marriage, Michael fled to British lines and the Grasses' property and furniture was seized and auctioned off as Margaret and her three young children watched. In a desperate attempt to support her family, Margaret sold some of Michael's belongings – "saddlers tools and Sticks for Nine gunnees, saddle bags and some sheep Sticks for two gunnees." However, when the Schenectady Committee of Safety learned of the sale, Margaret was ordered to return the money to the purchaser since the confiscated Grass estate belonged to the state. Unable to provide for herself, Margaret and her children had no choice but to seek permission to join Michael in New York City.[24]

There are other examples of Loyalist families struggling to survive in the face of great hardships. The sixteen-year-old daughter of John McDonell, a Scots Loyalist from Tryon County, "was obliged to hire herself to an Old Dutch woman to spin in order to prevent starving." A group of New York Loyalist women established rudimentary shelters and did some farming on the frontier, near Saratoga. In 1780 they petitioned the Patriots for permission to go to Canada, but the next year they were still on the frontier and regarded as a serious enough threat that they were ordered to move to the interior.[25] There was also the case of the Elizabeth Bowman, who squatted with her husband and six children on land along the Susquehanna River and later resettled in the Cataraqui area.

When the Patriots plundered her home and took away her husband and eldest son, Elizabeth was so distraught that she gave birth prematurely to her seventh child and was left in a weakened condition to care for her large family. She lived through the winter only because of the help of friendly Indians. In the spring, she moved to the Mohawk River and joined other Loyalist women in growing corn and potatoes to survive. When the British rescued them, just before the onset of another winter, there were five women, thirty-one children, and only one pair of shoes among them.[26]

Because Loyalist women were often deprived of the property and other possessions that formed the basis of their livelihood, their challenges went beyond coping to sustain their families within a familiar setting. Instead, they had to improvise and adapt against a backdrop of the uncertainties of committee decisions about the future disposition of their property and the fate of their families. The Revolution also drove a wedge between the women and their most valued relationships with friends, neighbours, and even parents.

But these Loyalist women were not only victims of the Revolution, they were also heroic actors in the drama. Left behind in enemy territory in the midst of a major theatre of the war, they displayed courage, ingenuity, and determination, whether in participating actively in the military side of the Revolution, struggling to care for themselves and their families, or, when all other options were closed to them, appealing to Patriot committees for permission to leave. Their public and assertive role in assuming what were generally considered to be male responsibilities was illustrated by the wife of the Tryon County sheriff, who, when an exchange was arranged for her Loyalist husband, undertook the negotiations with the British. Consider, too, Isabel Parker, who "aided and succoured his Majesty's Scouts on secret service by procuring them provisions and intelligence and encouraging Sundry persons to join his Majesty's service at her great expense, peril and risk." Isabel also interceded with the governor of Quebec on behalf of her son, who had been in the British secret service and had been arrested by the Patriots.[27]

Some Loyalist women even ventured into the political realm by petitioning those in authority about their dire circumstances. Petitioning was a long-established British constitutional device by which subjects could appeal to government, but before the 1770s it was almost unheard of for women to take an active political role by this means. The Revolution changed that for both Patriot and Loyalist women. Individual petitions from Patriot and Loyalist women, usually widows, were common. Group petitions, however, were rare and suggested a more overt form of political activity.[28] While an individual petition involved appealing to those in authority to address the specific circumstances of an individual family, group petitioners called attention to a generalized problem which those in authority were being asked to address.

Loyalist women in Tryon County addressed at least two undated group petitions to the local Patriot committees. One, signed by nine women – only two of whom could write their own names – was on behalf of "many others who are in the same Distressful situation who living at a distance is not able to subscribe their names." Margaret Hare, whose property had been looted and taken by the Patriots and whose husband had been killed at Oriskany, headed the list and her situation was typical. Margaret and the other women had been "left by our Husbands and our Effects sold" and they were "reduced to the greatest distress imaginable." Dire need was also the reason for the other petition from seven female Loyalists in Germantown who had been "left in the wretched State of Widowhood, with a number of Fatherless Children." Distress may have been more acute for Loyalist women in Tryon County because it was a major target for Loyalist-Indian raids, leaving the tolerance for Loyalists low, and an area where whole families were Loyalists, which made it harder for women left behind to get help from other family members.[29]

The Tryon County petitioners posed a problem for the Patriot committee members. The women were unable to provide for themselves and their children and they appealed to the humanity of the Patriots. One group of petitioners wanted "People of Christian Principle to behold the distresses of our hapless children" and the signers of the other stated that they were "humbly leaving our Selves, and our fatherless Children, to Your Honour's Goodness and Compassion." What the women wanted was either to be sent to their husbands or to be given "Relief," specifically provisions. As the second group declared, with "winter coming upon us ... we must certainly perish without some assistance."[30] The women petitioners effectively outlined the choices that the Patriots had: either the women had to be provided for, since knowingly allowing innocent children to starve or freeze to death was not acceptable, or the women had to be sent to their husbands.

The choice was not an easy one for Patriot leaders. Sending families to the soldiers would raise the morale of the troops and allow intelligence to be passed to the enemy. Women coming to British bases brought local newspapers, which sometimes contained information about where Patriot troops were located or where cattle were being hidden. On the other hand, the women and children posed a serious military threat to the Patriots by remaining in their communities to gather intelligence and assist Loyalist-Indian raiding parties. Moreover, some of the women were destitute and the Patriot fear was that they would become charges upon communities already struggling to fight a Revolution and civil war.

The ambivalence of the Patriots about what to do with Loyalist women and children in the 1770s was reflected in committee decisions. If Loyalist women applied to the local Patriot committee for permission to leave and join their husbands, usually the requests were granted and after 1777 there was a steady stream of Loyalist women to British bases in Canada or New York City. But there were instances in which such requests were denied or granted on certain conditions. Mary Herkimer, for instance, sought permission to join her husband, Johan Jost, after his escape to Canada. However, the local committee replied that only the governor could authorize her request and that she could leave only after Patriot prisoners being held in Canada were returned. Margaret Hare wanted to come to Canada after her husband was killed at Oriskany and her property destroyed, but, as she put it, "she was kept by one of the Rebel's Commiss. ... Says he stopped her as an hostage." Other women, especially in Tryon County, were used as pawns – the Patriots would allow them to go to Canada only in exchange for the release of Patriots held by the British. Such exchanges had to be negotiated with British officials who were not always anxious to have women and children at their bases, especially in Canada.[31]

There were several reasons why British officials might prefer to have Loyalist families remain in the colonies rather than having them at British bases. What British military leaders needed and wanted at their bases was able-bodied men who could raid the frontiers, build fortifications, or spy on the Patriots. What they did not need were women, children, and other non-combatants who had to be fed, clothed, and housed. There were shortages of essential supplies in New York City and especially in Canada, where housing had to be constructed and food often imported by way of the St Lawrence River, frozen for part of the year. For the British Loyalist families would be more valuable as spies behind enemy lines, where they could pass on intelligence or provide invaluable assistance to raiding parties.[32]

The governor of Quebec revealed his view of Loyalist women and children in a 1780 letter in which he mused about the possibility of a Patriot conspiracy which involved "taking advantage of [the] desire to rescue families." The Patriots, he feared, might be plotting to encourage exchanges so as "to pour into the Province a number of useless Consumers of Provisions." In calling women and children Loyalists "useless Consumers of Provisions," the governor was reflecting his view of them as "useless" since they could perform no useful military role in Quebec and at the same time consumed precious supplies. Rather than bringing destitute families to Quebec, the governor preferred sending money to them in the colonies. In the colonies, the families did not consume limited food supplies and were a military asset.[33]

So the Patriots might be negotiating with the British about exchanging Loyalist families for Patriot prisoners while the British were reluctant at best to bring the families to Canada. Sometimes unfortunate Loyalist families were caught in the middle; the Stuarts were one such family.

In 1775, just as the trouble between Loyalists and Patriots was brewing in Tryon County, the thirty-five-year-old John Stuart, missionary to the Mohawks, brought his young bride, Jane OKill, to live with him on the frontier. Stuart, with his impressive educational credentials as well as his love of the classics and fine music might have seemed out of place at the outpost of Fort Hunter, and Jane, from a prosperous Philadelphia family, certainly did not immediately blend into the surroundings. But John had come to teach and minister to the Mohawk and their support for him was wholehearted; as the tensions in the area mounted, they warned the Patriots not to harass the Stuart family. The warning was needed, because the Patriots were suspicious of an Anglican minister who continued to pray for the king, even after the Declaration of Independence. They watched him closely.[34]

Matters changed for the worse after the Burgoyne expedition, when the Mohawk were severely punished for their support of the British. The Stuarts did not escape the Patriots' violence. "My Church was plundered by the Rebels," John explained later, "the Pulpit Cloth [was] taken away ... it was afterwards imployed as a Tavern, the Barrel of Rum placed in the Reading Desk – the succeeding Season it was used as a Stable – And now serves as a Fort to protect a Set of as great Villains as ever disgraced Humanity." The Stuarts' home was also ransacked and John, Jane, their infant son, and their slaves were sent on parole to Schenectady. In July 1778 the local Patriot committee denounced the Reverend John Stuart as "a declared Enemy to the Liberties of America" and ordered the family to Connecticut. Although Stuart successfully appealed this decision, he remained miserable. His family was virtually alone – all but three families of his parishioners having joined the British – he was not allowed to preach or teach, and, living as they did on the frontier, they were in danger of being attacked by Indian-Loyalist raiding parties.[35]

During a trip to Philadelphia, a scuffle with a gang of Patriots probably convinced Stuart that returning to his home in Pennsylvania was impossible. More important, he was "fully persuaded" by November 1780 that he could not "possibly live here [Schenectady] secure, either in Regard to our Lives or Property ... this Place is likely to be a Frontier and will probably be burnt." Stuart went on to explain that he had already "lost a considerable Part of my Stock while in Philad. partly by public & partly by private Robbers." For these reasons, Stuart decided to apply for an exchange, which he was sure would be granted, so that he could move to Canada "to maintain my little Family." Stuart's plan was to leave in February or early March.[36]

Stuart's letters provide an intriguing and rare glimpse into the role played by his wife in the decision to leave. Jane had left her family and friends in Philadelphia in 1775 to follow her husband to the frontier. By 1781 she had three young children, she had been forced to move from one frontier location to another as the Patriots' hostility to her husband intensified, she had witnessed the ransacking of her home, and, while her husband was away in Philadelphia, a raiding party had come within miles of their residence in Schenectady. Then in 1780 John decided that there was no choice but to move to an even remoter base in Canada. In Novemeber 1780 Stuart wrote that his decision had the "full Approbation & Consent of Mrs. Stuart." A few months later, Stuart was less emphatic about his wife's support of the decision; he wrote, "Mrs. Stuart submits to it rather from Necessity than Choice, and I Cannot but lament the Necessity that puts her Affection to so severe a Trial." The Stuart marriage, like other late-eighteenth-century unions, was based on affection and respect: John Stuart cared enough about his wife to consult her about his decision and to hope that she supported it. But the relationship was still essentially patriarchal: it was John Stuart who made the decision and it was Jane's duty to "submit." Jane Stuart did not choose to go to Canada; she made her most fateful choice in 1775 when she married John Stuart.[37] She was probably typical of most Loyalist women.

Thus, by late 1780, John Stuart had decided to go to Canada and the Patriots were willing to let him leave under certain conditions; however, it was not obvious that the British wanted him in Canada. The exchange that Stuart had hoped would occur in February or early March did not materialize. Shortly after, Stuart was again hopeful that he and his family would be leaving within days, but his hopes were dashed. Then, in April 1781, he wrote expectantly that they would be leaving in May, but May came and went. The delay, it seems, was caused by the British. The key spy for the British in northern New York, Dr George Smyth of Albany (known by the code-name Hudibrass), had been found out and forced to flee, as had other Loyalists who passed on intelligence. John Stuart was a good choice to replace Smyth. He was intelligent, resourceful, and in a good position to pass on information. Moreover, the Patriots were unlikely to be too brutal to a minister. The rationale used to justify ignoring the Stuarts request to leave the colonies was made explicit in July 1781, when the governor of Quebec instructed Sir John

Johnson not to arrange an exchange for the Stuart family. "The esteem under which the former [Stuart] is held will save him from injury," the governor wrote, "and he may be of service, there are few left in the colonies that can be useful."[38]

Ultimately, however, Stuart's persistence produced results – the family left the colonies in September 1781 and arrived in Canada a month later – but the circumstances of their departure were unusual. Although their property on the frontier was confiscated, much of Jane's property in Philadelphia was retained by the Stuart family. In accord with the patriarchal practices of the late eighteenth century, it was John who managed and made all of the decisions about its disposition. The Stuarts were also allowed to bring their slaves and other personal property with them to Canada. Relative to other Loyalists who later settled in the Cataraqui area, the Stuarts had been treated well and this perhaps explains their greater tolerance for their political foes. On his departure, Stuart declared, "I leave behind no personal, altho many political enemies," and he later made fond references to prominent Patriots who had been friends. Also, unlike many other Loyalists, John Stuart acknowledged his refugee status on his departure. He knew that he would never return to the American colonies. In April 1781 he wrote to his best friend, "I mean to leave Nothing behind me here that may impose any Necessity upon me of returning to this Place (provided such a Thing possible) when the War is at an End."[39] John Stuart displayed insight uncommon to most Loyalists and it probably lessened the anguish he would experience two years later when the Revolution was over and Loyalists had to come to grips with the reality of their status as refugees.

The Stuarts were also fortunate since they did not have to endure the separation from each other that caused a great deal of pain for other Loyalists. There is evidence that some of the men in Quebec suffered severe psychological strain as a result of their separation from their families. Political dissenters who successfully escape to become refugees experience emotional stress of various kinds, often the most tormenting being the despair and guilt associated with having had to leave behind loved ones. Captain John McDonell probably spoke for many Loyalist men when he described his decision to join Sir John Johnson in 1777, leaving "my little property & which was Dearest of all, my weak family to the mercy of enraged Enemies ... "[40] In the context of the late-eighteenth-century patriarchal family structure, men would feel that in leaving their families they were abandoning their responsibilities as household heads. In addition, when Loyalist men spoke about their "weak" or defenceless families, they were expressing the commonly held view that women and children were fragile, dependent creatures who needed to be cared for. Many Loyalist men consequently experienced feelings of guilt.

Maintaining contact with families was one way of dealing with the guilt associated with leaving wives and children to the "mercy" of the Patriots. It was common for the men to steal off to visit their families during raids and letters were carried by scouts between the men and their families. With contact, however, came awareness of the plight of the families. When the men discovered how badly their families were being treated, their anxiety and guilt were heightened. John Munro, for example, was deeply upset by a letter he received from his wife in which she told of her betrayal by her family and pleaded desperately for help,[41] that he included it in his appeal to the governor for some action to rescue families left in the colonies.

Desertion was often the result of anxieties and guilt about the fate of families. A lieutenant in Sir John Johnson's regiment who had served loyally for over a year, upon "receiving Information of the melancholly and distressed situation" of his wife and children," was "induced to Resign his Commission in order to proceed to their Relief"; however, the Burgoyne expedition intervened and the Loyalist soldier was forced to return to Canada. Roger Stevens, a Loyalist who had joined Burgoyne and would later settle in eastern Ontario, applied to return to his home, but the request was denied; so he left anyway. The rebels would "not accept him," however, and he had to go back to Canada where he was arrested for desertion. A court of inquiry found that Stevens had a "sweetheart" in Vermont who caused his "folly," but he was given only a reprimand and a warning since it was decided that he "had no bad intention" in leaving. Thus, even hard-nosed British military officers had some understanding of the unusual emotional pressures that led men to leave the army and return to their families.[42]

Distress at the suffering of their families prompted Loyalist soldiers in Canada to petition the governor to act. In July 1778 John Munro, after receiving Mary's letter, joined with other anxious husbands in a joint petition. As was true of most Loyalist petitions in the 1770s and 1780s, the petition from the soldiers began with a pledge of their loyalty and an account of their devoted service to the British cause. The men had at "the risk of their lives and fortunes, engaged in His Majesty's Service with a view to assist in reducing the present Rebellion in America." The men continued: "Their chief cause of regret is owing to their having left wives and children behind them who are at present under the most calamitous circumstances, being robbed of their all, and left destitute of the common necessaries of life." Hopes of improvement were dim since "nothing is to be expected from the Clemency of our Enemies, but Insults added to distress." Guilt glimmered through references to the

"Sorrow" felt for "Connections" who are "so justly entitled to our tenderest regards." Appealing to the governor's "humanity," the soldiers requested that some "plan" be devised to relieve the families from their "present distress."[43]

A similar petition was sent from the men who had accompanied Sir John Johnson to Montreal in 1776. After outlining how they had "suffer'd much for our Loyalty" and the fact that "the welfare and safety of our Familys depends on their immediate Relief," the men portrayed the helplessness of their families and their own sense of responsibility. The women and children "cannot Subsist without our Aid," and it was the "Paternal Duty" of the men to find some way to rescue them. Another petition came from "late Inhabitants of Albany and Charlotte" counties, "desirous to obtain our Wifes and Little ones out of the Land of Rebellion," who requested a "flag of truce at their own expence."[44]

The paternalistic relationship between Sir John Johnson and his followers surfaced when some of them appealed to their former landlord for help and Johnson in turn pressed the governor for action. Johnson took up his men's cause in March 1780 when he expressed to the governor his mens' "disappointment" that "their families cannot be exchanged" and his own fears that there might be more desertions. Johnson offered to lead an expedition to rescue the families but the governor, although appearing sympathetic, managed to find excuses to delay the proposed rescue missions. What Johnson did get from the governor was an explanation for the repeated postponements. In July 1781 the governor wrote as follows to Sir John: "The necessity of saving provisions prevents anything being done to bring in the families of the soldiers ... " He went on to explain that his "fear of Scarcity" had "induced" him to allow some Patriot prisoners to return to the colonies.[45] In short, keeping the families in Quebec was an expense and inconvenience which the British wanted to avoid.

The McDonells from Tryon County were especially anxious about the treatment of their families and one of them, John McDonell, showed signs of suffering from severe emotional distress. The wives of John and Alexander McDonell had been left in the colonies and harassed by the Patriots since 1775, when the men had fled. Alexander had signed the 1778 petition to the governor and in February 1780 he and John again pleaded with the governor to send some form of relief to their suffering families. Then, after five years of separation, John McDonell was informed that his wife and children had arrived at St Johns. But, when he rushed to meet them, he found that they were not there. He had the "mortification of a disappointment" as well as the knowledge that they were "naked and starving." The heartbreak he experienced at finding that his family had not been rescued from their suffering in the colonies caused something to snap in John McDonell and he poured forth his innermost feelings and frustrations in a letter to the governor's secretary: "I wish you or any man of feeling may never experience what I suffered upon the occasion." Either he wanted an exchange to be arranged or he was willing to lead an expedition to save them or "perish in the attempt." However, "if nothing can be done to obtain their speedy deliverance," he begged "His Excellency to send a party of Savages to bring me their six scalps, tho' it may seem unnatural, yet I assure you I would rather see, or hear them dead than to linger any longer in misery." The anxiety and guilt about loved ones left behind, common to refugees, had apparently exacted a heavy psychological toll on John McDonell.[46]

The pressure from Loyalist soliders to rescue distressed families had minimal effects. In the late 1770s and early 1780s, exchanges were negotiated and flags of truce sent to the colonies to bring needy relatives to Canada, but priority was given to raids that had strictly military purposes. In November 1780 Captain John Munro reported to the governor that, on his recent military expedition to the colonies, he purposely avoided "striking first on Saratoga as directed" because of the "great number of Women & Children which were lodged in the Barracks and having their Husbands in my Detachment, would of course follow them."[47] The McDonells and other Loyalist soldiers might have wanted raiding parties to bring in their wives and children, but military considerations prevailed over humanitarian feelings.

Usually it was the Patriots instead of the British who decided when and if Loyalist women and children would leave home. When the women could no longer provide for themselves or stand the pressure, it was Patriot officials who scrutinized their petitions to join their husbands and laid down the terms of their departure. Often the decision to allow women to leave was prompted by concern about the financial cost involved in permitting them to stay. This concern was nicely summarized by the Albany County Commissioners for Detecting and Defeating Conspiracies, who permitted three Loyalist women to depart "it having appeared to us that those Women are become chargeable to the Districts in which they severally reside and that they together with their Families are subsisted at public Expence." Patriot officials, it seems, did not want communities to take on the burden of caring for indigent Loyalist families and were frequently quite willing to grant permission to such families to leave.[48]

It was just as common, however, for Patriot officials to *order* Loyalist women to leave or for mobs to force them out. During the Burgoyne expedition, the Vermont Council of Safety recounted the various ways in which Loyalist women aided the enemy by providing intelligence or

by housing, feeding, or supplying Loyalist or British soldiers and resolved that: "All such persons as have joined or may hereafter join the
British Troops (& left or may hereafter leave) their wives and families
within this State, Have their wives and families sent to General John
Burgoins [sic] Head Quarters, or some other Branch of the Ministerial
Army, as soon as may be."[49] In 1780 and 1781, as Loyalist raids on the
frontier intensified, so did pressure on Loyalist families. After a devastating raid, families or others associated with the raiders were sometimes driven from their homes. As one petition to the governor from
Loyalist soldiers in Canada stated, after Major Ross's raid near Johnstown in late 1781, "The Rebels finding Husbands and Friends were in
the King's Service here, were all ordered off their Places for their Loyalty
and have been at Skenesborough a Month past in a very distressed Condition, wanting almost every necessary of Life."[50] The Albany County
Commissioners wrote to the governor of New York in July 1780 asking
that "Women whose Husbands are with the Enemy may be sent to the
Enemies Lines" and again, in September 1779, requesting the removal
of Mrs Tuttle whose husband, Stephen, "has gone off to the Enemy
some time ago."[51]

Legislation authorizing the removal of women whose husbands had
joined the British was passed by most colonies. In 1777 the New Jersey
Council of Safety was authorized "to send into the Enemy's Lines such
of the wives and Children of Persons lately residing within this State,
who have gone over to the Enemy, as they shall think Necessary." In
1780, after the Patriots had retaken Philadelphia, Loyalist women left
behind by their husbands in Pennsylvania were also expelled. That July,
New York passed an act ordering the removal of families of those who
had joined the enemy.[52]

In most cases, orders to Loyalist women to leave were inspired by fear
of the military threat they posed to the Revolutionary cause. When Loyalist soldiers came to colonies such as New York to "gain Intelligence
and commit Robberies, Thefts and Murders," they were "concealed and
comforted by their respective Families." After months and even years of
trying to neutralize the military value of Loyalist women by relocating
them from the frontiers or other sensitive areas, charging them individ-
ually with aiding the enemy, and imprisoning or fining them, Patriot officials had to concede by 1780 that Loyalist women were important
enough to the success of the Loyalist-Indian raids that they had to be
moved *en masse*.

The acts expelling Loyalist women are interesting because they show
both the idea of familial guilt and the notion that the women *in their
own right, as individuals* were a threat to the security of the state. Familial guilt was behind the sweeping condemnation of all women whose

husbands had joined the enemy. If the male family head had shown his colours by joining the British, then it was assumed that his wife shared in his guilt and should be removed. Yet commissioners could and did consider individual petitions in which women asked permission to stay. The determining factor was the women's behaviour. Women allowed to stay were individuals who, according to the testimony of their Patriot neighbours, were of "inoffensive Characters who they do not in any Manner conceive dangerous to the Safety of the State." The same idea was conveyed in a later judgment by a New York committee allowing a woman to remain because she was "a person of an unexceptional Character and that they do not think that her remaining at her present Habitation will in any way injure the Liberties and Independence of this and the United States." These judgments were perfectly consistent with the New York act which stated that permits to remain could be given to women "of Good Character and not dangerous to the Liberties and Independence of this and the United States."[53] In other words, women who were forced to leave were those who had tarnished their reputations by *their own* actions. All women were suspect because of their husband's activities; yet those who could prove their innocence were spared. The enforcement of the act, then, recognized the independence of women to incriminate themselves, regardless of their husband's actions, and to be held accountable for their own treasonous behaviour. Women had become political beings in that they were deemed capable of treason and considered liable to be punished for their crimes. Patriot officials, ironically, recognized Loyalists women's contribution to the war effort and accorded them an independent status that they would never achieve once they reached British lines.

Once it was decided that the women were to be expelled, the terms for their departure were also specified and usually they were harsh. In 1780 in New York, all women whose husbands were with the enemy were ordered to leave the colony for British bases within twenty days, and appeals from this all-encompassing action had to be heard within the same period. Patriot committees drew up lists of the women to be removed and officials were designated to inform the women of their fate and of the consequences of ignoring the order. Section II of the New York act read: "That in Case any of the Persons aforesaid, shall, after the Space of twenty Days after such Notice, be found in any Part of this State; they shall and are hereby declared to be out of the Protection of the Laws of this State; and shall be liable to be proceeded against as Enemies of this and the United States." In short, the women would be considered to be guilty of treason. If the women went to British bases via a flag arranged as part of a prisoner exchange, then they had to pay their own way and bring their own food. A latter enactment in New

York allowed the government to sell Loyalist property to pay expenses. If the women went on their own, they were, of course, completely responsible for their expenses and care.[54]

No matter how they went, there were severe restrictions on what Loyalist women were allowed to take with them. In Vermont, Mrs Jeremiah French was escorted to the east side of Lake Champlain by Patriot officials who had ordered her out of the state, and the notice expelling her specified that she could take with her only "two feather beds and bedding not exceeding Eight Sheets, six Coverlids or blankets, 5 plates, two platters, two basons, one Quart Cup, & knives & forks if she has such things, her own & her childrens Wearing apparril." The rest of the "moveables belonging to sd. Estate" were to be sold to "Defray the charge of Transportation of her & family." What was left was to go to the state treasurer.[55]

Similar restrictions were placed on other Loyalist women leaving home. Alida Van Alstine, left behind with her relatives when her husband fled to join Burgoyne in 1777, applied in December 1779 for permission to join him in New York City. Her husband had written and advised her to apply to leave and, as she put it in her petition to Patriot officials, she had little choice because of her "inability of supporting herself and Family owing to the sequestration of her Husband's Estate." The permission was granted and Alida left for New York City accompanied by her three children, "1 negro boy Eleven Years old," presumably a slave, and another woman and child. She was allowed to take with her "Bedding, 2 Chests, 1 Trunk, 2 bbls. flour, wearing apparel and some household furniture."[56] Although the list was more generous than the one given to Mrs French, Alida's bundle of possessions was meagre for the long and tiring trip with young children and provided a slim foundation upon which to build a new life.

The harshest condition of all related to the women's children; boys over twelve had to be left behind to serve in the Patriot army. The anguish that this caused Loyalist families was enormous. When Loyalist soldiers at British bases pressed officials to allow expeditions to rescue their families, often they meant specifically their sons. Major James Rogers, commander of a Loyalist battalion, wrote in 1781 to a British official in Canada for permission to send to Connecticut for his son who he was "afraid may be pressed by the rebels." His wife, he explained, would "be sent in next summer, but the oldest boy will not be allowed to come with her, which makes him anxious to get him away before then."[57] Another Loyalist soldier, Henry Ruiter, was even more explicit. His wife was "greatly oppressed by the rebels" and wanted to come to Canada. His greatest concern, however, was for his two sons, "who will be pressed into the rebel service" if not brought to Canada. Ruiter's proposal was that he go to rescue his sons and "the rest of the family will afterwards be at liberty to come."[58]

Necessity also forced future eastern Ontario Loyalist women to abandon children, if only temporarily. The women generally had no say in the timing of their departure, and so the trip either south to New York City or north to Canada was often undertaken in winter when it was cold and treacherous. Since such a journey was not one that small children could make easily, some had to be left behind. When Richard Cartwright Jr's sister left Albany to marry a British officer at Niagara, her young daughter, Hannah, stayed with her grandparents and young uncle. Similarly, when Maria Young was ordered to leave New York, at least one of her children remained with his grandparents.

The case of Mary Cruger Meyers reveals the complexity of family relationships during the Revolution. After being betrayed by her husband's cousin, Mary was forced to seek permission from the local committee to leave and join her husband. The permission was granted, but she still had to make the long journey to New York City with seven children and one was only an infant. Her in-laws, despite their strong Patriot views and their at least passive complicity in the cousin's betrayal, offered to take the infant, Jacob.[59] One can imagine the mixed emotions Mary felt as she accepted the offer; she was probably grateful that her son would survive, something not at all certain if he had been taken on the trip, but also heart-broken to leave her child with people who had treated her and her family so callously.

Leaving home was a traumatic experience for Loyalist women. They were leaving behind their homes, most of their belongings, their friends, usually some family members, and precious memories. Simon Schwartz, whose father had been a tenant of Sir John's who fled with his landlord to Canada in 1776, aptly portrayed his mother's reluctance to leave her home. He wrote that she "would not come in [to Canada] before the House & builds were burnt."[60] Mrs Schwartz was likely typical of other Loyalist women. They left home only when they were ordered to or when desperation left them no other choice.

Eastern Ontario Loyalists who went to New York City have left no record of their journeys; however, one of the main difficulties of going south was that the Loyalists had to travel through enemy territory. Accounts have survived of the physically more challenging treks north to Canada and they depict something of the hardships faced by Loyalist women. There were two main routes to Canada. Some Loyalists, especially from New York, travelled overland through Indian country to the shores of Lake Ontario and from there they either crossed the lake at Oswego or followed the south shore of the lake to the Niagara River.

Others, mainly from Vermont, followed in Burgoyne's tracks by travelling along the Richelieu River-Lake Champlain route to Montreal.

A New York Loyalist, Philip Frey, described the dangers associated with making his way to Canada through Indian country. When he decided that he had to flee to Canada, Frey contacted Molly Brant, who provided him with supplies and an Indian guide named Tom. The route north was through the territory of the Oneida, most of whom supported the Patriots; however, Tom knew the Oneida who favoured the British and he conducted Frey and another Loyalist to the wigwam of Schuyler, a loyal Oneida. Schuyler treated them well and gave them asylum until nightfall, when they could travel safely through hostile country. Soon after their departure, they came to a small Oneida village and had to crawl past it on their hands and knees to avoid detection. Next, they came across a party of American dragoons but Philip and Tom managed to elude them by plunging into a swamp, with gunfire at their heels. Their other companion was not as lucky and was captured by the Patriots. Frey and Tom watched from a hill as their former fellow traveller was beaten, put on a horse with his feet tied, and taken away as a prisoner.[61]

After escaping from the Patriots, Frey and Tom were half way up a hill, three-quarters of a mile high, when they ran into a party of Oneidas. The chief drew a long tomahawk from his belt, raised it, threw it into the ground with such force that dirt flew up into Frey's face, and declared the path that they were on closed. Tom fabricated a story to the effect that Frey, the son of a Canadian merchant, had been going to school in Schenectady and was now returning home. The Oneidas let them pass, but knowing that their lie would soon be discovered, Tom told Frey that they had to abandon the one hundred pounds of supplies they had brought with them so that they could run fourteen miles to a friendly Onandaga village. At the village, a tent was erected for Frey replete with a red pole in front of it as a sign of distinction, a custom learned from the French and called "baton rouge." After resting for a week, Frey was assigned a new Indian guide to take him to Niagara and an Indian woman to carry his provisions.

The trip to Niagara was difficult since it was spring and the water was high. Three days from Niagara, they ran out of food. On their second day without food, they came upon a porcupine, hung from a tree by Indians for use by needy travellers. Although the creature had been dead so long that it was partly decomposed, they nevertheless boiled the remains, strained the broth through a blanket, and drank it. Frey finally reached Niagara safely, after a tiring and frightening journey.[62]

Richard Cartwright Jr, who at eighteen travelled along the Richelieu River-Lake Champlain route to Montreal with his young niece,

Hannah, described his feelings about leaving home and seeing the car-
nage left after the Burgoyne expedition. Of his departure, he wrote,
"The distracted Condition of my native Country, where all Government
was subverted, where Caprice was the only Rule and Measure of
usurped Authority, and where all the Distress was exhibited that Power
guided by Malice can produce, had long made me wish to leave it." The
two left in October in the company of some servants and a Major
Hughes. On the first day they rode fourteen miles on horseback over
muddy, bad roads. After stopping for the night at someone's home, the
party travelled to the scenes of some of the battles between Burgoyne
and the Americans. As Cartwright surveyed the battlefields, he thought
of the victims of the war and the survivors, "the weeping parent, distressed widow, wretched orphans and afflicted Friends." Making his
way among the remains of the buildings, "burnt" or "torn to Pieces,"
Cartwright reflected on "this once agreeable and delightful part of the
country" which "now displayed a most shocking Picture of Havock and
wild Desolation." Cartwright and Hannah were lucky. After reaching
Fort George, now reduced to ashes, they met a boat which took them to
an island in Lake Champlain. There they again were fortunate enough
to find a British detachment which guided them the rest of the way.[63]

Many other Loyalists were not as fortunate as Cartwright since they
did not coincidentally meet boats or British detachments to assist them
and the weather and terrain were much more hazardous. Because much
of the travel was along forest trails, Indian guides were essential. Por-
taging, often for long distances, was exhausting and virtually forced
Loyalists to travel in groups whose members could share the burden of
carrying boats and provisions. With no roads and only crude trails, refugees could use only pack horses, ponies, or hand and horse carts for
their belongings and provisons. "On the water, canoes, bateaux, skiffs,
and lake boats had to be brought, made, bought or hired." Some, like
Cartwright, might be lucky enough to make the trip in thirteen days,
but most took much longer. An expedition of women and children that
had to move slowly, was not lucky enough to make good connections
with boats, and experienced some bad weather could take from two to
three long and gruelling months to reach Quebec.[64]

The rugged country and poor to non-existent roads meant that travelling was hard on clothes. As one officer said, "The woods east and
west of St. John [were] so very bad to march through" that the men
"wear out a pair of Mocassins and return with their clothes torn every
time they are sent out." Another officer agreed that trudging through
the bush meant that many "wore out all their Shoes, Mockosins, Trow-
sers, Leggings, &c." Because the trip was so difficult and tiring, it was
not uncommon for parties to run out of provisions. One man who took

eleven days to make his way to Canada through the woods had to live on nuts and roots until a ship picked him up. Sir John Johnson and those who accompanied him to Canada in 1776 ate wild onions, roots, and the leaves of beech trees. The journey north was so taxing that some were unable to complete it. Isabel MacLeod's husband had left New Johnstown with Sir John in 1776, but the marching was so strenuous that he "went till he could go no farther" and then was forced to turn back. Weather forced the retreat of another group. Of twenty Loyalists who headed north from Vermont in 1780, fifteen turned back because they were not well enough clothed for the weather.[65]

There were still other hazards. Running across hostile Indians was a danger and the "rebels" were reported to keep "scouts constantly on the lake to keep Loyalists from coming down." Many Loyalists, driven from their homes by mobs, had no time to clothe or supply themselves properly and turning back was simply not an option for them. Considering that many travelled in wet or cold weather, through rugged terrain, and without adequate clothing and food, it is not surprising that they arrived ill and in need of quick care and attention.[66]

Lake Champlain posed an especially formidable obstacle to some Loyalists. Those going in summer had to wait for a boat to arrive to take them across the lake and bad timing could lead to distress. Women and children Loyalists forced from their homes in Vermont waited for over a month for help in completing their journey and were reported to be "wanting almost every necessary of life." In the fall of 1779, William Fraser got permission for his wife and children to leave for Canada and he hired a sled to take them. But when they reached Fort George, they had trouble crossing the ice. They had to spend a whole night on the ice during which time one boy's foot froze. The family then returned and got a wagon, hoping for a scouting party from Canada as soon as the lakes opened; however, in April 1780 the family was still waiting to be taken across the lake.

There were advantages to travelling in winter since it was often preferable to travel by sleigh over frozen lakes and rivers than to risk being bogged down in muddy wilderness trails. But crossing Lake Champlain in winter had its perils. While the weather could be very cold in the middle of winter, the ice could be unreliable in early or late winter. Justus Sherwood told of his trip in February when the ice was "bending" under the weight of his party and, although they made it safely, he swore that he would not return on the ice "for all the world."[67]

Lake Champlain was the scene of a great tragedy for the Freeman family, according to fourteen-year-old Thomas Freeman. Thomas's father had been a guide to Burgoyne and a battle in the 1777 Burgoyne expedition was fought at Freeman's farm, devastating the family's crops, cattle, and property. A British officer promised to compensate the family, but the officer was killed and, of course, the British expedition defeated, and so the Freemans decided to take General Burgoyne's advice and make their way to Canada. Eleven members of the family started out, but only three survived the trip. As Thomas recounted, his father, mother, four brothers, and two sisters "perished on the banks of Lake Champlain, through absolute want and Distress on their way to this Province," leaving Thomas and his two younger sisters in "a strange land and foreign country ... in misery and poverty."[68]

All in all, then, the journey from their homes in the colonies to the safety of British lines was one of the greatest challenges faced by many Loyalist women on their path to becoming refugees. The trip was long, physically exhausting, often dangerous, and probably emotionally draining. Although literally hundreds of Loyalist women made the trip, we know of the experiences of only a few.

For Sarah Sherwood, the trip to Canada was a harrowing experience. In October 1777 the Vermont Council of Safety gave her permission to join her husband and allowed her to take with her all of her clothing and one bed. She was to be escorted by a Patriot flag of truce to British territory; however, the plan went awry. In November she was taken in a wagon to Skenesborough and from there she was transported in a boat to a deserted Ticonderoga, the British garrison having retreated to Fort St John on the Richelieu River for the winter. Sarah's Patriot escort started to take her to the nearest British base, Pointe au Fer, at the north end of Lake Champlain, but about thirty miles before reaching the destination, the Patriot guides panicked and fled, leaving Sarah and her young family on the west shore of the lake to fend for themselves. They hid their belongings, walked the thirty miles through the bush, and then were taken by boat to St Johns. When Sarah made her epic trek, she had with her a slave as well as a child of three and a baby and she was seven months pregnant.[69]

Ann Peters's journey to Canada was just as difficult. After her husband, John Peters, deserted from the Patriot army in Montreal, Ann and her seven children, fourteen years old and under, were evicted from their home in early 1777 and sent to Canada by sleigh. Mrs Peters, "a small and delicate woman," had to take her young family 140 miles by sleigh to Ticonderoga, in the brutally cold weather of January. "Almost dead" when they arrived, the Peters were treated kindly by the "rebel" general at Ticonderoga where they were allowed to remain until April, when they were again sent on their way to Canada with three weeks provisions. Ann and her young family were left in a deserted house, miles from British territory, and had to wait eighteen days until they were discovered by a British boat which took them to St Johns. They arrived on

4 May, about four months after their departure, exhausted, "naked and dirty."[70]

Mary Munro had been forced to flee from her home in Shaftsbury following the defeat of Burgoyne and, after being rebuffed by her parents in Schenectady, a Patriot relative got her a pass to go to Canada. However, Mary had to figure out how to get her eight children to Lake George to join others *en route* to Canada. They lightened their load by discarding food and "most of their wearing Apparel." "After much difficulty," they arrived at Lake George and "lay in the woods Six days almost perished with Cold and Hunger" until three other families arrived. After they "prevailed on" the commanding officer at Fort Edward to give them a boat and a flag, they set off across Lake George. But they were "discovered by a party of Indians from Canada – which pursued them, and must have fallen a sacrifice had they not gained the Shipping before they were overtaken." As a result of the "excessive hardships they underwent," Mary and her children were "very sickly the whole Winter" after arriving in Canada. The toll the trip took on Mary was described poignantly by her husband, who said that "the children recovered [from their illnesses] but Mrs. Munro never will."[71]

The accomplishments of Loyalist women such as Mary Munro or Sarah Sherwood were remarkable. Traditional theories about women being dependent subordinates within a patriarchal family structure were dispelled by the realities of their actions during the Revolutionary War. Many played a military role in the war by supplying and protecting raiding parties and acting as spies. Within the household, many had to take over what was considered to be the male responsiblity of making decisions for the family and providing their children with food, clothing, and shelter. Eventually all had to face the stark reality that they had to leave their homes – their belongings, their friends, their families, and their communities. The women sometimes had to assume responsibility for negotiating with the Patriots about the terms and timing of their departure. Leaving home also meant facing the dangerous trip through enemy-held territory to New York, or the physically demanding and emotionally draining journey through the wilderness of the northern frontier to Canada.

Once the Loyalist women reached their asylum at British bases a formative phase of their refugee experience ended. While fighting the war, striving to cope with the uncertainties of the Revolution and caring for their families, the women were actors, scrambling to survive and carve out a future for their dependants. This was especially true of the Loyalist women on the frontiers of the American colonies who were a military asset to the British while they remained there. However, once at British bases, their military value came to an end, as did their power to decide and act for themselves. When most reached British lines, they were exhausted, sometimes ill, poorly clothed, ill fed, and impoverished. They depended totally on the British for the essentials of life. Considered to be of no military value, they took on the different, less noble, but more customary status of dependants within a patriarchal power structure. It was also during their exile that the Loyalists began the process of reinterpreting their past and assuming a new identity which left no place for the women and their accomplishments.

4 Exile

Exile is the emptiness – for however much you brought
with you, there's far more you've left behind.
Exile is the ego that shrinks, for how can you prove
what you were and what you did?
Exile is the erasure of pride.
Exile is the escape that is often worse than the prison.

Paul Tabori, *The Anatomy of Exile*[1]

On 29 November 1780, Barry St Leger, a veteran British officer stationed at an outpost on the frontiers of Quebec, wrote that a party of one man, thirty-eight women, and seventy-seven children, all belonging to Sir John Johnson's regiment, had arrived from the American colonies "in a very great misery indeed." "These poor creatures," who had travelled from New York to St Johns via Lake Champlain and the Richelieu River, "suffered greatly, particularly the children." St Leger had summoned "all the heads of Families" to the frontier "to succour and bring forward their respective people" and he had assigned some of the Loyalist troops to take care of those whose husbands and fathers were absent or dead. Their "wretchedness and unprotected situation," he explained, "induced" him to order in the governor's name two pounds of tea, ten pounds of sugar, and two pounds of chocolate and to make special arrangements for blankets since the children were unprotected in the cool November weather and "unable to proceed without them."[2] Even a seasoned British officer such as St Leger, writing a formal military dispatch, was obviously touched by the suffering of these women and children who were following the men in their lives into exile.

Similar to the women and children described by St Leger was a group that arrived at Niagara "almost naked"; they had "been so long hiding in the woods" that they were "almost famished." "It was distressing to behold them," the observer noted. Even more distressing was the news that "50 [more] are on their way, but so weak they can scarcely crawl." Another group at Crown Point *en route* to Quebec was "attacked with measles," threatening not only themselves but also others who would join them in making their way northward. Some arrived at St Johns on the Richelieu River in such a "distressed" condition that they were unable "to go from here without assistance." St Leger, in another dispatch, aptly summed up the plight of the Loyalist refugees when he called them "a set of poor forlorn people" who looked to British officials for relief, to "help forward those who cannot help themselves."[3]

Exile, which involved spending from one to eight years living in either temporary quarters in New York City or in camps in Quebec, was a formative experience for Loyalist refugee women and one that clearly set them apart from their Patriot counterparts. Like other refugees, the Loyalist women struggled with the day-to-day realities of life in a camp: overcrowding, disease, and inadequate food, clothing, and shelter. There were rivalries with fellow Loyalists, worsened by the necessity of living at close quarters, and conflicts with the local population or British officials. Refugee life also involved insecurity, anxiety, frustration, and, for the women especially, loneliness. Exile meant leaving everything associated with home and the familiar.

Exile also meant being reintegrated into a patriarchal, paternalistic power structure. At British bases Loyalists became subject to élitist, hierarchal, and authoritarian regimes. Within this framework, women, who so recently had broken through the constraints governing the responsibilities of their gender, were again cast into a traditional mould where femininity was associated with weakness and dependence. While Loyalist men became part of the patriarchal military system, Loyalist women had to appeal to the paternalism of those in authority.

Exile, finally, involved coming to terms with what had happened to their lives. Once in exile, the destitute Loyalists depended solely on the British and they had to persuade British officials that it was either their duty or in their interest to support the Loyalists. In the process of petitioning for British aid, the rhetoric about the Loyalists, which often bore little resemblance to reality, emerged. The Loyalists reinterpreted the past and took on a new and manufactured identity which was passed on to future generations. This view of the Loyalist experience, however, ignored or distorted the role of women during the Revolution and consigned them once again to the status of subordinate dependants within a patriarchal power structure.

In the late 1770s and early 1780s thousands of Loyalist families found asylum from Patriot harassment at the very different British military bases in New York City and Quebec. New York, before the Revolution, had been a prosperous commercial and political centre of about 22,000 people. When the British captured it from the Patriots in 1776, the civilian population had declined to somewhere between 500 and 3000, and soon afterwards a fire, allegedly started by the Patriots, gutted between 500 and 1,500 of the buildings.[4] But the city's fortunes quickly improved. During the occupation, the population swelled again with the arrival of British and Hessian troops and Loyalist exiles, and New York not only regained its commercial importance but assumed military significance as the main base of operations for British forces. Socially, the city was characterized by its cosmopolitan flavour and its stratified class structure. Ships came and went from around the world. Newspapers advertised plays and concerts as well as a wide variety of luxury goods – "chinzes, linens, silk ... ostrich feathers ... sattins," "old Genuine Madeira Wine" – at the same time as they described the schemes, such as lotteries, in place to help the poor.[5] In 1783 over 25,000 Loyalists were evacuated from New York City and some 400 of these sailed to Quebec and then made their way to the Cataraqui area.

Over 85 per cent of the Loyalists who eventually settled around Cataraqui spent their refugee years in Quebec, which was isolated, vast, and alien to them. Relative to New York City's size, Quebec was indeed huge, encompassing not only the area where most of the French Canadians lived – between Montreal, the main commercial centre, and the capital of Quebec City – but also, by virtue of the Quebec Act of 1774, the territory west to the Great Lakes and south to the Ohio and Mississippi rivers. Defending this vast colony was a major concern of the British, especially since an American army had invaded it with ease in 1775. As for the Loyalists, they had their own preoccupations, the main one being survival, and their view of Quebec was conditioned by their background in the Thirteen Colonies. Coming to Quebec was probably not an attractive prospect to them, since it was identified with the devastating French-Indian raids unleashed on their frontier communities during the Seven Years War. The French regime had also been notorious among American colonists for its arbitrary and oppressive government as well as its Roman Catholicism, described by some as anti-Christian "Romish bigotry."[6] Once in the colony, the Loyalists lived in an enclave, isolated as much as possible from the local French population and even the minority of English-speaking merchants. Estimating their numbers is difficult since they did not settle in one community but were scattered at bases all over Quebec and the colony's size made it easy to enter undetected. However, we do know that by 1780 British officials were feeding 6,000 regular troops and over 10,000 white and Indian Loyalists, many of them on their way to eastern Ontario.[7]

Whether Loyalists fled north to Quebec or south to New York City, they were faced with authoritarian, hierarchical military regimes. The Quebec Act of 1774 reinforced the authoritarian, hierarchical character of the French regime by establishing an appointed council, but no elected Assembly, and by restoring French civil law. With no *habeaus corpus* or trial by jury, people could be subjected to indefinite imprisonment.[8] Similarly, in New York City the civil government and courts that had been suspended by the Patriots were never fully restored. Instead the city was run by military officers appointed by the commander-in-chief. Trade, commerce, and prices were strictly regulated. Loyalists, accustomed to an elected assembly, were dismayed to find that firewood, gunpowder, or the price, quality, and weight of bread were being regulated "by order of the Commandant." Complaints about the lack of *habeaus corpus* and trial by jury fell on deaf ears. Military rule prevailed.[9]

The tone of the regime in Quebec from 1777 to 1784 was set by its governor, Frederick Haldimand, who was a career soldier. Born in Switzerland, he had served in the Prussian, Dutch, and British armies. His career in North America began with the Seven Years War and continued in the 1760s when he held various military and civil posts. Haldimand sympathized with the Loyalists and took a paternal interest in their well-being. In a 1778 letter to the colonial secretary, Lord George Germain, he wrote: "The distress of these poor people is so great that, I take for granted, the expence which must be incurred by relieving them will be judged unavoidable and be approved of."[10] Haldimand was also an able and fair administrator. But he was first and foremost a soldier who believed in hierarchy, obedience to authority, and order and who headed a totally male, authoritarian military administration. He epitomized the paternalism and patriarchal power structure that pervaded all aspects of the Loyalists' life as refugees.

Paternalism was fostered by the utter helplessness of the Loyalists and their total dependence on the British. When they finally reached New York City or Quebec most were destitute, having lost all of their property and most of their possessions. Few brought money with them and those who did soon found that the high cost of living quickly absorbed their cash. One Loyalist who brought £300 to Quebec had to petition the government for assistance. Another relied on friends for help but ended up appealing to the government for "daily subsistence support or employment for money." Others borrowed money and found them-

selves in debt. Daniel McGuin admitted his need of "support in the pe-
cuniary line," his desire to not be a "burden to government," and his
willingness "to serve in any line." Hugh Munro explained that he
needed money because he had "to begin the world again and shift for
myself ... [in] a strange country unacquainted with the language." Most
typical was Valentine Detlor's declaration that his family was "stript by
the Rebels of every individual thing belonging to them ... [leaving them
with] no subsistence except their bare provisions, being destitute of
Money, Cloathing and every other Necessary of life except a poor pittance."[11]

Many had no choice but to petition the governor for subsistence, rations, firewood, or shelter. The very act of petitioning for aid cast all
Loyalists in the role of supplicant; "the formulation of a petition," in
the words of Linda Kerber, "begins in the acknowledgement of subordination."[12] The language used in the petitions reflected the paternalism of the relationship between the Loyalists and those in authority.
One group, for example, spoke of fleeing to Quebec and taking "shelter
... under your Excellency's Gracious Protection" and ended by giving
"filial" thanks to Haldimand for his support. Another group of petitioners explicitly called on Haldimand as "our Father" for help. In New
York, refugees petitioned the Earl of Shelburne in the knowledge that
they "can trust their dearest interests in Your Lordships hands, convinced that You will manage them with judgment and knowledge." Deference and paternalism permeated their message: "Like mariners in the
most dangerous moment, they place their hope in the wisdom of their
Pilot, and far from disturbing his attention with their crys, with respect-
ful silence, they wait his directions, and stand ready to execute them."
A Loyalist officer summarized the situation when he wrote of the Loyalists' need "to take shelter again under your [Haldimand's] wing, with
a brood of unfortunate women and children." Paternalism and élitism
emanated from the other side of the relationship as Haldimand instructed one of his officers to care for the Loyalists since the "common
sort may not have sufficient judgement to know what may be best to
pursue, and therefore rely on the better understanding of their Superiors."[13] The language used reflected the reality that many Loyalists were
at the mercy of British authorities when it came to providing basic
necessities.

Women figured in the men's petitions as frail, dependent creatures
whose helplessness justified begging for government aid. A male Loyalist admitted his guilty feelings about being unable to meet his responsibilities as family head by earning a livelihood: "Being always brought
up to Business," he was "entirely lost having nothing to do" and he was
"really ashamed to be staggering about the King's Garrison as an idle

spectator." Only old men too feeble to work felt justified in petitioning for subsistence for themselves. Otherwise, men explained their petitions for aid by pointing to their "numerous and helpless family," their "small children," their "chargeable family," or their "large helpless family." A group of Loyalists appealed for better rations by citing their unwillingness "to hear the Cries of the Women and Children for Bread."[14] The vulnerability of women was used to evoke the paternalism of British administrators.

Faced with feeding, housing, and clothing thousands of refugees, British officials encouraged the men to enter the provincial corps. Loyalist soldiers, along with the Indians, raided the northern frontiers of the colonies, and in New York City Loyalist militiamen helped defend the area and the provincial corps raided the surrounding Patriot-controlled countryside. But the Loyalists were indifferent soldiers at best and were treated with disdain by British officers, one of whom wrote: "I declare, they are so unlike anything I ever saw under the appellation of soliders, that I am at a loss what to do with them."[15] The provincial corps may have been of limited military value, but the British had other reasons for wanting the men in regiments.

In April 1777 the governor of Quebec ordered that all refugees had to stay with the Loyalist regiments since it was improper for them "to straggle about the country." It was easier to control the men when they were organized into military units and ensure that they were not conspiring with the local French population whose loyalty was suspect.[16] The regiments also provided employment. From the beginning Loyalists were encouraged to earn their livelihoods so that they would not become government charges. But this was easier to do in New York City, where there were other sources of income such as privateering, than in Quebec. There the provincial regiments built fortifications, barracks, and other structures, constructed some of Canada's early canals along the St Lawrence, or transported goods and people.[17] Yet some of this work was of questionable value. Halidmand's secretary was horrified to discover in 1780 that, of the seventy-two batteaux men employed at Niagara, there were only enough men adequately trained and knowledgeable to operate two small batteaux.[18]

Joining the regiments satisfied destitute Loyalist men's basic needs. Loyalist soldiers received a small subsistence and usually rations, lodging, and clothes, and boys of fifteen or younger and old men were cared for in the regiments.[19] The regiments also provided many Loyalists with the status and pride that they had lost along with their homes and possessions. Loyalist soldiers were outfitted in brightly coloured uniforms, and many were given titles and told that they were serving his Majesty in defending British liberty in North America. What was crucial was that Loyalist men were making a tangible contribution to the British cause. This military service was cited by them to justify claims for support or compensation from the British.

Within the Loyalist regiments there was no place for women. White women, of course, could not fight and were given no role in military decision-making. They were attached to the regiments merely as dependants and were seen by the British as added and unwanted burdens. British officials tried to avoid the responsibility for caring for Loyalist women and children. When they arrived at outposts as destitute refugees, the women and children had their immediate needs cared for, but British officers quickly sent for their relatives whose duty it was to care for their dependants. Similarly, British officials resisted appeals from Loyalist officers for support for the families of Loyalist soldiers. Minimal, piecemeal aid was given only when there was severe distress or the governor was persuaded that the men "would not otherwise engage in the Service." Once again Loyalist women had reverted to the status of being mere appendages to their husbands within a patriarchal power structure. Sir John Johnson underlined the invisible quality of women in Quebec when he told the governor that his returns of Loyalists underestimated the women since he did not count the ones married to men in his regiment.[20]

The fact that women had no role within the Loyalist military framework is important because military service was a formative experience for Loyalist men, reinforcing aspects of their past and influencing the directions of their future. Most men who would later settle around Cataraqui served in one of the regiments for from one to seven years and many aspired to be officers. "Rank," Haldimand wrote, "is the Idol worshipped by all on this continent."[21] However, since officers did not receive their commissions until their battalions were full, the scramble for recruits led to abuses and Loyalist officers such as Justus Sherwood were frustrated at having to sort out the squabbles. Sherwood wrote to a fellow officer, "I think you and I have too long experienced the misfortune of being at the tail of the cow. Let us look about and try to get hold of the head horns."[22]

There was as well conflict between the soldiers and the French Canadians, who were suspected of spying for the Americans, especially after 1778 when France became an ally of the Thirteen Colonies.[23] There were complaints from French Canadians about troops damaging crops and other property and about robberies and riots. There were fights between soldiers and local residents and reports of disorderly behaviour by the soldiers, the latter incidents including "a nasty dirty disagreeable Drunken Squabble," "bestiality," and the selling of arms and clothing to inhabitants in exchange for liquor.[24] Soldiers annoyed French Canadians by ringing the church bell at Châteauguay at night; French Canadians, after the end of the Revolutionary War, attacked soldiers and erected a battery, with a cannon and gallows near it, to mock the defeated Loyalists. The fact that there was hostility and mutual suspicion between the Loyalists and the host population in Quebec probably made the Loyalists feel more separate and distinct and encouraged them to look to each other for mutual support.[25]

The provincial regiments, despite the squabbling over recruits, helped to counter the loneliness, isolation, and displacement common to refugees. Often refugees find life in camps to be "an imposed system aimed at replacing what the refugee must feel is irreplaceable, the sense of community and solidarity" of earlier days. "Uprootedness," in the words of another expert on refugees, is a part of life as an exile and leads refugees to "find a group with a similar outlook on life."[26] The regiments provided continuity in the otherwise totally disrupted lives of Loyalist men. Many joined in the colonies or immediately after reaching Quebec and tended to choose regiments in which there were familiar faces, whether they were family members, former neighbours, or men from the same ethnic background. The regiments gave them a sense of belonging, cohesiveness, and unity, reinforcing the ethnic or familial bonds of their past.

The cohesiveness of the regiments was reflected in the Loyalist soldiers' opposition to attempts by British officials to change their officers or units. The Irish-born Germans from New York were grouped together in one battalion and were upset when told that they were to serve under a former New Englander, Justus Sherwood. Another Loyalist soldier informed the governor's secretary that the men in his unit did not want to be separated from each other. A petition from a group of Loyalists expressed well the continuity provided by the corps. The petitioners had, in their own words, raised men at considerable "risk" and "expense" and "engaged their Honor to men that they should not be separated from their officers nor one another." After coming to Quebec, "attempts to drag these men into other corps has caused great alarm." The men were willing to be "annexed" to another department but only if they went as a unit.[27] A memorial from Albany County Loyalists who wanted to serve in Johnson's regiment stated that "Our Friends and Relations being already in said regiment ... Several of us having served last war under Sir William Johnson, we now look to his son as our protector and under whom we shall be more happy to serve."[28]

Hierarchy, élitism, and paternalism were evident in the regiments. The rigid hierarchy of the British military was reflected in Sir Guy Carleton's comment that the Loyalists' request to choose their own officers was "unjustifiable" and "indecent."[29] Also, older family members were often officers in the same regiment in which sons or nephews served further down the military ladder. In Johnson's first battalion, for instance, the senior officers included Sir John Johnson, Major James Gray, and Captain John Munro, while the lieutenants included Hugh Munro, son of John, Jacob Farrand, nephew of Major Gray, and William Claus, son of the deputy Indian agent Colonel Claus and nephew of Sir John Johnson.[30] From examples such as this it is clear that the hierarchical structure of the patriarchal family, in which the father and family head was owed deference and respect by his sons, was duplicated in the regiments.

The treatment of blacks also reflected support for the existing social hierarchy and traditional property rights. The British encouraged slaves to become Loyalists by promising them their freedom; however, once they reached British lines, blacks found that the promises were not always fulfilled. Some were taken prisoner and either claimed as property by their captors or sold. Others were returned to Loyalist masters. Only a few were allowed to serve. A very atypical Loyalist soldier wrote "about the sensible feeling I have for my fellow Creatures" and explained that blacks were often of great help to scouting and raiding parties; he then noted sadly that sixteen blacks he had brought in as recruits "for their loyalty ... now are rendered Slaves in Montreal." British officials consistently maintained that former slaves of Loyalists had to be returned to their masters.[31] The property rights of white Loyalists obviously took precedence over promises to blacks.

The hierarchical nature of society dictated the relationship between Loyalist soldiers and those in authority. Rank-and-file soldiers appealing to the governor for aid usually worked through officers such as Sir John Johnson, who was listened to because he had the proper social credentials in terms of status, education, and "breeding." Johnson, described by Haldimand as a person of "Rank, Influence, Knowledge, Activity and Perfect Honor," acted as a patron for his followers, just as he had done before the Revolution.[32]

But there was also a harsher side to British paternalism. Haldimand used the Loyalists' dependence on government to control them, as was shown in the story of a Loyalist officer who had been demoted. The "cruel, degrading change" had been made, according to the officer, in his absence but when he complained to Haldimand's secretary he was told that "I might starve if I refused captain's pay ... I should not be allowed rations if I refused, my subsistence being stopped." Having a wife and eight children, he had no choice but to "accept" the demotion without complaint or "perish." Even more brutal was the treatment of those who might "look suspicious" to an officer; they were immediately imprisoned.[33] Indians were treated no better. "Nothing will more tend to keep the Indian allies to their duty," Haldimand wrote to Germain, "than to make them feel a dependance upon the King, their father for such goods as have now become in some measure necessary to their existence." When the Mohawks refused to follow the directions of a British officer, the governor's secretary was quick to point out that "if they [the Mohawks] do not chuse to accompany his officers to war, he concludes they are no longer in need of their [British] assistance."[34] British paternalism was obviously a double-edged sword: for white and Indian Loyalists it meant support and assistance, but it also involved the often harsh assertion of unchecked power.

Thus, when Loyalist women reached British lines, they encountered a clearly defined social hierarchy – there were those who needed to be cared for and those responsible for administering the care, those in leadership roles and those who were clearly subordinates. This kind of society, in which deference to authority was expected, accorded women the most marginal of roles. Indeed, even more so than the civil administrations in the American colonies, the military regimes in Quebec and New York City had no place for women and even shunned them as extra mouths to be fed and families to be housed. Women could fit into such paternalistic and patriarchal structures only as subordinates.

This subordination was reflected in the Loyalist women's petitions for rations or subsistence. Some women did not even petition themselves, but had men request aid on their behalf. When Catherine Peck, wife of one of Sir John Johnson's tenants who had fled to Canada in 1776, arrived in New York City "in hope of getting a Passage to Canada" and found herself and her child "destitute of any Sort of Support," it was an Indian Affairs official who appealed to British officials to assist her.[35] Whether Loyalist women themselves petitioned or had others do it for them, what was stressed was their weakness, dependence, and suffering. The widow, Mary Deforest, described how she and her seven children had "suffered much" and were "greatly distressed"; in these "distressed Circumstances," she predicted, they "will become naked for want of cloathing." Helena McLeod, whose husband had come to Canada with Guy Johnson in 1775, described her inability to support herself and conveyed her helplessness by talking about "her fatherless child."[36] Feeble and helpless were the adjectives used most often by Loyalist women to describe themselves.[37] The Loyalist Jean McDonell, who wrote that she was "utterly destitute of any other support," summed up perfectly the notion of female incapacity when she described herself as "feeble" and added that she also had "a family of daughters."[38]

These professions of weakness were very much at odds with Loyalist women's recent experiences. The case of Phoebe Grant illustrates this point nicely. When her husband and son joined Burgoyne in 1777, the "rebels" seized his property and "effects" and turned her "and three helpless Female children Out of Doors destitute." She then had to "fly" to Quebec "for protection." Within days of her arrival in Quebec, her husband drowned and she was "obliged to provide for herself and her three children without an allowance from government which ceased on the death of her husband." After her husband's death she did "everything in her power to support herself," even though she was "in a country far from a single Friend and a stranger to the language." When Phoebe finally had to "most humbly throw herself and poor family at your Excellency's feet praying" for subsistence, she could not revel in her accomplishments and seek praise for even surviving such ordeals; all she could do was tell her story as a tale of suffering and depict herself as "a Feeble Woman."[39]

What is almost bizarre about Phoebe Grant's petition is the juxtaposition of facts reflecting courage, tenacity, and achievement with the language of enfeeblement. The contrast with men's petitions is striking. The petitions from males did not suggest weakness and suffering but conveyed the impression of decision-making, action, service, and sacrifice. Roger Stevens, for example, wrote about his decisions not to sign a Patriot oath and refuse a Patriot militia captaincy. He then described his imprisonment, his escape, and his extensive service under Burgoyne. Stevens's hardships were not portrayed as suffering so much as sacrifice in a noble cause; as he put it, he had "lost his all for his Majesty's Service."[40] The same impression was conveyed in officers' letters supporting the petitions of men in their regiments. Dan McAlpin, an officer, wrote about one of his men that in 1776 he "declared ... his Abhorence of the Rebellious proceedings," that he was "well qualified," that he had served extensively, and that he was "a good subject."[41]

The difference is in part a reflection of the language used. The power of language, particularly as it affects women, has been studied extensively.[42] In the American colonies from the mid- to late-eighteenth-century, the language used to describe male behaviour encompassed the positive traits of action, service, and decision making. There was no female counterpart to any of this. The language used to depict women was cast within the mould of weakness, submissiveness, helplessness, and suffering. During the Revolution, as Phoebe Grant's petition shows, women were forced by circumstances to become more assertive and independent and to take over duties that until then were widely accepted as the domain of men. However, while their actions might have changed, the language used to describe women did not. In other words, the women did not develop any new "script" which allowed their experiences to be interpreted as achievements rather than as suffering.

New language about women's capacities was even less likely to emerge under the British military regimes. Gender roles were rigidly defined by British officials. To them, military service meant formal enlistment in one of the Loyalist regiments. Because this was strictly men's work, at least in the case non-Indians, women, had nothing to offer the British which was of value. Not surprisingly, therefore, Loyalist women who outlined their "service" described the military accomplishments of their husbands. Helena McLeod was typical. She went into great detail about her husband, Captain Norman McLeod, who had joined Colonel Guy Johnson and the Indians on the Mohawk River in May 1775 and marched with them into Canada where he put himself under the command of Guy Carleton at Oswego. This was the service that she cited to explain why she deserved aid. The widow Loveless's story was even more dramatic. Her husband had been "very zealous and active" in the service and had been hanged. As a result of this service, Mrs Loveless was given a pension.[43] Clearly, the only way for women to appeal to the British was to cite their husband's valued services, rather than their own undervalued ones.

Not only did Loyalist women have nothing of value to offer to the British, they were also seen as dependants within a power structure in which there were clearly prescribed social roles. In contrast to the situation in the American colonies during the Revolution, where gender roles had been blurred, at British bases male and female responsibilities were starkly different. Men fought, women did not. Women were not useful, productive members of the society, but burdens who consumed scarce provisions and who had to be housed and clothed. Within this framework what was left to white women was their feminine frailty and dependence. When appealing to British officials for aid, they had to cite their husband's military service and invoke the paternalism of the military regimes by stressing their vulnerability, their need for protection, and their suffering.

The fact that Loyalist women never had the chance to speak with pride about their achievements set them apart from Patriot women whose contributions to the Revolution were publicly recognized. The attention paid in the American colonies to the clearly feminine task of spinning highlights this point. When the boycott of British manufactured goods in the late 1760s led to the wearing of homespun as a sign of patriotism, the stature of spinning was enhanced. Newspaper articles praised the efforts of women to increase the supply of home-made cloth. Spinning bees were widely publicized and became public events. The bees, in the words of Mary Beth Norton, "were ideological showcases" designed to "convince American women that they could render essential contributions to the struggle against Britain ... "[44] The status of Patriot women was enhanced by the publicity given to their work and there was some change in the language used to describe their efforts during the Revolution.

The fate of Loyalist women was much different. Their contributions went unrecognized and the women themselves never publicly proclaimed their accomplishments. Indeed, an article written by a woman in the *New York Gazette* in 1782 even suggested that it was not ladylike for Loyalist women to be active in politics. The author, Lucinda, was responding to *New York Freeholder*, which had advocated a moderate approach to the Patriots. Although she claimed to be "tolerably conversant in modern history, novels and plays," Lucinda explicitly shunned politics: "What lady of taste can be amused with musty politics?" She went on to claim that it was only Patriot women who demeaned themselves by dirtying their hands with politics. Involvement in politics "may do well enough for rebel Ladies, who are not very careful about female decorum, or preserving an easy cheerfulness of temper" but would never do for Loyalist women.[45] The idea that politics, like military service, was a preserve of males was perhaps one of the many reasons why Loyalist women's contributions did not become part of the language and public record of the Revolution.

Although white Loyalist women at Quebec were seen to be of no military value, this was not true of Mohawk women. Connected by "marriage and long intimacy" with the Indians at Caughnawaga (Kahnawake) near Montreal, who were believed to be disaffected, Mohawk women were active in keeping them from aiding the Americans.[46] Also, the Mohawk, when they came into the various bases along the Great Lakes-St Lawrence River system, were often helped and encouraged by Molly Brant and Sarah McGinnis. Both women spent some time at Niagara, but more at Carleton Island, near present-day Kingston, a base where Indian scouting and raiding parties wintered. When Sarah was there in 1782 "most of the Indians resorting to that place came to her House to visit and advise with her upon every occasion." Sarah served the British cause by giving them "her best advice" and by dividing "her provisions with them"; "sometimes when they come in hungry (as her place is chiefly their first resort) [she] even gives them the whole."[47] Molly Brant was also consulted by the Indians and obliged to share her provisions with them. One officer described her as the Indians "confidant in every Matter of Importance and [she] was consulted thereupon and prevented many an unbecoming ... proposal." The commanding officer at Carleton Island wrote glowing reports about her ability to keep order at the base: "The Chiefs were careful to keep their people sober and satisfy'd, but their uncommon good behaviour is in a great Measure to be ascribed to Miss Molly Brant's influence over them, which is far superior to that of all their Chiefs put together, and she has in the course of this Winter done every thing in Her power to maintain them strongly in the King's interest ... "[48]

While both women were active in the war effort, there was a dramatic difference in their treatment by the British. Molly Brant was considered demanding and even temperamental. Perhaps this was because she was torn between her various responsibilities. Within Mohawk society, she was looked up to for leadership, and so she felt keenly her obligations to her people. At this same time, because of the historic ties of the Mohawk and of her mate, Sir William Johnson, and her own desire to reclaim her ancestral lands, she was committed to the British cause. Added to this were her family responsibilities; she had six daughters who needed some education and reasonable doweries. The result was conflicting demands. When she went to Montreal at the request of the governor she found it "very hard ... to leave her old Mother & other Indn Relatives ... and live in a Country she was an entire Stranger in"; she worried about the expense of staying there and about being so far from the Mohawk at the outlying bases. When at one of the bases she complained about being "not at all reconciled to this place & Country, having two grown Daughters with her whom she would willingly see appear decent," by presumably being educated at Montreal.[49] Balancing the demands of family, kinship ties, and political loyalties was difficult.

Despite complaints about how excessive her demands were, British and Loyalist officers scrambled to accommodate Molly. In July 1779, when she was going to Lachine, the governor wrote to Sir John Johnson explaining that "arrangements" were being made for her "reception." At Fort Carleton, where Molly spent much of the period from 1779 to 1783, the commanding officer tried to please her by first digging her a garden and then building her a house a few hundred yards from the fort so that Molly, her daughters, and servants would not have to live in the barracks with the others.[50] Although Molly was considered demanding when it came to her family and "favourites," her wishes, the governor and other officers agreed, should be "attended to" since she checked "the demands of others for both presents and provisions" and kept the Mohawk "orderly and well disposed."[51]

Yet, for all of her stature and influence, Molly Brant was still treated by white men as a woman who needed care and protection. Several officers displayed an extraordinary concern that Molly's needs be met. Daniel Claus, Sir William Johnson's son-in-law, wrote to Sir John Johnson about getting a "yearly fixed income" for Molly and her many children, three of whom were "marriageable." The male members of the Johnson clan, it seems, felt a paternal duty to take care of Sir William's widow. But even the commanding officer at Fort Carleton, who was not related to the Johnsons, wrote to Claus about finding a way to make the governor aware of her "numerous family" and important service. There was also a suggestion that all three approach Haldimand on her behalf. What is interesting is that the three officers were writing to each other, not to Molly, about promoting her interests. Even Molly herself occasionally conformed to contemporary views about femininity when she spoke of her contribution to the war effort as her "little service." Molly had to have known that her contribution was enormous, but modesty to the point of self-deprecation was what was expected of eighteenth-century women.[52]

Sarah McGinnis's treatment was even worse. In 1777 Colonel Claus, of the Indian Department, observed that Sarah had served the British "without Expectation of Employ being at her ease"; in other words, when Sarah started helping the British she had sixty-two acres of land, given to her by her father, a house, barn, and "6 Negroes" and needed no payment for her efforts. After 1777, however, all of this had changed. Sarah and her family had been driven from their home and all of their property and possessions had been confiscated. Sarah was a penniless refugee in a strange land. But she did not have the connections of Molly Brant. For British officials such as Haldimand who thought in terms of status, position, and hierarchy, Molly had stature while Sarah did not.[53] By November 1778 Sarah was in Montreal in "dire need"; her married daughter was "so scantily lodged" that Sarah could not live with her. Even a request for firewood was denied. Claus wrote to Haldimand on her behalf, explaining that it was "very harsh to have no money or income except what [she and her daughter] can earn by the Needle." After an "easy way of life," the hardship "touches very sore."[54]

Sarah suffered such shabby treatment not only because she was not as well placed as Molly Brant but because she was a woman. Had she been a man she could have joined one of the provincial regiments or the Indian Department, perhaps even been an officer. But such choices were not open to women. Despite her treatment, Sarah again returned to Indian country in 1779 and in the early 1780s she worked with the Indians at Carleton Island, even though she was in her late sixties. Had she been a man she would have been eligible for a pension for her past services; even if she were the widow of a man who had performed such valuable service she would have had a chance for a pension. Yet because she was a woman, with no husband whose recent service she could cite, she was eking out an existence on "bare Rations" and "humbly" petitioning the governor for some supplies since she was sharing what little she had with the Indians who frequented her place.[55]

Other women also suffered poverty, many within the confines of refugee camp life. The most formative part of the refugee experience is life in camps, which, according to the literature on refugees, has several main characteristics. Typical camp life involves segregation from the "host population," a lack of privacy because of the need to share facilities, overcrowding, and "a limited, restricted area within which the whole compass of daily life is to be conducted."[56] The psychological impact of camp life is also great. Because of the regimention they are subjected to and their own "dependency," the refugees believe that "they have a special and limited status and are being controlled."[57] Camp life is a period of limbo, when refugees have time to reflect on what has been lost in the past and to consider the future. Out of the process, however, the refugees often come to understand what they have in common and to carve out a new identity for the future.[58]

A main feature of camp life is the refugees' utter dependance on government for the necessities of life. As Loyalists streamed into Quebec or New York City, providing for their immediate needs and long-term care was a massive organizational task for which the governments were unprepared. There were constant shortages of supplies, which led to unsuccessful attempts to regulate prices and calls for economy. Also, rather than clearly defined policies, there were regulations that shifted as supplies or the demands of war changed, leaving the door open to corruption. And since many decisions were made on an individual basis by officials such as the governor, status and connections were important in determining the level of aid one received.

The lack of privacy, overcrowding, and regimentation of camp life were reflected in the lodging arrangements made for the Loyalists. There were shortages of housing both in Quebec and, because so many of its buildings had been destroyed by fire, in New York City. The social hierarchy of the regiments carried over into housing arrangements. While rank-and-file soldiers lived in barracks or were billeted, an officer, in the words of one of them, regarded himself as "too great a Gentleman to Lodge in the Barracks."[59] Officers rented or bought quarters. In New York City houses abandoned by Patriots were assigned to Loyalists and permission was given to build on vacant lots, many in the burned-out area; however, because of the high cost of building materials and labour, few new houses were built and a canvas town of make-shift quarters for the poor took shape.[60] In Quebec, officers complained about being "in a very expensive and extravagant country." For one of them, the "expenses of being an officer" included renting a house and buying firewood, and these two costs alone consumed nearly one-third of his pay. Married officers were at the mercy of local inhabitants who, it was claimed, charged from $6 to $10 per month for a room and a small closet "not half so good as some of their kitchens at home." Even Sir John Johnson complained that his wife was at Quebec and "expensive to keep."[61] Houses, it seems, were also poorly built; for example, it was alleged that frost came as they were being built so that chimneys put up one day fell down the next.

The housing arrangements available to a Loyalist officer's family can be seen in the experiences of Captain Justus Sherwood, his wife, Sarah, and their three small children. After Sarah's arrival in Quebec in 1777, the Sherwoods were able to rent a small house at St Johns. But living in the privacy of one's own home was a luxury that even officers did not always enjoy. By 1779 Justus's relative, Thomas Sherwood, his wife, Anna, and their three children had arrived and were sharing the small dwelling. Then, in 1780, Justus's brother, Samuel, his wife, Rachel, and their daughter, Eunice, moved in for a while and an addition was put on the dwelling. Much of the time the men were away serving in the regiments and it was the women and children who shared quarters. But even sharing lodgings was expensive. In 1782, eight-year-old Samuel Sherwood was moved from the local St Johns school to what was considered a better school in Montreal run by the Reverend John Stuart. The school was expensive and to economize Sarah had to move from her house in St Johns to the Loyal Block House, a military fortification on the Quebec frontier, where Justus was in charge of scouting and intelligence. Safety was a problem here since wood from the large fireplaces often fell on the floor, risking a fire.[62]

Sarah Sherwood had three children within the first five years of her marriage, but had none for the ten years between 1778, when she arrived in Quebec, and 1788, when she had resettled in her new home. The same was true of Anna Sherwood, who had three children between 1768 and 1779 but none during her stay in Quebec. For both women, the absence of the men could be one explanation for the lack of pregnancies, but another could be the overcrowding and lack of privacy which may have restricted sexual activity.

The stratification apparent in housing was also reflected in social life. At Quebec, the governor and British officers set the tone for a dazzling whirl of balls, dinner parties, and plays staged by members of the garrison. Marriages still had to be approved by officers and the prevalence of patriarchy was revealed in comments such as those of Sir John Johnson, whose permission was requested for the marriage of his niece. Johnson wrote, "I shall never forgive her or own her as a Niece, if she does not immediately break off all correspondence or engagements" [with her suitor].[63] In New York City, there was a striking contrast between the wealthy who bought frivolous luxuries, attended numerous plays, teas, receptions, and balls and the poor who struggled to survive in a shanty town of canvas tents.[64] Virtually all Loyalists, however, scrambled to educate their children. In New York there were various schools including one for girls; at British bases Loyalists petitioned to have their chosen candidate paid as schoolteacher, and at Montreal the Reverend John Stuart tried to open a school "principally intended for the children of Protestants" – an effort that ran into opposition from Governor Haldimand, who insisted that "the children of the established religion of the country [Catholicism] should be as readily received and their education as carefully attended to as that of Protestants." The Mohawks ensured that the British tradition of supplying them with a schoolteacher was continued so that "the disturbances of the times" did not "prevent their children from getting instruction." As well, they had 1,000 copies of a Mohawk prayer book printed and in 1781 they were studying it and had nominated a clerk and schoolmaster to hold Sunday prayers and teach them English.[65]

The Mohawk were not part of the stratified white society and housing them was relatively easy. Although there were regular complaints about the cost of maintaining the Indians, Haldimand had to admit that "if a Calculation is made, the Warriors of the Six Nations will not appear to cost more than a like number of white men with their officers." While the Indians might demand expensive luxuries, they were much cheaper to house and feed than white Loyalists. After the devastation of the Indian lands and dwellings in 1779, over 2,000 arrived in Quebec "naked and starving." However, after their immediate needs were met, the Indians helped support themselves. At Lachine, where the Mohawk wintered, they built their own huts and cut their own firewood.[66]

The practice of billeting Loyalist soldiers with French-Canadian families, which originated because of the shortage of buildings, was initially common. However, it was disliked by the French Canadians and by British military officers, who wanted the soldiers together so as to keep track of them, enforce discipline, and isolate them from the habitants. As a result, barracks were built at locations within the central part of the colony and at strategic outposts, such as Carleton Island. When it came to housing Loyalist women and children, the initial reaction of British officials was to oblige families to support them. But the cost and shortage of housing made this unrealistic and by 1778 British officials had assumed the responsibility for housing women and children refugees.[67]

British officials thought in terms of regimented, communal living arrangements for Loyalist women and children since separate quarters for each family was expensive and there were security problems. At St Johns in 1776 and 1777 Loyalists were allowed to build their own homes within a few hundred yards of the fort; however, these same people were later caught selling liquor illegally and harbouring persons who had come to gather intelligence for the enemy. British officials wanted families living together in a supervised environment so that they could control their activities and minimize expenses. Some Loyalist families were put in a rented house in Montreal "formerly occupied by rebel prisoners," which was described by an officer as a "cheap residence for Loyalists needing assistance." The house, which rented for a mere $14 per month, housed four families and provided room for "distressed families that arrive and have no place to stay."[68]

The British approach to aid for Loyalists in Quebec was revealed in the 1782 "Regulations as to lodgings and allowances for Loyalists," the ideas of which were similar to British poor-house or relief policies.[69] First, like their counterparts in Britain, officials in Quebec thought in terms of the deserving and undeserving poor. Loyalists able to work, the undeserving poor, "on first coming into the province" were to "give an account of the trades or professions [they] have been brought up to" so they "may be sent to places where they are most likely to get employment." Those deserving public assistance, according to the regulations, were "the sick, infirm, women with young children and those who from their situation can not go out to service." The second principle, characteristic also of British relief policy, was to provide only a bare subsistence and minimize costs. The needy were to live together in one or two buildings so that money could be saved in providing them with food, firewood, and medical care. The third idea borrowed from British relief thinking was that the needy should work for their assistance so as to avoid indolence. Loyalists being lodged at public expense were to be employed making "blanket coats, leggins at cheaper rates than the [French] Canadians." Control, regimentation, and impersonal detachment were at the core of the regulations which stated that all Loyalists including women and children were to be mustered each month so that they could be inspected and those able to work denied further support.[70]

Loyalist women, in a further example of their dependency and lack of control over their own lives, were told by British officials where they would live. Although some women were allowed to stay in barracks at Carleton Island, most were not allowed to remain with their husbands. While Sir John Johnson, an officer, was allowed to live in Montreal, his men were quartered at various places around Quebec and their families were in barracks at Lachenaye and later Machiche. The families of men "in the upper country" – Niagara and Detroit – were ordered to the central part of Quebec, where it was cheaper and easier to care for them. As of July 1779 needy Loyalists were being provisioned around the colony; there were 209 at St Johns, 27 at Chambly, 208 at Montreal, 126 at Pointe Claire, 196 at Machiche, and 87 at Sorel and Nouvelle

Beauce. As more barracks were built, families were also moved to other locations, such as Verchères, Trois-Rivières, Lachine, Yamaska, and Coteau-du-Lac.[71]

Many Loyalists were unhappy about the separation of family members. In 1780 Haldimand's secretary found that women and children at Niagara were being added to regimental returns and ordered that the corps were not "a nursery for women and children who can be as well taken care of, and at much less expense to Government in the lower parts of the province."[72] The men, it seems, were doctoring records in a vain attempt to keep their families with them. There was also evidence from St Johns that some fifty Loyalists were being provisioned without official returns being filed, suggesting perhaps that families were being cared for unofficially there as well.[73] Sir John Johnson also tried to intervene on behalf of his men to reunite them with their families who were living in barracks at Machiche. In March 1780 Johnson asked Haldimand if his men "could go into cantonments with the women until the river opens," when they presumably would return to their work elsewhere; Haldimand replied that there was no point moving the men since the ice was nearly broken up. When that tack did not work, Johnson tried another one in July when he suggested that the women be moved to where the men were, to which he received the cryptic response that the "families of the men ... will have permission to leave Machiche when the service shall permit." Even someone of Johnson's stature could not move Haldimand from his cold, impersonal, military approach to housing Loyalist families.[74]

Officials did not brook opposition to their plans to move Loyalists to specific locations. Although it was easier to care for Loyalist families in the central part of the colony, it was also cheaper to house them outside Montreal. In 1780 there was a plan to move Loyalist families from Montreal to Saint-Ours. However, there was resistance to the idea, perhaps because it was easier for Loyalist families to hear from friends and relatives when they lived in the bigger centre and Montreal was a more lively and interesting place. The unwillingness of the Loyalists to follow instructions about where they were to live was dealt with in a summary fashion. An order was issued that all able bodied Loyalists who refused to move to Saint-Ours were to be struck off the provision list.[75]

Many of the Loyalist women and children who later settled in and around Cataraqui lived in a camp-like setting at Machiche, present-day Yamachiche. In September 1778, Conrad Gugy, who had been born in the Netherlands of Swiss ancestry and served in the British army and in the government at Quebec, proposed to Haldimand that he settle women and children Loyalists on one of his seigneuries. Haldimand, needing quarters for Loyalist families and wanting them separated from the French population, agreed to the project, which cost the government about £1,300. Gugy was empowered to establish regulations and require services of his charges and he was advised to discipline those who disobeyed by cutting off their provisions. The buildings were constructed in a month by French Canadians from neighbouring parishes doing corvée labour – a seigneurial duty requiring habitants to work on public projects. By November 1778, twelve buildings were completed but, since there were no beds and blankets, the Loyalists were to "stay with habitants," although many moved into their quarters anyway. As well as the supplies brought in, Gugy looked to the local population to provide fresh food – although he had made a garden and a pasture for fifty cows – and clothing; on 20 December 1778 he took the Loyalists to a habitant who was to make them moccasins.[76]

Gugy called the quarters houses or apartments, but they were more like the barracks constructed for Loyalists in other parts of Quebec and were occupied mainly by women and children. Over 82 per cent of the adults were women and there were 2.4 children per woman. By December 1778 there were 12 buildings and 196 people, by 1779 21 buildings and over 400 people, and in 1780 between 327 and 355 people. Besides living and sleeping in the quarters, the Loyalists also did their cooking there since twenty-four pots and eight frying pans were supplied by Gugy in 1778. Except for December 1783, when many Loyalists were preparing to move to their new homes, there was usually between fifteen and twenty people living in each buildings, and the dimensions of these structures were only eighteen by forty feet. The quarters would have been cramped, especially in winter, with four or five families in each small building and ten people per room.[77]

The Machiche Loyalists, according to Haldimand, were treated well, but were "discontented and troublesome." In the eyes of British officials, the Loyalists were taking out their frustrations by striking out at the very government that was taking care of them. Gugy wrote that it was difficult to please "Messieurs Les Loyalists," while[78] another officer was more direct: "if you give them [the Loyalists] provision[s] they would have you put [them] in their mouths."[79] There is evidence that the Loyalists were quarrelsome, demanding, and complaining. Some Loyalists complained that the site for the quarters was a "drowned bog without water" until there was an investigation which showed that the "location for an establishment of this nature was the best available." Moreover, in 1778 the government agreed to a Loyalist request to pay for a teacher, Josiah Cass.[80]

But there were substantive complaints, common to other Loyalist refugees. One was that officials administering aid were heartless or cor-

Table 3
The Loyalist Settlement at Machiche

Loyalists Living at Machiche				
Dec. 1778	Oct. 1779	Sept. 1781	Jan. 1782	Dec. 1783
196	442	327	355	265
Number of Loyalists in Each Building				
Dec. 1778 (12 buildings)	Oct. 1779 (21 buildings)	Sept. 1781	Jan. 1782	Dec. 1783
16.3	21	15.5	16.9	12.6

Return of Clothing for Loyalists and Families Attached to the Different Corps at Machiche, 14 December 1781				
Men	Women	Children over 12	Children under 12	Total
21	97	60	184	362

Source: HP, 21,824

rupt. The use of public offices for private advantage was a frequent occurrence in the late eighteenth century and, when it came to dealing with the Loyalists, this practice was made easier because of the problems involved in supervising the officials responsible for supplying the refugees; regulations varied from place to place, and with many of the recipients of aid being illiterate it often happened that they signed for supplies they never received. In both New York and Quebec there were loud complaints about officials administering relief. In 1780 at Machiche, Loyalists made thirteen charges against Gershom French, a fellow Loyalist in charge of supplying them, for misappropriating funds and supplies. A board of officers' investigation concluded that the charges were "groundless" and called the complaints "idle, ill supported and malicious." Haldimand blamed the "irregularities and infinite trouble" at Machiche on the men who were in the camp intended only for women and children. He moved the men and ordered that troublemakers be taken off the provision list. However, in 1784, when the prominent New York Loyalist, Stephen DeLancey, was in charge of Machiche, he reported severe distress and complaints coming from "the best characters among them [the Loyalists]." He also concluded that French was guilty of "neglect and cruelty" and that the suffering at Machiche was the result of the "cruel treatment of the Loyalists" by French, who had abused them with "ill language" and took "cloth and linen" designed to clothe the poor women and children and cut it up to make carpets and sheets for his own use. Unfortunately, DeLancey's report came in May 1784 after the women and children had left Machiche.[81]

Discontent was also caused by provisioning problems at Machiche and elsewhere. Supplying food to the exiles was a constant problem in Quebec and New York. In both places the population was swelled with the influx of Loyalists, troops, and Quebec also had to contend with the arrival of large numbers of Indians. Attempts to regulate food supplies resulted only in a blackmarket, shortages, and a dramatic increase in the price of food. It is estimated that in New York City food prices increased by 800 per cent from 1776 to 1777 and rationing was common. Both centres relied on food imports from Great Britain, which was risky since the lack of refrigeration caused spoilage and because of the activities of privateers.[82] The problem was especially severe in Quebec, where the long distances between the widely dispersed population centres meant that transporting food was very haphazard. As a consequence, there were regular attempts to economize and to grow food locally. Farmers at bases such as Niagara and Detroit were urged to grow their own provisions, as were the Indians; even Loyalists stationed at remote bases such as the Loyal Blockhouse had cows and horses. On Carleton Island, ploughs were sent in to allow wheat to be planted; Indian crops, such as beans and pumpkins, were grown. Still, grasshoppers destroyed the potatoes and the dependence on imported food continued.[83]

Food shortages and the destitution of refugees arriving at British bases meant that many Loyalists, especially women, had to be provisioned at public expense. Many women fleeing to New York City or Quebec were the families of Loyalist soldiers and theoretically were to be fed by their husbands; however, because the military subsistence was small and families large, large numbers of these women were provisioned. Others were either the wives of unincorporated Loyalists, unconnected to any regiment, or widows, eligible for pensions based on their husband's military service. Typical of the last group were the widows Crothers and McLaren, who each received pensions of £20 per year. The sum was small when one considers that £30 per year was considered the minimum upon which a family could survive without assistance. Also, the schoolteacher at one of the Loyalist bases was paid £80 per annum and the Reverend John Stuart, who taught as well as ministered, received almost £300 annually. Also, widows lost their pensions if they remarried and, in some cases, the new husband was unwilling to provide for children from the former marriage.[84]

Provisioning statistics reveal a high percentage of women. In two returns of Loyalists being provisioned in 1780 and 1781, there are more women than men; in group one there were 308 women and 262 men, while in the second there were 367 women and 89 men. Women represented 54 per cent of the adults in the first group and 81 per cent in the second. These statistics are especially striking when it is considered that only between 25 and 30 per cent of those Loyalists who settled in and around Cataraqui were women. Also noteworthy is that, while the numbers of male and female children under twelve were quite close, there was a significant disparity between the male and female children over twelve. In the first group there were 242 females and 195 males over twelve, and in the second 323 females and 256 males. What these figures show is that many young boys over twelve joined the Loyalist regiments and were provided for just as if they had been men. Joining the regiments, in which they were clothed, housed, and fed, was an option open to male Loyalists. Women, on the other hand, were denied this opportunity and hence had no choice but to petition humbly for provisions. Consequently, it was much more common for women than for men to undergo the feelings of dependency and helplessness associated with being a refugee relying on government provisioning.

Table 4
Loyalist Provisioning

	Return of Loyalists Receiving Provisions in the District of Montreal from 25 October to 24 November 1780	General Return of Unincorporated Loyalists and Families Receiving Provisions Gratis from 25 May to 24 April 1781
Men	262	89
Women	308	367
Male children under 12	175	181
Female children under 12	186	178
Male children over 12	195	256
Female children over 12	242	323[85]

Source: HP, 21,826

The British approach to provisioning, as to so much else, was paternalistic and hierarchical. Need was obviously a criterion in determining the level of support, but so was one's former status in the colonies. The reasoning was, according to Haldimand, that "families who have been least used to difficulties, are least able to contend with them" and therefore "need help." Loyalists petitioning for aid cultivated these notions of hierarchy. One widow was described as a "genteel woman" in a petition for a pension. Ebenezer Jessup wrote of coming to Quebec in 1777 "with a Brood of unfortunate Women and Children," "many of which were possessed of very good livings at their homes." Sir John Johnson's corps was described as containing "many" women "who formerly lived in Affluence & were totally unable to exist upon the Ration of their Husbands."[86] Such descriptions might have persuaded British officials to provision Loyalist women whose husbands were in the corps, but they bore little relationship to reality. To state that many of Johnson's men had "lived in Affluence" was simply untrue. What one can see developing in these assertions is the myth of the upper-class origins of the Loyalists.

The allocation of rations was haphazard and open to abuse and the amounts distributed inadequate. One ration included a pound of flour and beef or twelve ounces of pork, and in theory each man received one ration, each woman one-half, and each young child one-quarter; however, there were variations from place to place and some rations were somehow distributed without being counted. Also, since each individual had to petition for rations, enormous power rested with officials who approved the requests. In New York City, decisions about food and firewood were made by the inspector of the claims of refugees, Colonel Roger Morris, whom Loyalists claimed was ignorant of the "character of the refugees," "austere," and inhumane. There were repeated requests for his removal and in 1782 commander-in-chief Guy Carleton replaced Morris with a board which made decisions about relief and established pensions of £20 per year instead of rationing and providing firewood. There were also allegations that officials profited by paying little to those supplying or transporting food, but charging exorbitant prices to the army. Allegations that the well placed were well supplied were also common. Equally serious was the chorus of complaints about the inadequacy of the rations. Loyalists complained that the men were too poorly fed to work effectively, that women and children did not get enough to eat, and that disease and even death was caused by poor and insufficient food. Such claims took on compelling credence when made by officials in charge of the Loyalists. In 1778 Conrad Gugy expressed concerns about the children at Machiche; one-half a ration, the standard for children over six, was simply not enough food for a six-year-old "who runs constantly"; mothers, he reported, were depriving themselves and giving some of their rations to the children. Gugy was so worried that he sought Haldimand's approval for increasing the flour to children to one full ration and giving infants one-half instead of just one-quarter of a ration.[87]

A poor diet was one cause of the many illnesses which plagued the Loyalists. By the late eighteenth century, colonial American families were used to a diet that included fresh meats, vegetables, and dairy products.[88] At British bases, salt provisions were much more common. In 1780, for example, the Indians requested five days of fresh provisions and two of salt because they were getting half of each and suffering from diseases, such as scurvy. Yet, because they hunted, the Indians were often better off than the whites. The lack of milk and "root greens" was cited as the cause of illness and the prescribed remedy for an outbreak of measles was a vegetable diet, which was unavailable. Bad water, provisions, and even bad rum were also believed to cause colds and flus.[89] Other ailments included malaria, caused by mosquito-infested swamps, smallpox, and inflammation of the lungs.[90] Remedies, which included drinking vinegar, wine, or spruce beer, were crude, as was the medical care offered by local French-Canadian doctors or ill-trained army surgeons. Consequently, illness was common and so was death. On an average evening in New York City it was reported that seven or eight people would be buried, usually having died of disease, and on an especially bad night there were seventeen burials. Illness and death were great levellers; no family was immune. In 1778 Sir John Johnson wrote that he and his wife were "trying all they can to relieve" their son, "poor little John," who was "declining fast with worms."[91]

The distress caused by the quality and quantity of provisions became severe after 1780 when cuts were ordered. Cutting people off provisions as a punishment or a means of forcing them to obey orders had always been common. But as the war dragged on, supplies became shorter and shorter and concerns were expressed that the Loyalists were coming to rely on government aid and were becoming indolent. As a result, in 1780 and 1781 there were orders to reduce the provision lists and force able-bodied Loyalists to work. All healthy males, "who shall refuse to be employed in any Situation where his Excellency may think his Service useful to Government," were to be struck off the provision list.[92] Haldimand's order that those of "superior rank" not in dire need "will voluntarily decline" provisions showed the thinking of the regime – *ordering* someone to do something *voluntarily*.[93] Blacks also suffered in that slaves and servants were not to be provisioned since "those who can afford to keep Servants cannot be considered ... proper Objects of that bounty." The reasoning was solid but did little to help slaves and servants. At this time, interestingly enough, Molly Brant's slaves were being provisioned at Carleton Island, which may merely show Molly Brant's influential connections.[94]

Many of the cuts were directed at women. Those whose husbands were in the provincial corps were to be "struck off the provision list" as of August 1781. Others were compelled to work for their rations; Loyalist women receiving rations were ordered to wash for officers and soldiers at four coppers a shirt and do similar work at comparable rates or be "struck off the provision list." The British concern with status, position, and hierarchy was, again, reflected in the cuts. All unmarried women thirteen to forty who refused "going into service when offered customary Wages and good treatment" were to be denied provisions "unless they can make it appear that their *Birth* and *former condition in life* was above such menial employ." The reasoning behind the cuts was that there were at places such as Machiche "many young women ... able and hitherto accustomed to earn their bread by labor who are now passing their times in idleness." The paternalistic concern was that "a habit of idleness [was being] encouraged which must be very fatal to the happiness of these people in the future." It was supposedly for their own good that these women were being deprived of their rations.[95]

Women and children suffered greatly because of the cuts. In statistical terms, many more women than men were cut off provisions, as the table below illustrates. In August 1781 twice as many women as men were cut off provisions.

Table 5
Return of Loyalists Struck off the Provision List,
1 August 1781

	So-rel	St John's	La-chine	Point Clair	Rivière-du-chen	St Gen.	Mtl	Côteau-du-Lac	Ver-chère	Ma-chich
Men	9	13	3	2	–	5	4	–	5	–
Women	14	9	4	8	1	9	10	3	2	22
Total:	Men – 41				Women – 82					

Source: HP 21,826

In addition, the suffering caused by the cuts hit women and children harder. One Loyalist soldier complained that his two sons, thirteen and fourteen, and a thirteen-year-old orphan girl for whom he was caring had been deprived of provisions which they needed to attend school. Stephen DeLancey reported from Machiche that those over twelve were being cut from the provision lists but were "not able to get employ;" thus, there were more "sickly" and "deaths" from "the want of provision and cloathing." Similar reports came from Montreal, where a 1782 list of distressed families included four men, thirty-two women, and fifty-seven children.[96] Women and children suffered most because it was assumed that their husbands and fathers could and should take care of them, an assumption that was often untrue. Also, cutting boys over twelve off the provision list was one thing, since any able-bodied male could join the provincial corps, an honourable occupation in which his basic needs were satisfied. But girls and young women were cut off the provision list on the assumption that they could earn their own livelihoods; however, there often was no work for them to take. They had to look for some menial job – such as washing clothes – and if that was not available they had literally to beg British officials for aid or suffer silently.

Stress is an inevitable part of life in exile and is especially acute in refugee camps. "It is during the camp experience," an expert on refugees explains, "that the enormity of what has happened finally strikes home to the refugee. The focus is on what has been lost." Because exile is a "transition" period, it is, in the words of another expert, a "stressful" time with "high frequencies of psychological disturbances."[97]

Among the Loyalists, family relationships showed the strain of war and uncertainty. Marriages collapsed. Stephen Tuttle, a Loyalist soldier, wrote to the governor's secretary about his wife who had left him, taking £100 with her and running up bills in Quebec; Tuttle warned that she would probably request assistance and requested that the governor "send her home." Another soldier who did not return from Yamaska was believed to have committed suicide because his wife had had a baby by another man. Then there was the case of Joseph Bettys, a Loyalist soldier and a married man, whose open affair with the daughter of a habitant created a scandal in Quebec.[98]

Some Loyalists broke down because of the heavy burdens they bore. There was at least one incident of infanticide at Carleton Island where a mother was believed to have killed a newborn. There were as well references to people losing their senses and having to be watched constantly by neighbours and friends or to "insane Loyalists" being sent to the hospital in Quebec. And at least one Mohawk leader who had been sober before the Revolution developed a drinking problem because of the stresses of the war.[99]

Death and tragedy surrounded the Loyalists, as the story of Mrs Buck shows. Her husband and a son were killed in battle during the Burgoyne expedition, and then another son died of illness in Quebec. Her daughter-in-law remarried, but both she and her second husband died. The widow Buck was asking for aid because she was left with the responsibility of raising her three grandchildren. Orphans such as the Buck children could not look to institutions for care but had to turn to other family members.[100] As well as anxiety and anguish, Loyalist women suffered from loneliness. A Loyalist officer writing to his wife in the colonies told of a woman relative in exile who had just given birth and had "wished for no more in the world than your being here." There were times such as birthing when women traditionally looked to their closest relatives and friends for help and to be without them was very hard. Another example of loneliness was the case of Jane Stuart, wife of the Reverend John Stuart. Jane's married life had been difficult. She left her home in Philadelphia in 1775 when she married John Stuart and moved to the Mohawk River. Immediately after her marriage she became pregnant and had another child the next year, when her mother also died, leaving an estate over which there was a prolonged wrangle. Then the Revolution turned the Stuarts' lives upside down. They experienced the hostility of the community, the threat of violence, the moves from one location to another, and then the trek to Quebec. Jane Stuart endured life as an exile on a remote frontier far removed from friends, family, and familiar surroundings. Her husband wrote that she was "reconciled" to the changes, but he also knew that long after they had reached Quebec Jane's "heart is still with her friends in dear, dear Philadelphia."[101]

Leah Moore, who in 1780 married Joel Stone, the founder of the St Lawrence River community of Gananoque, was the only Loyalist woman to write about her emotional upheaval during the Revolution. Leah was the daughter of a prosperous New York City mariner who was obviously accustomed to a comfortable life; when she married Joel, her family gave the newly-weds the use of a house as well as furniture and £100 per annum. She could write a decent letter, which is noteworthy since most of the Loyalist women covered in this study were illiterate, and reading was one of her interests. The men in her life portrayed her as being demanding and temperamental, but this might have reflected her less than happy family life.[102]

Leah's father, William, was hardly the ideal family man. His own brother left him nothing in his will, which referred to "my ungrateful brother William," and only left money to William's children on the condition that it be "free from his control." He virtually abandoned his family, going to sea for seven years and not even communicating with his wife for two years. Leah wrote to him in 1781 – in a letter with the salutation "Honoured Papa" and the ending "Your dutiful Child" – about the "Anxiety of mind your long Absence gives me & the family." Leah warned that it "will soon bring her [Leah's mother] to the Grave for she takes it to heart & grieves continually ... which has thrown her into a deep decay." Then Leah's mother, Mary, did die in 1782 and William professed his overwhelming grief but also married a nineteen-year-old whom he had known for a month.[103]

Leah's marriage to Joel Stone was not a happy one, perhaps because of the strain placed on it by the Revolutionary War and its aftermath. After Joel escaped to New York City from a Connecticut prison, he scrambled to make a living in a city teeming with people trying to do the same. He prospered from privateering for a while and when that failed he tried unsuccessfully supplying the army. He was plagued by repeated bouts of an unknown but devastating illness. Then in 1783, when the war was over and it was clear that he would not be able to recover his property and debts in Connecticut, he went to England to seek compensation from the British government and to fight a legal battle over a handsome legacy left to Leah and her two brothers by their uncle. The legacy was Leah's, but she was not very interested in it, perhaps because, within the patriarchal world of the late eighteenth century, legal and financial matters were left to women's husbands. Joel's trip to England lasted three years.

From Joel's point of view, he was being a dutiful husband, carving out a secure financial foundation for the family's future. To be sure, he did take care of his family. Before leaving, he arranged for Leah to be cared for by relatives and friends. He wrote regularly to his wife, sent her gifts and money when he could, addressed her as "My Dear," and closed his letters with "affectionate husband." But Leah did not answer his letters, despite his pleas to hear from her. She was of little or no help in his struggle to document the claims to her legacy. And then in June 1785 he received a stern letter from her father – beginning not with "Dear Son," as an earlier one had, but with the curt greeting "Dear Stone" – saying Leah's "behaviour is so most unaccountable that it is not in my power to do anything for her." Leah's father, displaying again his unwillingness to take responsibility for his family, asked that Joel either return home or send Leah to England or to his family in Connecticut. Leah Stone was a married woman and Joel's responsibility.[104]

Joel's behaviour was perfectly acceptable by eighteenth-century standards. Leah's was not. Joel was the family head, on whose shoulders fell the responsibility of providing for its future, and that was what he was doing in England. He explained to his father in Connecticut: "Am Sorry to leave my Pleasant family so long, but Business demands it of me"; it was his duty, he believed, "to effect some plan for future provision for myself and Dear family ... "[105] Joel Stone had the qualities expected of a good husband of the time; he was responsible, hard working, dedicated, even affectionate. He had probably tried as hard as he could to be a good husband.

Leah's behaviour is more understandable by twentieth- than by eighteenth-century standards. As Joel put it, he was used to "hardship" but his "young wife" was "never in the least accustomed to such" and was under "the necessity of participating in all my woes." Leah was married in 1780 when she was still very young, in very unstable and trying circumstances. Her mother, to whom she was very close, died in 1782. The same year, Leah had her first baby and she was three months pregnant when her husband left in 1784. The second baby died in infancy. At the same time she was being buffetted from one male protector to another. Joel's brother, Leman, had her in Connecticut; next she was sent to New York where she was with a family friend for a while, and then her own family tried to manage her. Leah Stone was experiencing enormous stress and it was being reflected in her behaviour. Joel's family called her "Black Bets" (Joel sometimes called her Bets), an intimation of deep depression, and stories about her uncontrollable behaviour suggest a mental breakdown.[106]

Leah poured forth her feelings of abandonment and betrayal, feelings often experienced by refugees, in a 1785 letter to her husband. After acknowledging receipt of his last letter, she complained of receiving "no satisfaction respecting your Business nor of your Returning home." For Leah, Joel was the negligent one, for "it seems as if you have forgot you ever had a family." She continued: "For my part I am in a miserable starvation, I have not a shilling nor a home to go to and what will become of me this winter God only knows ... " In fact, Leah was reasonably well provided for in a material sense, but she was in desperate straits emotionally. She always had a place to live in but never a home and one confrontation with her brother, which fueled the notion of her uncontrollable behaviour, was over her allegedly reckless spending; according to her brother, she "had gone and purchased Furniture to keep House with."[107] What Leah yearned for was the security and stability of having a home, a husband, and a family.

By 1785 she was deprived of all three. She didn't have a home, her husband was away, and she lacked emotional support from her family. To make her situation still more difficult, her remaining companion was taken away by her father. When Leah's behaviour became "unaccountable," her father asserted his patriarchal power and sent her son, William, away to boarding school even though he was only three and his own mother wanted to keep him with her. This only worsened her mental state; "It makes my heart ake," she wrote, "wehn I think of him [Dear Bill] he was all the comfort I had But now I must be separated for him." Her remaining brother, Lewis, was also preparing to leave. "Then," she lamented, "I shall be quite alone." Leah concluded her letter to Joel with a desperate plea for help: "For god Sake come home to your Distressed Family who wishes much to se you ... I am very unhappy."[108] The stress of the Revolution had taken its toll on Leah Stone. Whether her behaviour was caused by severe depression or a mental breakdown, she suffered terribly. We will never know how typical her tale was.

As well as being a time of stress and hardship, the exile period was formative because it was when Loyalists had to explain the significance of their experiences and the bonds that held them together. Once safety has been reached, refugees' "attitudes and sentiments felt in earlier stages ... crystallize and are articulated." What also often emerges is the outlines of a group identity. Refugees share a common experience; all were harassed, forced to flee, and live as exiles. As they begin to explain why they were treated in this way, certain common threads, which later coalesce around a well-defined group identity, become apparent.[109] In the case of the Loyalists, arrival at British bases began a process of self-definition because so many had to petition British officials for aid or support and in the petitions the meaning of their experiences had to be articulated.

A recurring theme in the petitions was their signers' declarations of loyalty. One wrote of his "love of my King;" another said that he was imprisoned "for his loyalty and attachment to his Majesty's interest"; and still another spoke of being "a prisoner for his loyalty."[110] By the time they reached British bases, Loyalists had been harassed, they had lost their property, many had been imprisoned, and they were living in often desperate circumstances in a strange land. Why had these misfortunes befallen them? To say that they had followed their leaders, friends, neighbours, or relatives into battle was not very satisfying. More rewarding was the explanation that they had all been persecuted because of a principled attachment to the British cause. Alan McDonell proclaimed that from the beginning of the "rebellion ... Principles of True Loyalty" prompted him and his fellow Scots to put themselves under the "direction of Sir John Johnson to stand in defence of their King and Country." Similarly, a Loyalist from Orange County New York proclaimed that from "Principle and Duty" he "was always firmly attached to his Graceful Sovereign and Government."[111] What these declarations convey is the idea that Loyalists made a conscious choice, from pure motives, to support the British empire and king.

Not only were their motives noble, but the Loyalists had also proved their dedication by their service to the crown. "My Loyalty to my King, my respect to the just Laws and Government of Great Britain, and my abhorrence of the unnatural Rebellion and revolt in America," Solomon Johns declared, "induced me very early in this contest to transmit my Name to His Excellency Sir Guy Carleton, offering my feeble Services."[112] Johns's motive was loyalty, and his noble intentions were demonstrated by his service in a Loyalist regiment. Men petitioning for government aid could easily prove their service by naming the regiment in which they served and describing their service and time of enlistment. Typical was William Lamson, who declared that he was "amongst the

first of those [who] came to Canada in 1776 with Major Jessup." Another wrote that he had been "repeatedly sent back into [Charlotte]
county to bring in royalists and procure intelligence." Certificates of
loyalty and service, affirming Loyalist men's loyalty and dedication,
were provided by officers of the Loyalist corps, such as Edward Jessup
or Sir John Johnson, whose background and status gave them auto-
matic credibility with British officials. The war had exacted its toll on
Loyalists such as Edward Foster, who was incapacitated because of "old
age" and "severe service" in the military, or Hugh Munro, who referred
to "my bleeding wounds." Military service also was the formal, recognized contribution which Loyalist men made to the Revolution and was
cited to justify their demands on the British for aid.[113]

Loyalists stressed their sacrifices, too. James Robbins spoke for many
Loyalists when he declared that he was "sacrificing his all for his Attachment to government." Imprisonment or the need to abandon families were mentioned as sacrifices, but the most consistent references
were to property losses.[114] Some had supplied Loyalist-Indian raiding
parties; John Fraser, for instance, had supplied "a large New England
oxen, 1 bull, 12 sheep, 6 hogs" and some "English cheese."[115] More
common was John Ryckman's claim that the "rebels seized his house,
land, cattle, stock, household goods and implements," or Ranald Mc-
Donell's statement that he was "by birth and education a gentleman"
whose "considerable property" was lost "because of loyalty."[116]

Loyalty, service, and sacrifice, as defined in Loyalist petitions, were all
male concepts. Loyalty involved the political decision to choose the Loyalist side and the realms of both politics and decision-making were male
preserves. Service usually meant military service in the Loyalist corps, in
which there was no place for women. And sacrifice was defined in terms
of loss of property or other assets which were owned and controlled by
the male head of the household. Thus, as the Loyalists groped during
their years in exile to explain their past and carve out a new future, they
spoke in terms that left no place for women and their accomplishments.

The exile experience was crucial for Loyalist women and set them
apart from their Patriot counterparts because it undermined so much of
what the women had done in the earlier stages of their lives as refugees.
The women's role in supplying Loyalist-Indian raiding parties, in spying, in enduring harassment, in supporting their families, in making
their way into exile – all of these achievements were lost during exile.
When the women reached British lines they fitted into a patriarchal, paternalistic power structure as burdens – mouths to be fed, bodies to be
clothed and housed – whose own accomplishments were irrelevant.
Rather than citing their contributions to the Revolution, Loyalist
women had to point to the loyalty and military service of their hus-

bands. Rather than pointing to their sacrifices, it was the property, assets, or even pensions of their husbands that they claimed. The only thing left to women was their feminine frailty, helplessness, and suffering. What the women were losing was the public record of their accomplishments and of their history.

5 Resettlement and Redemption

At last we are preparing to leave forever this land of my birth. The long weary years of war, followed by the peace years, that have been to us worse than the time of fighting, are over. As soon as it is possible we shall set foot on our travels for a new land of promise ... When I leave this beautiful Mohawk Valley and the lands that I had hoped we would always hold, I shall hear no more the words "Tory" and "Parricide" ... Our grandparents little thought when they sought this new land, after the rising of Prince Charlie, that a flitting would be our fate, but, we must follow the old flag wherever it takes us. It is again "The March of the Cameron Men" and wives and children must tread the hard road.

Nancy Jean Cameron, New York, 15 May 1785.[1]

In May 1784 Governor Frederick Haldimand ordered Loyalist refugees to move from their camps scattered around Quebec to Sorel, to be mustered and provisioned for their voyage to the new settlements in and around Cataraqui. Stragglers and doubters were brought into line by the threat that their provisions would be cut off if they refused to comply. At Sorel each man and boy over ten was issued a coat, waistcoat, breeches, hat, shirt, blanket, shoes and shoe soles, leggings, and stockings. Women and girls over ten got two yards of woolen cloth, four yards of linen, one pair of stockings, a blanket, and shoe soles, while small children qualified for one yard of woolen cloth, two yards of linen, stockings, and shoe soles. There was one blanket for every two children and five people were to share a tent and one cooking kettle. After being mustered and outfitted, the Loyalists were sent to Lachine to begin their treacherous trip along the St Lawrence River to Lake Ontario.[2]

At Lachine they were loaded onto batteaux specially constructed to traverse the rapids of the western St Lawrence River. The flat-bottomed batteaux, from twenty-five to forty feet long, took four to five families and their belongings, which ranged from the grandfather clock that one family had brought all the way from the New York frontier to the meager bundles of others who did not even have bedding. Once the batteaux, manned by four or five French Canadians, were loaded, they assembled in brigades of twelve, usually comprised of others from the same corps, and set out, being powered variously by oars, poles, or sails. The trip was slow and trying. Rapids along the way forced the passengers and their belongings out of the batteaux, which had to be dragged and pulled with ropes through the churning waters. During the day, it could be cold on the open waters, so that the crowding together of the passengers was almost welcome. Winds, currents, and mosquitoes made the trip long and uncomfortable. And at night the passengers had to sleep in make-shift tents pitched by open fires used for cooking.[3]

The ten- to twelve-day journey ended when the Loyalists reached their new settlements whose "strickingly beautiful" scenery was broken only by "the bark-thatched wigwam of the Savage, or the newly erected tent of the hardy Loyalist." After unloading their belongings, seeds, tools, supplies, and two huge full grown bulls sent to take care of the 200 cows driven overland on the north shore of the river, the Loyalists pitched tents and prepared to begin their lives again. Behind them was the persecution and fighting of the Revolution, the misery of the years in exile, and the agony of defeat. Ahead of them was hard work and hardship, but also the companionship of family, kinsmen, and comrades-in-arms who either had come with them or poured into the new settlement from every direction. Within a few years, they would transform the "howling wilderness" into "a very respectable frontier settlement" and they would later proclaim their experiment in the wilds of Canada "a compleat success."[4]

Cataraqui and its surrounding area was from the beginning seen as a special place settled by special people. It owed its creation to the paternalism of the British government, which had assumed its responsibility to provide for the Loyalists after the Revolution was lost. Although located on the frontier, it was a structured society with clear social distinctions, an authoritarian political system, and conservative values. Most important, it was settled by refugees who had lost a civil war and needed to justify their actions and find a new sense of meaning and purpose. They were not just ordinary settlers, they were Loyalists, who had been motivated by principle to make great sacrifices in a noble cause.

This was the view of their past which they would pass on to later generations of myth-makers and historians.

The women, once beyond the reach of Patriot committees and the supervision of the British government, faded from the historical record, which is almost silent about their new lives. As was true during their exile, they once again had to fit into a structured framework in which there were those who were recognized as leaders or decision-makers and those who were treated as followers. There was no Loyalist counterpart to the anti-patriarchal, republican views of the American Revolution which gave more scope to women and promoted more egalitarian family relations. Instead, the conservative ideas and institutions of their society merely reinforced the patriarchal power structure of the newly reestablished Loyalist households. And in the myths about the Loyalists and their heroism, the women's role was either neglected or distorted. The success of the new settlements may have redeemed the Loyalists' defeat in the Revolution, and as individuals many Loyalist women may have found peace and prosperity. Nevertheless, Loyalist women as a group vanished from the public record and lost their rightful place in history.

During the war, the defeat of the British and the achievement of independence by the American colonies was unthinkable to most Loyalists, and it was only slowly that they came to accept their fate. In retrospect, the defeat of Cornwallis at Yorktown in October 1781 signalled the end; but this was not apparent to the average Loyalist, who received little accurate news about the war despite the existence of several newspapers in New York City and the bilingual *Quebec Gazette*.[5] The newspapers were filled with advertisements – usually occupying over half the space – official proclamations or notices, news from abroad, debates in the British parliament, intercepted Patriot correspondence, or excerpts from other newspapers. Political articles sounded more like propaganda than information; for example, in September 1782 a New Yorker claimed that Congress did not speak for Americans who shared the "almost universal desire of their country for the return of peace with the reunion of the empire."[6] There were also official documents written in almost unintelligible legal and diplomatic language. For example, the articles of capitulation following Cornwallis's defeat were reprinted in one New York newspaper on 5 November 1781 and in another a month later, while the *Quebec Gazette* reprinted the articles of peace on 8 and 15 May 1783. Illiterate Loyalists had to rely on public meetings where the documents were read or on intelligence from scouts. Quebec, because of its isolation and its preoccupation in 1782 with the threat of an invasion, was even more out of touch than the more cosmopolitan New York City.

By 1782 some Loyalists in New York City painfully considered the unthinkable and spelled out to Sir Guy Carleton their vulnerability. Emotions seeped through the otherwise stylized petitions when the authors conceded that it was "impossible for us to express the Consternation with which we are struck, even on the probability of so calamitous an Event [independence] taking place ... we cannot suppress our Feelings." As in earlier petitions, the Loyalists reiterated their sense of identity. They were Loyalists, "engaged by the purest motives ... to vindicate the Dignity of your Crown" and the unity of the empire. Their service and sacrifice had been great; they had not "hesitated ... to step forth and hazard ... [their] Lives and Fortunes" for the cause. But now, with the prospect of the war being lost, they were dependent on His Majesty's "paternal Goodness." The British had to ensure in any treaty with the Americans that the Loyalists' "Persons and Properties" were protected and some "Asylum prepared for such of us as cannot remain in this country."[7]

Other Loyalists exhibited behaviour typical of refugees when they refused even to countenance the prospect of defeat. Refugees often deny that there is a serious threat to their future and the Loyalists were no exception. The defeat of Cornwallis, for example, was brushed aside by one Loyalist writer with the comment that "such accidents" happen; a "melancholy atmosphere" was not justified since the "spirit of the nation [Britain] was too high, its resources too many .... [it will] revenge his [Cornwallis's] fate."[8] Another writer in the *Quebec Gazette* acted like a typical refugee, indulging in self-delusion and the longing to return to a normal life. On 2 January 1783 this poet described a fanciful peace where all would be happily mended after seven long years of war: "In this quarrel never mind, who first was to blame, / But in oblivion let all animosities cease / And most heartily join, to establish a peace / A quarrel made up, between friends often proves / A renewal of amity, friendship and love." A similar unwillingness to face reality permeated the 1782 statement by a New York Loyalist that the "American Loyalists wish for nothing else than that their country may be flourishing and happy under the auspicious rule of their rightful and most amiable Sovereign; and in a constitutional union with the Parent State."[9] Such delusions did not last for long.

Within months many Loyalists knew that they had lost the war and that Britain had not gained any guarantees for their property and persons in the peace treaty. Captain Justus Sherwood described being on the Quebec frontier in April 1783 where Patriots "Naughtily boast that they are Independent, that this is their Ground & that they shall have possession of it by the middle of May"; he thought the taunts were merely "the mad sallies of Vulgar fools" until he learned of the peace terms from a Patriot newspaper. In June 1783 Haldimand reported a "sulkiness of disposition in this people [the Loyalists in Quebec] which can not be described." Carleton portrayed the New York Loyalists as a "people in grief" and the city as being in mourning, with "multitudes embarking and on the point of leaving the place of their nativity, their habitations and their friends foreever."[10]

The Indians, whose lands in the Ohio region and elsewhere had been ceded by the British to the Americans, were especially bitter. Haldimand kept the peace terms from them for as long as possible and worked hard to placate them. An eloquent Indian probably spoke for others when he said in 1784: "We do not think they [the Americans] have beaten us, our minds are still strong and determined to carry on the war. The disgrace is almost killing us." The depth of the Mohawk's grief was conveyed by Sir William Johnson's son-in-law, who observed that they had "lived at their ease upon a rich Tract of Country, left them and possessed by their Ancestors from time immemorial." In leaving their lands, the Mohawk were losing their history since "they chiefly by the natural Monuments of that native land of theirs, such as Rivers, Woods, Mountains, Rocks and its Environs preserved the thread or recollection of their General History handed down from Father to Son" and they were leaving "the graves of their deceased Friends and Relations to be demolished and abused by their Enemies." Another cause of sorrow for them this was internal divisions; many Six Nations Indians remained neutral in the war and later decided to remain in the United States.[11]

Some Loyalist refugees tried to return to their homes. As early as 1782 there were reports of low morale among the Loyalist corps and problems with desertion. By 1783 desertion was so common in Quebec that those who were suspect were sent to Niagara and Indians were posted at bases to catch deserters. "The longer the war lasts," an officer observed in 1783, "the more does the attachment of the royalists lessen and they must be watched."[12]

For most, returning home was impossible since they had been attainted and had had their property confiscated; others attempted to go back but shared the experience of Joel Stone who, on returning to Connecticut in 1783 to collect debts and recover property, received "a solemn warning from the mob, to leave the province within forty-eight hours." Although there was the occasional sign of good will – such as an article from the *Connecticut Journal* reprinted in *The Quebec Gazette* which argued that Loyalists should be allowed to return since the war was over and animosities should cease – more typical was an article in the *New York Packet or American Advertiser*. It advocated that an *Association* be formed against returning Loyalists – described as "abominable Wretches," "Robbers, Murderers and Incendiaries" – "to render their

Situation by every means in our power so unhappy that they will prefer a voluntary banishment to the proposed return, let it be a Crime abhorr'd by Nature to have any communication with them."[13]

Persecution was the main reason why Loyalists could not return to the colonies and why so many continued to move northward after the war, as was shown in "The Tory's Soliloquy," written in New York in 1783:

To go – or not to go – is that the question?
[the choice was to go to a bleak Canada]
Or stay and cringe to the rude surly whigs,
Whose wounds, yet fresh, may urge their desperate hand
To spurn us while we sue – perhaps consign us
To the *kind care* of some *outrageous* mob,
Who for their sport our persons may adorn
In all the majesty of *tar and feathers*;
Perhaps our necks, to keep their humour warm,
May grace a Rebel halter! – There's the sting!
This people's, the bleak clime, for who can brook
A Rebel's frown – or bear his children's stare
When in the streets they point and lisp "*A Tory?*"
The open insult, the heart-piercing stab
Of satire's pointed pen or worse, – far worse –
Committee's rage – or jury's grave debate
On the grand question: "shall their lives forsooth
or property – or both – atone their crimes?"
Then let us fly, nor trust a war of words
... Let's lose our fears, for no bold Whig will dare
With sword or law to persecute us there.[14]

Loyalists were not attracted to Canada for its own sake; the area around Cataraqui was dubbed a "howling wilderness" by more than one Loyalist. They were refugees fleeing from persecution and Canada was repeatedly referred to as their "Asylum," their refuge from the bitterness, rancour, and defeat of the Revolution.[15]

One Loyalist woman who left Johnstown, New York, in 1785 for New Johnstown (present-day Cornwall) to escape persecution expressed her feelings about the departure. Nancy Jean Cameron wrote to a relative about the physical and financial hardships of leaving. Their lands had been confiscated and cash was short since "it is hard to raise money at forced sales." The journey, she knew, would be "long and hard"; they would be on the road for weeks, trusting to Indian guides to lead them "through the forests" and living in a wagon drawn by four horses. There was obvious sadness in leaving "forever this land of my birth," "this beautiful Mohawk Valley and the lands that I had hoped we would always hold." And the decision to go was clearly not hers to make. Within the patriarchal family structure, it was the "Cameron Men" who were on the march again and the duty of the "wives and children" was to "tread the hard road" by following.

Leaving her home was obviously emotionally difficult for Nancy Jean Cameron, but it was also a relief. She made the surprising point that the "peace years" were "worse to us than the time of fighting." Why? There was the "taunting among the elders" and the "bickering among the children." But with her departure "bitter feelings are gone foreever"; she would "hear no more the words 'Tory' and 'Parracide'." Nancy Jean Cameron probably spoke for other Loyalist women when she confessed that what she loved was "friendship and neighborly kindness." Despite the lack of material comforts, in an emotional sense leaving was healing the wounds of the Revolution and restoring the unity of the family and community. And Nancy Jean did not go alone. She went with her family – with the children, excited "to start off," her kinsmen, "many of Scottish origin [who would] form the band of travellers," and a Catholic priest. She was taking the most important parts of her past with her.[16]

When Nancy Jean Cameron spoke of Canada as "a new land of promise" what hopes was she conveying? Canada was an asylum to which she could flee to escape hatred and division. It was not a place where she went to create something new or different; as she wrote to her relative in Scotland, they "hope[d] to found in the new land a new Glengarry ... [which would] lack the mountains which you see from your home." It was where she wanted to reunite her family, restore the harmony of her community, and recreate the kind of society she had always known. What she wanted most in Canada was peace, and she probably got it.

Groups of Loyalists such as the Camerons continued to move into the Cataraqui area in the 1780s to join family and friends. In the spring of 1784 a British officer reported that "many people [were] coming in daily" who were "persecuted" and were "seeking an Asylum under the King, their loyalty to whom has been the cause of their suffering." Over the winter of 1784 some 250 sledges arrived in Quebec from Albany and people continued to pour in during the spring.[17] A group of twenty-two that arrived at St Johns on 15 June 1784 were all from the same community – Noble Town in Albany County – and all but one were originally from Hanover in Germany. The Wiltse family was eventually reunited in Canada. Benoni Wiltse came in 1784 and built a shanty along the St Lawrence; he was joined soon after by this brother, James, and half-brother, John, who were in turn followed by their sons; finally, in 1793, their father completed the group. The clustering of the Loyalists in units with familiar faces and dialects was reinforced by official policy. In 1784 Haldimand ordered that those coming from the United States had to be informed "that if they wish to settle in the Province upon the King's land it must be with their corps and connections."[18]

The largest group of Loyalists to come to Quebec in 1783 were the approximately 300 Associated Loyalists. Although similar in background to the earlier arrivals, these people, many of whom came from southern New York and New Jersey, tended to have more American-born and more Dutch Loyalists. They were also different in that, while farmers represented the largest group among them, there were more artisans, merchants, and professional people. There was also a higher percentage of women among the Associated Loyalists, who had slightly fewer children per woman (2.3 versus 2.5). While there was not the same sense of community among the Associated Loyalists as there had been among those who had come before, there was some cohesion provided by the Associations in which friends, neighbours, or comrades-in-arms joined together to arrange the terms and conditions under which they would emigrate and resettle.

Table 6
Cataraqui and Associated Loyalists, 10 July 1784:
A Sociological Comparison

	Total of Cataraqui Loyalists	Associated Loyalists
American born	45%	61%
Dutch	5%	23%
Farmers	75%	46.5%
Artisans	5%	17.9%
Merchants	3%	12.8%
Professionals	3%	5.1%[19]
Women	571	76
Adults	1,943	202
Women as a percentage of adults	30.4%	37%
Children	1,412	172
Children per woman	2.5	2.3[20]

In the chaotic last days of British rule in New York, Associations were useful in uniting people around well-placed leaders who negotiated with British authorities. Beginning in late 1782 New York Loyalists made plans for their departure. There were advertisements aimed at "Loyal Refugees" enticing them to resettle on the Island St John (Prince Edward

Island), sales of "household furniture, plate," or "elegant household furniture." One such advertisment placed by Michael Grass notified Associated Loyalists that their request to settle at Cataraqui had been granted and plans were being made for the departure.[21]

The ships, which left for Quebec in July and August, travelled in convoys and conditions on them could be difficult. Overcrowding was a problem as thousands of refugees and their families had to be evacuated in a period of months. Several families slept in the same cabin and the night was interrupted by the cries of children or the retching of ill Loyalists. The trip, which took from one to three weeks depending on the weather, could be dangerous: one ship evacuating Loyalists sank off the American coast, while another *en route* to Sorel ran aground just before reaching its destination. Crowded conditions and a poor diet, consisting of "flour, oatmeal, butter and peas," contributed to illness, and there were even some deaths and burials at sea. There were outbreaks of measles, fever, and smallpox on a ship which arrived in Quebec on 12 August. A doctor was rushed to Sorel to care for the twelve children and four adults who had smallpox. Although the afflicted were put in isolation at hospitals in Sorel and Machiche, the disease spread and by 28 August there were six deaths reported.[22]

The Van Alstines were one of the families affected by illness. By the time Alida Van Alstine arrived in Sorel in 1783 she had travelled a long way from her patrician origins in Kinderhook. When her husband, Peter, was forced to flee to the British in 1777 and join a Loyalist regiment she was left with three young children. Soon after another child was born and died and then she lost her property. In 1779 destitution forced her and the children to join Peter in New York City, where they lived on a paltry eight shillings a day in a "Small Rebel House and ten acres of Land the house in such bad condition that the Repairs alone have cost ... more than all the Emoluments of the House and Ten acres of Land for the present year have been Worth ... " Disaster struck again in 1782 when their residence on Long Island, where Peter had been transferred, was raided and they were stripped of everything, even their clothes.[23]

The misfortunes of the war and the family's reduced circumstances weighed heavily on Peter Van Alstine, who seemed by mid-1783 to be depressed and overwhelmed by his problems. He obviously took his role as household head and provider within the patriarchal family structure seriously. In a July 1783 petition requesting compensation for losses under Burgoyne, he described himself as "encumbered with a family" and went on to confess that his inability to provide for it was an "Embarrassment" which was causing "Tortures of the Mind." Van Alstine continued to petition British officials for compensation and to lament his poverty. In fact, he had three servants and was able to have his land in the new settlements cleared for him. Nonetheless, his distress was probably real. As well as suffering a decline in his material circumstances, he was also experiencing the stress associated with being a refugee and household head who could not live up to his obligations to provide for his family.[24]

By May 1784 it was Alida who was suffering. She was "exceedingly ill," probably having contracted the smallpox which had come to Sorel with the Loyalists from New York and had also afflicted Loyalist families already in Quebec, such as the Sherwoods. Poverty and an inadequate diet were cited as factors in her declining health by her husband, who wrote that "the Rations are not suficient to Support a sickly famely." It was true that fresh provisions were difficult to get and many Loyalists did without such staples as milk, sugar, and oatmeal. As the Loyalists prepared to move into the interior in May 1784, Alida was too ill to accompany them and permission was granted for her and the children to be quartered and provisioned at Sorel. Peter had asked to stay behind with her; but Haldimand, the career soldier with no family, had replied that Peter's duty lay with his men who looked to him for leadership. He was to lead his men to the new settlements, begin to clear the land, and then return to his ailing wife. Following his orders, Peter left Sorel for Montreal in late May; however, by early June, Sir John Johnson, in charge of relocating the refugees, had heard about Alida's ill health and Peter was allowed to return to Sorel. When he arrived he found that, not only was his wife ill, his children had the measles. Peter, it seems, stayed with his family for two months, hoping desperately to restore their health, but to no avail. The children recovered, but Alida did not. She was one of many Loyalist women who never completed the journey to a new life in the interior. Her journey ended in Sorel, where she was buried on 3 August 1784.[25]

The utter dependence of Loyalists such as the Van Alstines on the British intensified the paternalistic relationship that had developed during the war. At war's end, as the Loyalist corps were disbanded and hopes of recovering former property faded, the Loyalist men's livelihood disappeared and they were, in the words of one group of soldiers, in "desperate circumstances ... having naught to depend on but the clemency and generosity of government ... "[26] The keys to future prosperity rested with British officials who controlled land grants, appointments, and other sources of income. British officials accepted the idea that the Loyalists deserved compensation because of their loyalty, services, and losses and took a paternalistic approach to resettling them and establishing the framework for the new communities.

The new settlements were seen as an asylum for those of proven loyalty. Guy Carleton, commander-in-chief at New York, was one of many

British officials who accepted the view that the Loyalists were "driven from their estates" and had "suffered ... on account of their Loyalty and Services."[27] The value placed on military service was illustrated in Haldimand's reply to a petition from the Associated Loyalists – whom he incorrectly believed had not fought during the war – in which he asserted that Cataraqui was planned for Loyalists "who had served during the war ... [and] are naturally entitled to any preference ... [the Associated Loyalists being] only mechanics ..." Loyalty and service were important criteria in evaluating individual Loyalists; praise was reserved for those "of approved Loyalty ... [who had always been] forward in the service of government," those who had "Sacrificed much property and rendered good service to government," or those who took an "early and hearty part with government."[28] Land was to be granted only to those of "approved loyalty" who had taken a "loyalty oath," and the British accepted their responsibility for compensating Loyalists for their losses since because of "their Loyalty to Your Majesty and Attachment to the British Government ... [many Loyalists] are reduced from Affluence" to distress. The British, obviously, had accepted the Loyalists' version of their past and the obligation to secure their future.[29]

Haldimand felt a special duty to provide for the Mohawk, who had rendered great "services," been "firm in their Allegiance to the King throughout the War," and deserved "indemnification for their losses," especially since they had been betrayed at the peace table.[30] He even allowed 114 of them to settle on the Bay of Quinte separate from the main Mohawk settlement on the Grand River. This group, under Captain John Deserontyon, had been settled at Lachine during the war and included a very high percentage of women, which suggested the heavy toll of warfare on the Mohawk men. As Captain John explained later, he wanted to settle on the Bay of Quinte far from the Americans because "I thought I could not live in peace so near those people ... The Americans are like a worm that cuts off corn as soon as it appears."[31] Haldimand gladly supported British retention of the interior posts, granted to the Americans in the peace treaty, to placate the Indians and he granted them 7,000 acres of land, advising them that more was available if they needed it, as well as paying for a minister and a schoolteacher.[32]

Haldimand took a paternalistic approach to settling the other Loyalists: he would decide what was in their best interests and in return for government benevolence he demanded deference and obedience. After he had decided that it was best for the Loyalists to settle at Cataraqui where the soil and climate were good and they were separated from the French Canadians, he would not tolerate any opposition. During the winter of 1783, overcrowding, illness, and shortages of provisions fanned discontent, and so did uncertainty and anxiety about the future.

Table 7
Loyalist Women: The Case of the Mohawk

Return of the Mohawk Village Near Lachine,
24 January 1783

Men	Women	Children	Total
36	41	37	114

Women as a Percentage of the Adult Loyalist Population

All Loyalists	Mohawks
30.4	53.2

Source: HP, 21,798, Barnes to Mathews, 10 June 1784

Rumours were rampant; some Loyalists began to settle elsewhere and others complained about the conditions. They were described by one official as the "most Jealous, Disatisfied and Troublesome people in the world ..." Haldimand dealt swiftly with the discontent. Those who complained were told that they could go to Nova Scotia, those who had relocated on their own were to be denied provisions, and the rest were simply ordered to move into the interior.[33]

The British established the material and institutional groundwork for the new colony, which differed in important ways from other frontier societies. British aid and planning minimized the material discomforts associated with frontier settlements. British officials purchased the land from local Indians and surveyed it in advance; they transported the Loyalists to their land; they provided equipment and tools including axes, hoes, froes, and drawing knives; and they issued a wide variety of seeds – potato, Indian corn, onion, turnip, cabbage, celery, carrot, radish, parsley, peas.[34] The Loyalists also continued to be provisioned until 1785; initially the rations were to be cut by the summer of 1784 to two-thirds but protests forced Haldimand in July of that year to restore full rations.[35] Fort Frontenac was rebuilt; a sawmill, grist mill, wharf, and storehouse were constructed, and lumber was cut and squared for other buildings. In 1786, when a school was established at Cataraqui, the British government "built a convenient house for the purpose" and paid the teacher's salary. And when the Loyalists wanted another wharf built in 1788, they petitioned British officials.[36]

The British also laid the foundations for a hierarchical and élitist social structure, which, again, was quite at odds with notions of frontier egalitarianism. Blacks, although in theory entitled to land grants for their military service, were treated like property and were provisioned only because they were needed to help the Loyalists clear and cultivate their land. Hopes of regaining his own slaves prompted Sir John Johnson to welcome a 1783 Patriot proposal to return Patriot slaves.

Conflict between "Master and Servant" resulting from "Severe Correction" of slaves by their masters was seen by a British official as the "most material" of the "Disputes" in the new settlement. And Loyalists such as Richard Cartwright Jr were willing to take legal action to prevent their "Negroe" men from claiming their freedom.[37]

British officials had the power to establish a social and economic hierarchy since they determined the conditions under which land would be held, Loyalists would be compensated for losses, pensions would be granted, and appointments made. Land grants varied according to one's rank in the Loyalist corps: in 1783 privates got 100 acres, captains 700, and field officers 1,000 acres, with grants to officers increasing in 1788. Officers were also given half pay. Similarly, when Loyalists were financially compensated for their losses during the Revolution, the amount given was based on their rank and property holdings before the Revolution, which had the effect of restoring former social and economic distinctions. The British practice of appointing rather than electing civil and military officials also fostered an élite; as well as having larger land grants, half pay, and more generous compensation, Loyalist leaders became militia officers, members of the land boards, magistrates, judges, and councillors.[38] Within a few years, the élitism and notions of hierarchy that had underpinned British decision-making during the Loyalists years in exile were firmly entrenched in the new settlements.

The authoritarianism of the refugee camps was also reflected in the political framework. In the early 1780s there were no civil or judicial institutions in the Loyalist settlements west of the Ottawa River, except appointed magistrates. The Quebec Act of 1774, which provided for an appointed Council but no elected Assembly and for seigneurial rather than freehold land tenure, was supported by Halidmand, who contended that the Loyalists had "suffered too much by Committees and Houses of Assembly" and did not want an elected Assembly.[39] The Loyalists may have suffered from committees, but they had also suffered from the authoritarian military regimes in Quebec and New York City and they were accustomed to having an Assembly. They wanted their former civil institutions restored. Also, land tenure was very important to them. Many had been tenants in the colonies, others had experienced uncertainty over land titles, and all had been promised land, presumably under freehold tenure, when they joined the Loyalist corps.

The Loyalists respected order and authority, but the Quebec Act went too far. Although there were some divisions in the 1780s, when rank-and-file Loyalists complained that their former military leaders were being too secretive and arbitrary, Loyalists united to oppose an act that denied their shared expectations and was a threat to their common futures. Traditional leaders again used the familiar practice of petitioning to seek changes on behalf of the Loyalists.

In their petitions opposing the Quebec Act the Loyalists reiterated their sense of identity and revealed their conservatism. Loyalty, service, and sacrifice were again called upon, this time to justify demands for political institutions similar to those that had existed in the colonies. The "British Constitution" was added to the list of things that Loyalists had fought for. One group of petitioners hoped to enjoy "the benefit of that mild & Lenient Government, for which we have so long & nobly contended & for which we have at least sacrifised our all"; the fact that many had been tenants was overlooked, as the group requested that land be held "in fee Simple as we have hitherto held our Lands under the Crown." The reality of the past eluded another group, which pressed for freehold land tenure on the grounds that they should hold their lands "on the footing of British Subjects on the terms they held their Possessions and Lands in the Colonies." While pressing their case, the Loyalist leaders were also deferential and profuse in their expressions of loyalty and gratitude to the British government. They had "a high opinion ... of the British nation ... [and of] the tender care it has taken of them"; they were "devoted to His Majesty's Interest and willing to sacrifice their Lives, and their Properties in defence of his Crown and the Rights of the Nation."[40] The petitions, it is clear, were cast within what was becoming by the 1780s the standarized version of the Loyalist past. Motivated by loyalty to the British crown, empire, and constitution, the Loyalists had served in the military and sacrificed valuable property; their loyalty and sacrifices obliged the British to comply with their requests for the restoration of familiar British institutions in Canada.

The emphasis in the petitions was on restoring former rights and institutions and fitting the new colony into the imperial *status quo*. One group of Loyalists leaders requested the establishment of civil and legal institutions similar to those enjoyed in the past, and it went on to try to fit the new colony into the regulated economic framework of mercantilism by asking for bounties for the raising of hemp and flax seed. There was no idea that the Loyalists were beginning again in a frontier setting where there should be experimentation with new institutions. On the contrary, the Loyalists stressed preserving past rights, re-establishing former institutions, and even opposing change. Seigneurial tenure was criticized because it was "so different from what they have been used to," or, according to another group, "so different from the mild Tenures to which they have ever been accustomed." Another group opposed "any innovation of their Rights." The Quebec Act forced Loyalists to clarify their sense of their own past and their vision of the future. They had fought the Revolution, they believed, to preserve the British empire and institutions. What they wanted in Canada was an asylum or refuge in which they could restore the institutions of the past, reunite their families, and enjoy peace, order, and good government.[41]

The Loyalist settlements of the 1780s were not a frontier in the sense of being communities in which there was social levelling, an individual-istic ethos, or a democratic impulse. On the contrary, to British officials who planned the communities and established their institutions, Can-ada was their second chance in North America, their opportunity to provide an asylum for Loyalist refugees and to establish societies that would avoid the pitfalls of the American colonies. It was by design, then, that the settlements had a stratified social order, a group-settle-ment pattern, and a conservative, even authoritarian, political system. Conservatism was also the hallmark of the Loyalists who sought to pre-serve former institutions, restore established rights, and reunite families and communities. Upper Canada, as it was called after 1791, was not the kind of place where women could expect any changes in their tra-ditional roles within the family and society. Gone were the extraordi-nary days of the Revolution, when women, separated from the men in their lives, participated in the war, took charge of their families, or en-dured harassment and life in refugee camps. With families reunited, communities re-established, and familiar institutions restored, women once again had a well-defined place within the family and society.

The extent to which Loyalist women's horizons were not expanded as a result of the Revolution can be seen by comparing them with their Pa-triot counterparts. First, although there were similarities in the role played by Loyalist and Patriot women during the Revolution, there were also important differences. Taking charge of families, managing farms or businesses, enduring persecution by opponents, or participating in the Revolution in various ways were activities common to both Patriot and Loyalist women. Patriot women, however, had the advantage of na-tion-wide campaigns, such as the fund-raising drive they organized dur-ing the war, and organizations like the Daughters of Liberty, which con-tinued after the Revolution. They also participated in the Revolutionary political debate, in which they honed their writing skills and, more im-portant, left a written record of their participation.[42]

Secondly, the status of American women was affected by economic and social changes which coincided with the Revolution. Even before the Revolution there is evidence that women were restive and less will-ing to accept the dominance of husbands and fathers. In New England, for example, there was a dramatic increase in female education and lit-eracy in the eighteenth century. At the same time, an increase in pre-marital pregnancies has been seen as symptomatic of a "breakdown in the orthodox moral code," with the suggestion that "young people" may have been "asserting their autonomy by taking control of their sex lives."[43] Moroever, the shift from a subsistence to a commercial or market economy, which began in the late eighteenth century, allowed more scope to women. There were opportunities for income from, for example, the marketing of garden produce or even wage labour. Also, the separation of home and workplace, which accompanied the growth and diversification of the economy, allowed women to assert control over their households.[44]

Republicanism also eroded patriarchy and changed the structure of power and the language of American society. It should be emphasized that American women's legal status as *femmes coverts* and their exclusion from the political process did not change.[45] What did were ideas about power. Gone was the reverence for the British father-king, the emphasis on being obedient children to the mother country, and the respect for the supreme authority of parliament. Rather than power being concentrated in one source, the British parliament – just as it had been concentrated within the family in the hands of the male, household head – power in the United States was dispersed. The separation of powers, the written constitution, and the Bill of Rights were all ways of checking or dispersing the power of the state. The language of obedience, deference, and respect for authority was replaced by a language that stressed voluntary consent, mutual dependence, and the virtue of autonomous individuals.[46]

The language of republicanism spilled over into descriptions of women. The idea that women were more virtuous than men, which dated to classical times, became central in American rhetoric after the Revolution. In a republic, where the success of the polity depended on the virtue of its citizenry, the status of women, who were seen as the "source of virtue in the society," was elevated. Moreover, individual women challenged ideas of female helplessness and inferiority and questioned prevailing values, such as the sexual double standard. The written word also heralded the change. For instance, in the 1780s and 1790s magazines about women were published which proclaimed women's accomplishments and challenged traditional views of them. In the long term, according to Mary Beth Norton, the change in language was formative since "the egalitarian rhetoric of the Revolution provided the women's movement with its earliest vocabulary ... "[47]

Changes in the language used to describe women were accompanied by similar shifts in women's experiences in the family and society. Women were given more access to higher education, spinsterhood became more common and accepted, and more egalitarian familial relationships developed. Marriage was increasingly seen as being based on affection and mutual consent, rather than on male dominance, and motherhood was exalted in status. Childhood came to be seen as a distinct stage in life during which reason, example, and persuasion became more important than harsh authority in children's upbringing. The home increasingly became the women's sphere and "patriarchal will breaking" was replaced by "mother love" as the "linchpin in a new method of socializing children."[48] In sum, rhetoric and reality worked together to alter the former view of women as helpless subordinates within a patriarchal family structure.

Republican ideas also changed the relationship between mothers and their sons. Since the success of the republic was believed to depend on civic and individual virtue, the "domestic realm," which had been "peripheral," became central and women's role as mothers of future generations of leaders assumed a key importance. One reason why women gained easier access to higher education was the belief that mothers had to be educated so that they could teach "morality and patriotism" to their children. In the past, women had developed warm and close relationships with their daughters, but their relationships with their sons had been more distant. Sons, once they reached the age of seven, came under the tutelage of their fathers who prepared them for their future careers and made major decisions for them. After the Revolution, however, older sons became closer to their mothers, whose duty it was to instruct them "for a future of service to the republic."[49] This closeness between mothers and sons was one of the signs of the decline of the patriarchal family.

In the case of Loyalist women, there is no comparable evidence that patriarchy was eroded and women's status enhanced or that new language to portray women developed. One basic problem is a shortage of sources; no Loyalist women penned their sentiments about their early years in present-day eastern Ontario. However, a glimpse into the world of these women was provided by an English immigrant, Anne Powell, who wrote about her 1789 trip through the Loyalist settlements. Of Indian women, Powell wrote, "I fear they are not like the women of other Countries." She described an Indian ceremony in which "the old women walk'd one by one with great solemnity and seated themselves behind the men." The "respectable band of Matrons," she wrote, "preserve a modest silence in the debates ... but nothing is determined without their advice and approbation." The "best compliment you can pay a young Hero is saying he is *as wise as an old woman*." In contrast, she described the misery of a lovely young white woman who had made the mistake, at the urging of others, of marrying, at fourteen, an indebted old, half-pay officer. Her husband, "old, disagreeable and vicious," "practiced" such a "series of cruelties" on his poor wife that she "should have great pleasure in hearing her Tyrant was dead, the only means by which she can be released."[50] These observations suggest that women's role had not really change; they are consistent with what we know about the status of Indian and white women in the colonies before the Revolution.

There was no compelling reason for the Loyalists to change their views about family relationships or the role of women in their communities. Unlike their Patriot counterparts, Loyalists did not reject the father-king, turn their backs on their mother country, or renounce their allegiance to the British parliament. On the contrary, whatever the motives of individual Loyalists may have been, by the 1780s the public record – in the form of Loyalists' petitions – showed that they had became Loyalists because of their allegiance to the British king, mother country, and parliament. Respect for authority, deference, and an acceptance of hierarchy remained basic to the language used in Loyalists' public addresses. Moreover, their experiences as refugees had strengthened rather than weakened their respect for the British government because they were imbued with gratitude to the British for assuming the responsibility for the Loyalists after the Revolution was lost. "Our gracious King gives us Land gratis and furnishes Provision and Clothing, farming utensils & c until next September," wrote the Reverend John Stuart in 1785. Richard Cartwright Jr described the "benevolent intentions of the British Government towards the Colony" and a second-generation Loyalist stated that she had "often heard my father and mother say that they ... were always thankful to the Government for their kind assistance in the hour of need."[51]

Not only did most Loyalists vocally support the established, hierarchical institutions of the British empire, they also accepted the British design to create conservative political institutions and a deferential society. In 1791 the Quebec Act was replaced with the *Constitutional Act*, which met Loyalist requests for freehold tenure and an elected assembly. Afterwards, protests ended, even though the institutions established were still more élitist than those that had existed in the American colonies. The 1791 act provided for an established church, which would inculcate morality and public virtue in its citizens, and the appointed branches of government were made more powerful than the elected. There is also some evidence that Anglican ministers imposed codes of acceptable behaviour in the new communities; one minister, for example, wrote that "I have refused churching two women because they refused to kneel."[52] And in terms of social life, the existence of a British garrison at Cataraqui lent a certain élitist tone to social events. By the 1790s the foundations had been laid for an hierarchically graded social structure, a deferential community, and a conservative political ethos, and there was no sign of widespread Loyalist discontent with the *status quo* as designed by British officials.

Just as former, established institutions went unchallenged, so did patriarchy in the society and family remain largely unquestioned. Obviously women could not hold public office or vote; nor did they receive the same higher education, outside the colony, which was open to some men. Their lack of participation in public life is further evidenced in the court records of the region. In 1788, civil courts (courts of common pleas) and criminal courts (courts of quarter sessions of the justices of the peace and of oyer and terminer and general goal delivery) were created. The records of their activities — some of the criminal court records were lost in 1921,[53] but the rest are available — reveal the role of courts as important local institutions and give an idea of the issues that concerned citizens. For our purposes, what is interesting about these records is the lack of female participation in court cases. In the civil and criminal records covering the years from 1788 to 1818 there were only three women litigants. Elizabeth Thomson's case to recover the cost of selling cheese was dismissed with the plaintiff being required to pay costs. The other two cases involved women who had in different ways violated orthodox standards. One was launched by Elizabeth Vansickler; she could not provide for her children, who were then bound out to work for others in return for care. Vansickler's case against the church wardens who took her children was successful; however, her children were returned on the grounds that "after receiving the said children [she] do depart this district by the first convenient opportunity, or at furthest by the 20th day of November next" (1789). Vansickler not only ignored the court order, she also had the gall to reappear before the court six months later as one of two female witnesses for Charles Justin McCarty, "a vagabond, imposture and disturber of the peace" who was found guilty. The other case was a paternity suit launched against Henry Bird by Katherine Brown. Bird acknowledged his paternity of the "Bastard Child" and was ordered to pay ten shillings per month until the child reached the age of twelve.[54] Neither Vansickler nor Brown could be called typical women. Usually other family members cared for children if the parents experienced hardship, and it was not common for illegitimate pregnancies to result in court cases. Thomson's case, then, stands out as the only shred of evidence that women might have had an independence uncharacteristic of a patriarchal society. By itself, however, it points merely to the existence of an exceptional woman, not to a trend.

The absence of women in local court cases stands in contrast to their frequent appearances in records during the Revolution. What this fact signifies is, on the one hand, the importance of women in the main events of the war years. When raids on the American frontier were a major part of the British war strategy, women left on the frontier had important roles to play in quartering, provisioning, and protecting raiding parties or in gathering intelligence. On the other hand, the records show that women, once removed to the area around Cataraqui, lived in communities with different concerns. Leaving aside the cases involving violence, drunkeness, or similar offences, the subjects covered in the court records included the appointment and payment of local officials – none of whom could be women – the granting of licences to run public houses or ferries – none of which were given to women – disputes centring around the cost or quality of goods and services – none of which were provided or paid for by women – or disputes involving property or other assets, such as cattle – which again did not involve women. The records therefore suggest that men obviously returned to their former status as the main linchpin between the family and the legal, commercial, and political world beyond the household.

The only Loyalist women to appear in public records were widows. The British government usually fulfilled its obligations to widows – deemed helpless because their male providers were gone – by granting them pensions, which were as much as 50 per cent less than those given to men since women's expenses were assumed to be less and none had served in the Loyalist corps.[55] At war's end, however, there was pressure to grant land to widows. In 1783 Edward Jessup, probably reflecting the concerns of families who would have to care for widows, advocated that widows and their eldest sons be granted land. Haldimand responded to the requests of widows such as Sarah Buck for land by stating in April 1784 that widow Buck could be taken care of until arrangements were made for her return to the United States, but nothing "permanent," presumably land grants, could be done. A few days later Justus Sherwood wrote that a determined widow Buck was going to settle in Cataraqui and her name appears on a list as one of forty women landholders.[56]

Widows such as Sarah Buck who settled in the Cataraqui area were usually supported by other family members. Of the forty women landholders in the new settlements, twenty-six or 65 per cent had others with the same surname living in the same or the neighbouring township.[57] Even this underestimates the extent to which widows had families nearby. In the case of widow Livingston, no other Livingstons appear on the list; however, in her claim she makes it clear that her son was living with her. While only one other Cryderman is recorded as living in New Johnston, widow Cryderman in fact had three daughters living with her and four sons in the same community. It was also very common for widows to remarry. The widow Hare, whose husband had been killed at Oriskany, remarried before resettlement and lived on her new husband's land. And in 1785 the widow Buck married David Beverly.[58]

The pattern of women owning land was firmly established in the 1780s. As well as widows, there were female orphans for whom there were claims for compensation in land. Martin Middaugh made a land claim as uncle to the Bush children, whose parents had died in 1779 and 1780 at Machiche; another uncle, John Cameron, claimed land for the orphans of Robert Dixon and his wife who died in 1785 and in 1786; and James McDougal requested land on behalf of his wife and her sister. The idea that male and female Loyalist children were entitled to compensation in land persisted, and in 1789 all Loyalist children were granted land as a recognition of their special lineage. Moreover, some Loyalist men gave land to their daughters as well as their sons. Although the fact that women did own land was an important crack in the patriarchal power structure, land grants to women were usually seen as doweries, reflected by the condition on grants to Loyalist children that females, unlike males, could acquire their land when they married.[59]

Noble motives, disinterested service, and heavy sacrifices were the mainstay of Loyalist petitions designed to wring more assistance out of guilt-ridden British officials. At the same time, the myth of the upper-class origins of the Loyalists, which had surfaced during the war, became more pronounced after 1783 as petitioners described themselves as "persons of property in the colonies," people who had "left considerable free property," "owners of large freehold estates," or individuals who had lived "in a state of ease and contentment" in the colonies.[60] In fact, however, the petitions are misleading both about the Loyalists' motives and about their social standing in the colonies. Most Loyalists were subsistence, tenant farmers, not men of property. A variety of factors other than loyalty to the British empire – such as family or ethnic ties, or the promise of freehold land – had led Loyalist men into the regiments. And some Loyalists told different versions of the past to American and British authorities. John Freel, the tenant farmer who had accompanied Guy Johnson to Canada in 1775, told a Patriot committee that he had been forced, with the threat of flogging, to go to Montreal where he had worked as a taylor. A decade later he told British officials that he had "to the utmost of his power and abilities served his Majesty since the beginning of 1775."[61]

What the petitions do tell us is the extent to which Loyalists had by the 1780s defined in clear and consistent terms the meaning of their refugee experience. They were not like other settlers. They were Loyalists, motivated by principle, who had been attached to the British crown, empire, and constitution. They had proven their loyalty through military service, which had led to property losses and suffering. It was the duty of the British government to reward these people for their noble contribution to the British empire.

The widows' petitions differ from the men's in important ways. Some women were more vague about the financial aspects of farming, suggesting that they were not active in decision-making. The widow Buck testified that her husband "had Lands in Pownal, cannot say how much, thinks 50 acres," while the widow Hogal, when describing the improvements to the farm, could say only that her husband "had laid out a great deal." Other women did not even present their own petitions, but had others speak on their behalf. The widow Obenholdt had her son present her case, while Lydia Van Alstine's petition was given by her second husband, Isaac Crowther. Having others present women's petitions suggests a lack of confidence – either by the women themselves or by men – in the women's ability to present a convincing case.[62]

What is striking about the women's petitions, in light of Loyalist women's contribution to the war, was that the Revolution was portrayed through men's eyes. Rather than discussing themselves, the women cited their husbands' ethnic origins, loyalty, and service. Margaret Huffnail, formerly of Charlotte County, said nothing about her background or role in the war, but she testified that her husband was a native of Germany who had come to Charlotte County twenty-three years ago and had joined "Jessups Corps" in 1780 and "served during the war." Another widow stated that her husband was "a Native of America ... [who] was very active from the first in support of the King's Cause – joined Genl Burgoyne he was taken Prisoner after Burgoyne's Defeat." Catherine Cryderman described her husband as "a Loyalist, very true to King George," while saying nothing about her own view of the Revolution. Property losses were cited but the property involved – whether land, buildings, cattle or equipment – was described as belonging to the husband. One widow stated that "Her Husband had 3 Farms on Rancellors Manor," while another claimed that "Her Husband had 150 acres [of land]" as well "2 good houses – 2 cows, 2 calves, 18 Sheep, 16 Hogs, furniture, utensils." When the women did speak about themselves, they stressed their suffering. The testimony of Jane Glassford of Tryon County was typical: after her sons had joined the Loyalist regiments, "the Rebels came in 1779 & plundered them and stript them of every thing – she was almost starved in her own house."

Even the petition of the obviously determined widow Buck followed the pattern. She testified that "her late Husband Brier Buck was a native of America, lived at Pownal, he joined in 1777 – He served with Sir John till his Death ... " Assets were also assumed to be his: "He had Lands in Pownal ... 2 Cows, a yoke of Oxen, 2 Horses, little Cloaths, Grain." Only the suffering was shared; everything "was taken by the Rebels after her Husband had left home in order to join the British" and when her husband and his son and daughter-in-law died, she was left to raise three children.[63]

Why did Loyalist women cite their husband's loyalty, service, and property while describing their suffering? It was expected of them. This view of the past reflected their status within a patriarchal power structure and it was consistent with the language of enfeeblement. The decision as to whether or not to become a Loyalist was a political issue left to the male household head. Women did not comment on their own loyalty because it was accepted that the decision about loyalty had been made for them. They made no reference to their own role in the Revolution because what was valued by British officials was formal military service in the Loyalist regiments. Property losses were losses to the men since they owned and controlled family property. Men suffered material losses; women were expected only to suffer emotionally.

There was so much emphasis on the women's suffering because this was consistent with contemporary views about femininity and it was the only way that they could appeal to the paternalism of British officials. According to accepted views of the time, women, it should be stressed again, were seen as frail, helpless, dependent creatures who had to look up to males to care for them. Since Loyalist men could not care for their families, it was the duty of the British to act in a paternal way to protect weak, dependent beings such as women, children, the old, and the infirm. Suffering was part of the lot of the weak and helpless and it even strengthened their claims for British aid. While the strong, independent, courageous men fought, the weak, helpless women suffered; and while men received just rewards for their loyalty, the women were cared for by the British because of a paternal sense of duty to care for the weak.

Sarah McGinnis's claim for compensation shows the pervasiveness of the language of enfeeblement. The evidence given to support Sarah's claim did refer to her considerable services in the war. However, the first page of her claim, in which she was introduced herself to the commissioners and set the stage for her case, was cast in the standardized form of other women's petitions. She identified herself in relation to her husband as the "widow of Captain McGinn who was killed last War under the Command of the late Sir William Johnson, Bart. near Lake George." She next cited her son's military service and his inability to perform his manly duty of caring for his mother: she "has a Son (being her only Son now living) Lieutenant in the Six Nation Department who was wounded in the Knee in this unnatural Rebellion and his having a helpless Family renders him unable to give her any assistance." Having established the fact that the males in her life could not provide for her,

Sarah next underlined her helplessness: "She is aged and very infirm." Finally, she described her suffering: "The Rebels have destroyed, plundered and taken almost all her Property ... "[64] If a woman as atypical as Sarah McGinnis had to cast her claim within the standardized framework of male military service and female helplessness and suffering, this view of the Loyalist past must have been firmly entrenched by the 1780s. Even before the first Loyalist history was written, women had been marginalized, consigned to the role of suffering, and firmly entrenched within the mould of the language of enfeeblement.

Women were subordinate not only in the society but also within the family. Resettlement meant the reunion of families and the return to traditional patterns of authority. Patriarchy means that the male household head has power to make decisions, but also responsibilities to provide for his dependants. During the Revolution, both broke down. Being absent from their homes, Loyalist men had, of necessity, to relinquish some of their decision-making power, and they also were unable to live up to their responsibilities. At British bases, it was government officials who took care of their families by provisioning, housing, and clothing them. John Munro felt guilty and frustrated for having "sacrificed a good estate and brought ruin on a numerous family," while another group of Loyalists complained in 1783 that they were "waisting away the bloom and strength of our days ... [instead of] acquiring something for the future support of ourselves and families."[65] Once reunited and resettled, however, the household head was again able to assume his responsibilities to provide for his dependants and exercise his authority.

The return to patriarchy was facilitated by the subsistence economy of the new settlements in which the household coincided with the main unit of production. As was true in the American colonies before the Revolution, the dominance of the male household head in a subsistence economy was unmitigated. Women lacked alternative sources of income, and with no separation of household and workplace they could not even assert their control over the domestic realm. A glimpse of a Loyalist household was provided by a second-generation Loyalist who remembered, "Mother used to help chop down Trees, [she] attended the household duties and as the children grew up they were trained to Industrious habits." The children, who were "very useful" to the mother, "attended the cattle, churned the butter, making cheese, dressing the flax, spinning, made our own cloth and stockings." It was the father, however, who "collected our Butter, Cheese and spinning, taking them in a Batteaux to Kingston, which he traded off for salt, Tea and Flour ..."[66] Transactions between the household and the outside world were still handled by the male household head.

There were, of course, exceptional women such as Molly Brant, who received a pension for her "early and uniform fidelity ... [and her] attachment and zealous services rendered to the King's Government ... " She also had a house built in Cataraqui for her and was accepted as part of the local élite. Sarah McGinnis, also extraordinary, was not as fortunate as Molly Brant; she lived out her days in obscurity in Cataraqui, although she had been given a plot of land at Ernestown, and was buried in 1791, at the age of seventy-eight, in an unmarked grave. Barbara Heck became a famous female Loyalist not because of her role in the Revolution, but because of her leading role in establishing Methodism in Canada. Barbara, along with other Palatines, established the "nuclei of the first circuits in what would become the Canadian Conference of the Methodist Episcopal Church." In 1909 a monument was erected to her at the Blue church cemetery, near present-day Prescott, at a ceremony attended by over 2,000 people. Similar ceremonies and tributes to Barbara Heck continued into the twentieth century.[67]

Equally unusual were women whose marriages collapsed. Maria Young, whose husband, Henry, had been a tenant on Rensselaerwyck and had joined Edward Jessup in 1776, had a hard life after her husband's departure. Her home was raided and stripped of everything and in 1780 she was ordered to leave it. Although she made an appeal to stay, it was rejected. When the war was over, her family, like many others, was split. Her oldest daughter who was married stayed in the United States and her two sons were with their father in Quebec. In 1783 Maria along with her four youngest daughters left New York City with the spring fleet for Nova Scotia. It appears that she went on to Quebec. However, in 1784, when the Young family moved into the interior to take up their land, Maria was not with them. She had, it seems, returned to the United States, perhaps to live with her oldest daughter.[68]

The turmoil of the Revolution placed enormous strain on the marriage of Joel and Leah Stone. In 1786, after spending three years in England seeking compensation for his losses, Joel was ready to return to North America and to his wife, who had suffered severe stress and had pleaded with him to return earlier. Ever conscious of making his way in the world, Joel jumped at the opportunity to have Leah come from New York to Quebec with the wife of William Smith Jr, chief justice of Quebec, about whom Joel wrote that his "influence will be great" and his "good graces may be of material Service." Joel was disappointed when Leah was not able to make the necessary arrangements. Then Joel disappointed Leah by scolding her for buying furniture, which was very expensive to transport, when he had already brought furniture from England; she could, he conceded, bring "whatever Light valuable articals you may have" but what was essential was all of his books, "Writings," and his small sword. By mid-1787 Leah had moved from the bustling, cosmopolitan city of New York to New Johnstown, on the Canadian frontier, and she was again pregnant. A daughter was born with only Joel and a servant girl in attendance in February 1788, but within months the marriage had collapsed. A formal separation agreement of May 1789 had specified the "subsistence" and "support" Leah was entitled to and "her place of abode"; however, when she violated the agreement by remaining in Montreal, Joel published a document notifying possible creditors that he would not pay her debts.[69] Leah's unhappy life ended in 1793.

Joel continued to chart a path to prosperity and prominence in Upper Canada with a second wife, who was an astute business partner, but his family life was still far from happy. His son, William, who had spent much of his early life boarding in either New York or Montreal, and his daughter, Mary, were basically raised by his family in Connecticut. A 1797 letter in which Joel regretted being unable to visit them or send the money he had promised reflected his preoccupation with business and success. Although his children eventually came to Upper Canada, William died prematurely of consumption and Mary was debilitated by a mental handicap. Joel Stone was probably always an ambitious man. But he was also a Loyalist and a refugee who had lost a civil war and, like many other refugees, he exhibited an "intense need to succeed," even, in his case, if it was at the expense of his family life.[70]

The more typical family life of Loyalist leaders is reflected in the correspondence of the Stuarts, Sherwoods, Joneses, and Cartwrights. The letters of these families, although somewhat stylized and formal, are not cold and austere but warm and affectionate. Mary Jones ended a 1798 letter to her father, Solomon, this way: "Please give my duty to Mama & Grandma & love to my Brothers and Sisters ... & accept my Duty yourself, believe me to be your Dutiful Daughter."[71] Yet the affection could not mask the essentially patriarchal nature of the relationships. Female children still felt the need to get permission from their parents before venturing into the world. Sophia Sherwood, youngest daughter of Justus and Sarah, wrote to her future husband in 1810 "that I will never change my name without the consent of my mother" (Justus had drowned in 1798 and Sarah was a widow). Sophia explained that she "deserved not happiness for disobeying the best of mothers" and she could "never be yours but with a parents blessing."[72] The lively Sophia Sherwood married Jonathan Jones, but died three years later at twenty-two. Hannah Cartwright, who also died very young, could not leave Montreal for her home in Kingston until she heard from her father to whom she had written "for leave to accompany Mr. and Mrs. Jones to Kingston."[73]

As Hannah's letter reflects, the correspondence was between children and fathers. This was not because Loyalist women were illiterate; for example, we know that Magdalen Cartwright, wife of Richard Jr, was literate. Fathers wrote the letters because they still made the major family decisions. Surviving correspondence gives no inkling of a closer relationship between mothers and sons, similar to that found in the United States. On the contrary, fathers directed family life and charted the family's fortunes by establishing the futures of both male and female children. For girls, fathers arranged for some basic education, if affordable, in drawing, music, and other feminine subjects, and concentrated on ensuring that they married well.

Sons were of greater concern to their fathers. The Reverend John Stuart spoke for other Loyalist fathers when he wrote in 1804, "I have straightened myself, at Home, for many years past, to promote my Grand and Leading Plan of placing my sons, as early in Life as possible, in such Situations as may give them some weight in Society."[74] It was the father's duty to provide his sons with an education or training and to use his influence and connections to help them secure a prominent and rewarding position in society.

An intriguing and tragic father-son relationship is revealed in the correspondence between Richard Cartwright Jr and his oldest son, James. There could be no doubt about Richard's affection for his son or the peripheral nature of the relationship between mother and son. In an 1803 letter that ended as the rest did with "Your affectionate father," Richard wrote "God bless you my dear boy" and added "Your mother embraces you most cordially." While literally hundreds of letters between the father and his sons have survived, there are none between the mother and her sons. In his letters, Richard supervised almost every aspect of James's life. James was sent to Montreal to study the law, even though he did not want to be a lawyer, and to learn French. Richard wrote to his son at least every two weeks. He told his son what to read, whom to cultivate, and how to spend his money and time. He even demanded that James keep a daily journal in which he described in some detail how he spent his days from the time he got up until he went to bed; the journal was then sent to the father for his scrutiny.[75] One can only imagine the devastation of the father when James and his second son, Richard, died prematurely in 1811. Richard Cartwright was a patriarch and a Loyalist refugee who felt an intense need to guide every move of his son and to ensure that defeat in the Revolution was redeemed by the success of his male heirs.

Just as it was important to Cartwright that his family succeed, it was crucial that Upper Canada – the deferential, conservative, patriarchal society established to vindicate the Loyalists – be proclaimed a success.

Relative to other refugees, many Loyalists did fare well. Unlike most refugees, the Loyalists had new settlements established for them in areas where there was no need to accommodate a host population with a different language or culture.[76] Further, the adaptation of refugees is made easier when they settle in groups or enclaves of familiar people. This was the case with the Loyalists, who moved from one frontier to another and lived close enough to their former homes to allow continued contact with family members. Many Loyalists asked to be allowed to settle together; for example, Johnson's first regiment settled in five townships, with Catholic Highlanders in the first, Scots Presbyterians in the second, German Calivinists in the third, German Lutherans in the fourth, and Anglicans in the fifth. They wanted to settle together, as one group explained, because "they have always been ... together, so they may still continue to be able to aiding and assisting each other in their present Circumstances."[77] In material terms, many exchanged small tracts of rented land for larger amounts of freehold land and some benefited from government appointments. The Mohawk on the Canadian side of the border settled in groups and retained their sense of unity and community, while their brothers and sisters who remained in the United States had their lands taken by whites and their communities were fragmented.[78] Given all of this there was substance to the idea – shared by Cartwright and many others – that the Loyalist settlements had succeeded.

In the early years, some Loyalists, like the Reverend John Stuart, doubted the wisdom of their choice. In a 1785 letter to a friend in the United States Stuart mused about his former home Philadelphia, but added that he had to "banish" pleasant thoughts of the past and "make a virtue of Necessity." "Perhaps," he concluded, "I could not live so happy, even in Philada as at Cataraque – I'll endeavour to persuade myself to it." By the end of the next decade, Stuart was at peace with himself. "Some years ago I thought it a great Hardship to be banished to this wilderness, and wou'd have imagined myself completely happy could I have exchanged it for a Place in the Delightful City of Philadelphia," he wrote in 1798, but "now the best wish we can form for our Dearest Friends is, to have them removed to us."[79]

Proclaiming the achievements of the new settlements was closely tied to the need to justify the Loyalists' past actions. More specifically, for Loyalists such as Stuart, their defeat in the Revolution could be redeemed only if Upper Canada could be unequivocally regarded as a success. First-generation Loyalist leaders, such as Richard Cartwright Jr, were very conscious of their Loyalist origins. In articulating their sense of the meaning of Upper Canada, they perpetuated the myths about the Loyalists which had begun to develop during their years in exile. "The origin of our settlements," Cartwright wrote in 1789, "took its rise from motives more noble than views of commercial advantage; namely to provide a comfortable asylum for the unfortunate Loyalists reduced to poverty and driven into exile by their attachment to Britain." In 1811 Cartwright responded to a critic of the colony who had branded the Loyalists as "a set of needy Adventurers, in quest only of Pay and Plunder." Taking the myth of the Loyalists' upper-class origins to new heights, Cartwright asserted that the Loyalists were "gallant men," "men of property; and some of them the greatest Landholders in America." The rest of his version of the Loyalist past also unfolded as earlier accounts had. The Loyalists had "hesitated not to hazard their lives and fortunes in the attempt to put down Rebellion and preserve the Unity of the Empire." Upper Canada was created as "an Asylum" by a "generous Sovereign and Nation" obliged to grant land and pay compensation for "the Fortunes which they [the Loyalists] had sacrificed in their Cause." Upper Canada had prospered in material terms, with the "wilderness" being "converted" into "fruitful fields" and "extensive and well cultivated farms," and it had been built on the sturdy foundations of British laws and its "unrivalled constitution." "It must gladden the heart of our venerable Sovereign," Cartwright proclaimed, "to know, that his paternal care of his loyal American subjects, settled in this remote corner of his Empire, has been crowned with such compleat success."[80] There was no longer any need for bitterness; Upper Canada, the Loyalists' asylum, had succeeded.

The Loyalists' version of the past, which ignored the contributions of women to the Revolution, was perpetuated by later generations. Loyalist children and grandchildren were the first to pass on the legends about their noble and hardy ancestors. According to one Loyalist descendant, her "forebearers only crime was loyalty to the Government they had sworn fealty to"; her grandfather, she believed firmly, "had done his duty to God and to his country." Another wrote that her parents were "thorough Loyalists." Similar statements were made by other Loyalist descendants who claimed that their forefathers had "determined never to side with the Republicans" or that the male family head had been "a strict Loyalist ... [who] took up arms in defence of his Sovereign, which he maintained to the last." The other main ingredients in the reminiscences were idyllic depictions of hardy pioneers carving a future out of the rugged Canadian wilderness. Their forefathers, in the words of one Loyalist descendant, endured many hardships but "we never thought of these privations but were always happy and cheerful." A similar unreality characterized the descriptions of Loyalist women's lives in the new settlements. An idealized image of women in the subsistence economy was reflected in portraits of happy women spinning, who, according to one tale, were "like the Princesses of old, they gloried in their occupation."[81]

The first amateur history of the Loyalist settlements, written in 1869, reflected perfectly the view of the past created by the Loyalists, who were aptly dubbed "the fathers of Upper Canada." "There cannot rest upon the mind of the honest reader of unbiased history," William Canniff declared, "a doubt as to the motives of the Loyalists." They had "faithfully adhered to the old flag [and] possessed all the ardor of a lofty patriotism." The Loyalists, a "devoted band of firm adherents to the British crown," had fought to maintain "the unity of the British empire." The myth of their upper-lass origins was again advanced; the Loyalists represented "the great bulk of the educated and refined, the religious classes, especially the clergy, the leading lawyers, the most prominent medical men ... " The theme of redemption was extended even further by Canniff, who proclaimed that the Loyalists' exile had "led to the establishment of a nation to their [the Americans'] north, which will stand, even after the union lies in fragments."[82] The Loyalists would have approved of Canniff's "unbiased" view of history.

Women were portrayed by Canniff as frail, helpless creatures who suffered but played no major role in the Revolution. The suffering of women was cited as evidence of the Patriots' brutality. One Loyalist woman, it was reported, was about to give birth when the Patriots stripped her of her bedclothes and even her bed. There were also the hardy women pioneers trying to feed their starving children and making maple syrup. Most astonishing was Canniff's portrait of Molly Brant. She was nowhere to be found in lengthy descriptions of frontier warfare featuring Sir John Johnson, the Loyalist regiments, and Joseph Brant. She figured in the piece only as Sir William Johnson's live-in "housekeeper." Canniff, reflecting the Victorian view that a woman's morality was her most prized asset, hastened to reassure readers that, even though she was not legally married to Johnson, she was a "faithful spouse" and "virtuous woman." In Canniff's history, the role of Loyalist women was minimized and distorted. Moreover, because there was no "script" for their past, they were the playthings of historians who could, like Canniff, interpret them in whatever way was consistent with contemporary views about women.[83]

The Loyalists cast a long shadow over the history and literature of Upper Canada and Canada. The French Revolution and the War of 1812 reinforced Upper Canadians' antipathy to republicanism and to the United States and their attachment to the British empire and conservative values. Loyalty became central to the early-nineteenth-century political system and to the success of individual politicians. By the late nineteenth century, imperial federationists, who advocated closer ties between Canada and the British empire, looked to the Loyalists as the founders of English-speaking Canada. Along with an attachment to the British empire and conservatism, the Loyalists gave to the Imperial Federationists a sense of mission and power. Also, in 1896, the United Empire Loyalist Association was founded to preserve historic records and keep "bright the spirit of loyalty in the inheritors of so noble an ancestry." And in New Brunswick, the Loyalists were esteemed for establishing "those institutions and principles regarded as the cornerstones of Canadian nationality." By the turn of the century, the Loyalists had achieved exalted status as the founders of English-speaking Canada.[84]

The legacy of the Loyalists, which had a major impact on the development of Canadian society in the nineteenth century, left no place for Loyalist women. Just as the Loyalists themselves had stressed that they had been motivated by loyalty to the British crown, empire, and constitution, later generations identified them with loyalty. But well into the twentieth century, loyalty was a male concept in that it was associated with political decision-making – a sphere from which women were excluded. The same can be said of the idea that the Loyalists bequeathed conservative values and British institutions to later generations of Canadians: women have had no role in fashioning political values and institutions. The notion that the Loyalists were the founders of a nation had obvious and unequivocal gender implications. The amateur historian William Canniff was right when he equated the "founders" with the "fathers."

The themes that began with the Loyalists and were perpetuated in the nineteenth century were passed on to twentieth-century historians. It was not, of course, that historians accepted at face value the Loyalists' selective view of their past and decided to leave Loyalist women out of their histories. It was just that the Loyalists, no matter which colony they resettled in, had been so successful in painting a clear and well-defined portrait of themselves that historians had to probe the various aspects of that portrait. The Loyalists' assertion that allegiance and political ideas had motivated them led to many studies of ideology and motivation.[85] It was some time before historians dispelled the myth of the upper-class origins of the Loyalists and this was achieved only after there had been many studies of their social and economic origins.[86] The usefulness of the Loyalist petitions themselves was debated. Some historians used them in studies of the Loyalists' motivation, while others pointed out that when people petition for compensation they often exaggerate their principles and assets.[87] And just as the British and the Loyalists saw military service by whites in a very narrow way as involving enlistment in one of the Loyalist regiments, histories of the white Loyalists' military role focused on the Loyalist regiments.[88] The Loyalists were masters at recreating history and obscuring our understanding of the past. They had played tricks on historians.

History bypassed the Loyalist women who settled in and around Cataraqui, but their experiences were not unique. Other Loyalist refugee women suffered a similar fate. In part this was because there were many similarities in their backgrounds. All Loyalist white women existed within a patriarchal family and society, which was not eroded, as it had been for Patriot women, by anti-patriarchal, republican ideas and language. Many other Loyalist women also lived in a subsistence, agricultural economy where household patriarchy prevailed. Their ethnic origins and the fact that so many were tenant farmers, it is true, set the group of Loyalists in this study apart from other groups. These factors along with their isolation from the mainstream of the Revolution help to explain their Loyalism. But what was typical was that many factors, such as family, ethnic, and community bonds, were more important in explaining their actions than was an undying devotion to British institutions.

What all Loyalist women who left the American colonies to settle in other parts of the British empire also shared was a common refugee experience. The American Revolution was a civil war in which many women were drawn into the fray in one way or another. In the case of the women in this study, the fact that most lived in a strategic location on the frontier meant that they played especially critical roles in the war effort. However, most other Loyalist women also experienced harassment of some kind, as well as the need to care for their families in the absence of male household heads, and they all had to undergo the dislocation and tragedy associated with leaving their homes, families, and communities.

Exile was also a formative experience for all the Loyalist women who left the colonies. Most had to spend up to eight years in exile, awaiting the outcome of the Revolution. Whether in Quebec, at New York City, or at some other British base, they had to live within a patriarchal, paternalistic power structure in which they were seen not as military assets but as burdens. It was here that their experiences during the Revolution were distorted to accommodate British officials. While male Loyalists could fit into the patriarchal British power structure by serving in the Loyalist regiments, women could appeal to British paternalism only by stressing their feminine weakness and helplessness and by recounting their suffering. Loyalist women, whether they were petitioning British officials in Quebec or elsewhere, became accustomed to citing their husbands' military service and casting their own experiences within the language of enfeeblement. Even before the Revolution was over, Loyalist women had begun to lose their place in the written records.

The identity and view of the past created by Loyalists who resettled in and around Cataraqui was also common to Loyalists who settled in other parts of the British empire, such as New Brunswick and Nova Scotia.[89] During their exile and resettlement, Loyalists everywhere explained their fate by taking on a well-defined identity – they were people of unswerving loyalty who had fought courageously for the crown and suffered much for their principles. This identity served to persuade British officials of their obligation to reward and provide for the Loyalists and it gave them an exalted place in the history of English-speaking Canada.

The role to which women were relegated within the Loyalists' version of the past was nicely illustrated in a poem written by William Kirby, a nineteenth-century writer who romanticized the Loyalist experience. His poem, entitled "The Hungry Year," followed the standardized Loyalist script. The Loyalists were those "who had kept their faith to England's Crown, and scorned an alien name." Their material losses were great, but they retained "their honour, and the conscious pride/ Of duty done to country and to King." The myth of their upper-class origins surfaced in estimates of their property losses – "Broad lands, ancestral homes, the gathered wealth/ Of patient toil and self-denying years,/ Were confiscate and lost; for they had been/ The salt and savour of the land ... " A telling passage referred to women in terms typical of other views of their role: "They [the men] left their native soil with sword belts drawn/ The tighter, while the women only wept/ At the thought of old fire sides no longer theirs,/ At household treasures reft, and all the land/ Upset, and ruled by rebels to the King ... "[90] In these few lines, Kirby aptly summarized the "bag of tricks" that had been played on Loyalist women refugees. All of their contributions to the war effort, their achievements in shepherding their families through the ordeals of persecution, exile, and the drudgery of refugee camp life, had been dismissed with the trite phrase that Loyalist men had acted heroically "while the women only wept."

Notes

PREFACE

1 In French the quote is "Ce n'est pas après tout, qu'un ramas de tracasseries qu'on fait aux morts." It can be found in a letter from Voltaire to de Cideville, 9 February 1757, included in *Complete Works of Voltaire* (Banbury, England: Voltaire Foundation 1971), vol. 101:448.

2 Bernard Bailyn, *The Ordeal of Thomas Hutchinson* (Cambridge, Mass.: Harvard University Press 1974); Robert M. Calhoon, *The Loyalists in Revolutionary America* (New York: Harcourt, Brace Jovanovich 1973); Mary Beth Norton, *The British Americans: The Loyalist Exiles in England, 1774–1789* (Boston: Little, Brown 1972).

3 Neil MacKinnon, *This Unfriendly Soil: The Loyalist Experience in Nova Scotia, 1783–1791* (Kingston and Montreal: McGill-Queen's University Press 1986); Esther Clark Wright, *The Loyalists of New Brunswick* (Fredericton, N.B.: privately printed 1955); David G. Bell, *Early Loyalist Saint John: The Origins of New Brunswick Politics, 1783–1786* (Fredericton, 1983); Ann Gorman Condon, *The Envy of the American States: The Loyalist Dream for New Brunswick* (Fredericton, N.B.: New Ireland Press 1984); James W. St. G. Walker, *The Black Loyalists: The Search for a Promised Land in Nova Scotia and Sierra Leone, 1783–1870* (New York and Halifax: Africana Publishing with Dalhousie University Press 1976). On Loyalism in eastern Ontario, see Marla Susan Waltman, "From Soldier to Settler: Patterns of Loyalist Settlement in 'Upper Canada,' 1783–1785," (MA thesis, Queen's University 1981) Eula C. Lapp, *To Their Heirs Forever* (Picton: Picton Publishing 1970); Hazel

C. Mathews, *The Mark of Honour* (Toronto: University of Toronto Press 1965).

4 See, for example, Mary Beacock Fryer, "Sarah Sherwood: Wife and Mother, an 'Invisible Loyalist'," in *Eleven Exiles: Accounts of Loyalists of the American Revolution*, eds., Phyllis R. Blakely and John N. Grant (Toronto: Dundurn Press 1982), 245–64; Mary Beth Norton, "Eighteenth-Century American Women in Peace and War: The Case of the Loyalists," *William and Mary Quarterly* (hereafter WMQ), 3rd Series, 33 (1976): 386–409; Elizabeth Evans, *Weathering the Storm: Women of the American Revolution* (New York: Charles Scribner's Sons 1975); Paul Engle, "Those Dashing Ladies of the Opposition," in *Women in the American Revolution* (Chicago: Follett 1976), 107–62; Katherine M.J. McKenna, "Treading the Hard Road": Some Loyalist Women and the American Revolution, (MA thesis Queen's University 1979); Beatrice Spence Ross, "Adaptation in Exile: Loyalist Women in Nova Scotia after the American Revolution," (PhD thesis, Cornell University 1981); Katherine M.J. McKenna, "The Life of Anne Murray Powell, 1755–1849: A 'Case Study' of the Position of Women in Early Upper Canadian Elite Society," (PhD thesis, Queen's University 1987).

5 Wallace Brown, *The King's Friends: The Composition and Motives of the American Loyalist Claimants* (Providence, R.I.: Brown University Press 1965); Leonard W. Labaree, "The Nature of American Loyalism," *Proceedings of the American Antiquarian Society*, 54 (April 1944): 15–58; Mary Beacock Fryer, *The King's Men: The Soldier Founders of Ontario* (Toronto and Charlottetown: Dundurn Press 1980); Wallace Brown and Hereward Senior, *Victorious in Defeat: The Loyalists in Canada* (Methuen: Toronto 1984).

6 Janice Potter, *The Liberty We Seek: Loyalist Ideology in Colonial New York and Massachusetts* (Cambridge, Mass., and London: Harvard University Press 1983).

CHAPTER I

1 "The Loyal North Britons, a Highland March," *Quebec Gazette*, n.d., War Office 28 [hereafter WO 28] B2862, vol. 4, National Archives of Canada [hereafter NA].

2 Robert William Venables, "Tryon County 1775–1783: A Frontier in Revolution," (PhD thesis, Vanderbilt University 1967), 124; Earle Thomas, *Sir John Johnson: Loyalist Baronet* (Toronto and Reading, England: Dundurn Press 1986).

3 Sir John Johnson to Daniel Claus, 20 January 1777, Claus Papers, C–1478, vol. 1, NA.

4 Ibid.

5 Mrs Johnson to General Washington, 16 June 1776, in Peter Force, ed., *American Archives* (Washington, D.C., 1837–53), 4th Series, vol, 6:930; Johnson to Claus, 20 January 1777, Claus Papers, C–1478, vol. 1.

6 Dothe Stone Diary, 1777–92, Joel Stone Papers, Archives of Ontario [hereafter AO]; Joy Day Buel and Richard Buel Jr, *The Way of Duty: A Woman and Her Family in Revolutionary America* (New York and London: W.W. Norton 1984); John J. Waters, "Family Inheritance and Migration in Colonial New England: The Evidence from Guilford Connecticut," *WMQ*, 3rd Series 39 (1982): 64–86; Robert V. Wells, "Quaker Marriage Patterns in a Colonial Perspective," in Nancy F. Cott and Elizabeth Peck, eds., *A Heritage of Her Own: Toward a New Social History of American Women* (New York: Simon and Schuster 1979), 81–106; Carl N. Degler, *At Odds: Women and the Family in America from the Revolution to the Present* (New York: Oxford University Press 1981), 7–8, estimates the age of marriage of women in Revolutionary America to have been twenty-three; Mary Beth Norton, *Liberty's Daughters: The Revolutionary Experience of American Women 1750–1800* (Boston: Little, Brown 1980), 71–2.

7 Norton, *Liberty's Daughters*, 3–14; Laurel Thatcher Ulrich, *Good Wives: Image and Reality in the Lives of Women in Northern New England, 1650–1750* (New York: Alfred A. Knopf 1982); Stone Diary.

8 Stone Diary, 22 October 1783, 5.

9 Stone Diary, 30 May 1784, 11.

10 Gerda Lerner, *The Creation of Patriarchy* (New York and Oxford: Oxford University Press 1986), 239; Philip Greven, *The Protestant Temperament: Patterns of Childrearing, Religious Experience and the Self in Early America* (New York: Alfred A. Knopf 1977), 242; E. Anthony Rotundo, "Body and Soul: Changing Ideals of American Middle-Class Manhood, 1770–1920," *Journal of Social History*, Summer, 1983: 23–38.

11 Alexander McDonell to his wife, in "Letters Extracted from the Letter Book of Capt. Alexander McDonell of the Royal Highland Emigrants written from Halifax, Windsor and Cornwallis between the years 1775 and 1779," Fraser Papers, MG 23 B33, NA.

12 Stone Diary, 22 October 1783, 5; 3 December 1783, 8.

13 Stone Diary, 22 October 1783, 5; 24 October 1783, 6; 3 December 1783, 8; 10 December 1783, 9.

14 Mary to Joseph and Rachel Fish, 6 August 1769, Noyes Family Papers, New Canaan Historical Society, 39–47, quoted in Buel, *The Way of Duty*, 62–3; Mary to Joseph and Rachel Fish, 30 May 1772, privately owned, quoted in ibid., 67; Norton, *Liberty's Daughters*, 118–24.

15 Joy Parr, "Nature and Hierarchy: Reflections on Writing the History of Women and Children," *Atlantis*, 2 (Fall 1985): 43.

16 Lerner, *The Creation of Patriarchy*, 239; Linda Kerber, *Women of the Republic: Intellect and Ideology in Revolutionary America* (Chapel Hill, N.C.: University of North Carolina Press 1986), 120; Joan R. Gundersen and Gwen Victor Gampel, "Married Women's Legal Status in Eighteenth-Century New York and Virginia," *WMQ*, 3rd Series, 39 (1982): 114–34; Marylynn Salmon, *Women and the Law of Property in Early America* (Chapel Hill, N.C.: University of North Carolina Press 1986).

17 Toby L. Ditz, "Ownership and Obligation: Inheritance and Patriarchal Households in Connecticut, 1750–1820," *WMQ*, 3rd Series, 47 (April 1990): 257; Toby L. Ditz, *Property and Kinship: Inheritance in Early Connecticut, 1750–1820* (Princeton, N.J.: Princeton University Press 1986); Philip Greven, *Four Generations: Population, Land and Family in Colonial Andover, Massachusetts* (Ithaca, N.Y.: Cornell University Press 1970); Christopher M. Jedrey, *The World of John Cleaveland: Family and Community in Eighteenth-Century New England* (New York, London: W.W. Norton 1979).

18 Rotundo, "Body and Soul," 29; Melvin Yazawa, *From Colonies to Commonwealth: Familial Ideology and the Beginnings of the American Republic* (Baltimore and London: Johns Hopkins University Press 1985).

19 Yazawa, *From Colonies to Commonwealth*, 89.

20 Janice Potter, *The Liberty We Seek: Loyalist Ideology in Colonial New York and Massachusetts* (Cambridge Mass. and London: Harvard University Press 1983), 39–62, 107–32.

21 Return of the Loyalists, Haldimand Papers [hereafter HP], MG 21, B168:100, NA, quoted in Marla Susan Waltman, "From Soldier to Settler: Patterns of Loyalist Settlement in 'Upper Canada,' 1783–1785 (MA thesis, Queen's University 1981), 33.

22 Eugene R. Fingerhut, "Uses and Abuses of the American Loyalist Claims: A Critique of Quantitative Analyses," *WMQ*, 3rd Series, 25 (April 1968): 245-58.

23 Alexander Fraser, ed., *Report of the Bureau of Archives for the Province of Ontario* [hereafter AO *Report*] (Toronto: Queen's Printer 1904), 1268, claim of John Curtis, who admitted to being "obliged to turn out once with the American Militia & served with them three months at Mount Independence"; see also Andrew Garetville, 1283–4.

24 Ross to Mathews, 7 July 1784, quoted in E.A. Cruikshank, *The Settlement of the United Empire Loyalists on the Upper St. Lawrence and the Bay of Quinte in 1784* (Toronto, 1934), 132–3; Waltman, "From Soldier to Settler," 58; AO *Report*, 1904, claim of Daniel McGuin, 952–3, James Parrott, 95.

25 Waltman, "From Soldier to Settler," 59–62.

26 Jane Goddard Bennett, *Hans Waltimeyer* (Cobourg, Ont.: Haynes Printing 1980), 96–8; Mary Beacock Fryer, *John Walden Meyers: Loyalist Spy* (Toronto and Charlottetown: Dundurn Press 1983).

27 Waltman, "From Soldier to Settler," 69; Walter Allen Knittle, *Early Eighteenth Century Palatine Emigration: A British Government Redemptioner Project to Manufacture Naval Stores* (Baltimore: Dorrance 1937); Lapp, *To Their Heirs Forever*.

28 G.S. French, "Barbara Ruckle Heck," *Dictionary of Canadian Biography* [hereafter DCB], 12 vols to date (Toronto, Buffalo, and London: University of Toronto Press 1966–), 5: 728–9.

29 W.D. Reid, "Johan Jost Herkimer, U.E. and His Family," *Ontario Historical Society Papers and Records* [hereafter OHSPR], 31 (1936): 215–26; Ernest Green, "Frey," *ibid*, 33 (1939): 45–74; Venables, "Tryon County, 1775–1783," 145–6.

30 Venables, "Tryon County, 1775–1783," 84–8; Waltman, "From Soldier to Settler," 71.

31 Wiltsee Family Geneology, Blanchard Papers, AO.

32 Alice P. Kenney, *Stubborn for Liberty: The Dutch in New York* (Syracuse, N.Y.: Syracuse University Press 1975), 1, and "The Albany Dutch: Loyalists and Patriots," *New York History*, 42 (1961): 331–50.

33 William H. Nelson, *The American Tory* (Boston: Beacon Press 1961), 89.

34 Kenney, "The Albany Dutch," 336–7; Henry John Van Allen, "The Van Allen Family in America," *The New York Genealogical and Biographical Record* 5 (1950): 4–17, 113–22, 179–84, 243–5: Larry Turner, "Peter Van Alstine, Michael Grass and the Associated Loyalists of Upper Canada, 1783–1784," (MA thesis, Queen's University 1984).

35 Ruth M Keesey, "Loyalism in Bergen County, New Jersey," *WMQ*, 3rd Series, 18 (January 1961): 558–71; Adrian C. Leiby, *The Revolutionary War in the Hackensack Valley: The Jersey Dutch and the Neutral Ground, 1775–1783* (New Brunswick, N.J.: Rutgers University Press 1980); AO *Report*, claim of Gilbert Bogart, 1256, 1266.

36 Bernard Bailyn, *Voyagers to the West: A Passage in the Peopling of America on the Eve of the Revolution* (New York: Alfred A. Knopf 1986), 26; Waltman, "From Soldier to Settler," p. 52.

37 Ned C. Landsman, *Scotland and Its First American Colony, 1683–1765* (Princeton, N.J.: Princeton University Press 1985), 45; Ian Charles Cargill Graham, *Colonists from Scotland: Emigration to North America, 1707–1783* (Ithaca, N.Y.: Cornell University Press 1956); Hazel C. Mathews, *The Mark of Honour* (Toronto: University of Toronto Press 1965); Waltman, "From Soldier to Settler," 76; Bailyn, *Voyagers to the West*, 583.

38 Nancy Jean Cameron to Margaret, Broadalbin, New York, 15 May 1785,

Mrs D.J. MacPherson, Private Papers, NA; Graham, *Colonists from Scotland*, 106–7.

39 Governor Frederick Haldimand to Captain Alexander Fraser, 12 November 1779, HP, 21,788; Haldimand to Colonel Guy Johnson, 10 October 1781, HP, 21,766; Haldimand to Germain, 28 November 1780, HP, 21, 774.

40 Barbara Graymont, *The Iroquois in the American Revolution* (Syracuse: Syracuse University Press 1972), 17, 21, 22–3.

41 Ibid., 47; Barbara Graymont "Molly Brant," in *DCB* 4: 416–19; H. Pearson Gundy, "Molly Brant: Loyalist," *OHSPR*, 45 (1953): 97-108.

42 G.A. Rawlyk, "The Reverend John Stuart: Mohawk Missionary and Reluctant Loyalist," in Esmond Wright, ed., *Red, White and True Blue: The Loyalists in the Revolution* (New York: AMS Press 1976), 55–72.

43 John Jay to Gouverneur Morris, April 1778, quoted in Potter, *The Liberty We Seek*, 2; Jon Butler, *The Huguenots in America: A Refugee People in a New World Society* (Cambridge, Mass.: Harvard University Press 1984).

44 Nelson, *The American Tory*, 89.

45 Waltman, "From Soldier to Settler," 39–42.

46 Bailyn, *Voyagers to the West*, 7, 10.

47 Waltman, "From Soldier to Settler," 43–7.

48 Bruce Wilson, *As She Began: An Illustrated Introduction to Loyalist Ontario* (Toronto and Charlottetown: Dundurn Press 1981), 13.

49 Bellesiles, "Life, Liberty and Land: Ethan Allen and the Frontier Experience in Revolutionary New England," unpublished manuscript, chapter 2, quoted in Gregory H. Nobles, "Breaking into the Backcountry: New Approaches to the Early American Frontier," *WMQ*, 3rd Series (October 1989): 648; James A Henretta, "Families and Farms: Mentalité in Pre-Industrial America," *WMQ*, 3rd Series, 35 (1978): 3–32; Allan Kulikoff, "The Transition to Capitalism in Rural America," *WMQ*, 3rd Series, 46 (January 1989): 120–44; Ditz, "Ownership and Obligation"; Mary P. Ryan, *Cradle of the Middle Class: The Family in Oneida County, New York, 1790–1865* (Cambridge, England: Cambridge University Press 1981).

50 "Further Evidence on the Claim of the Children of Mary Brant," AO Report, 1904, 472; claim of Sarah McGinnis, Audit Office 12, vol. 28: B1161, NA; claim of Peter Fitzpatrick, AO Report, 1904, 1076; claim of William Orser, Audit Office 12, B1161, vol. 28:144; claim of Elinor Maybee, widow of Joseph Hoffman, Audit Office 12, vol. 28:B1161; claim of John Lawrence, ibid.

51 Waltman, "From Soldier to Settler," 55; some Loyalists who later settled in the Cataraqui area protected themselves by having both New York and New Hampshire titles.

52 H.M. Jackson, *Justus Sherwood: Soldier, Loyalist and Negotiator* (Kingston, 1958); Mary Babcock Fryer, *Buckskin Pimpernel: The Exploits of Justus Sherwood, Loyalist Spy* (Toronto and Charlottetown: Dundurn 1981); Ian C.B. Pemberton, "Justus Sherwood, Vermont Loyalist, 1747–1798," (PhD thesis, University of Western Ontario 1973).

53 Claim of John Munro, John Munro Papers, AO; J.K. Johnson, "John Munro," *DCB*, 4:566–7.

54 "Narrative of John Peters," in H.M. Robertson Papers, AO.

55 Charles A. Jellison, *Ethan Allen: Frontier Rebel* (Syracuse, N.Y.: Syracuse University Press 1969), 63; Wilbur Library, *Wilbur Photostats*, N.3180, quoted in Chilton Williamson, *Vermont in Quandry, 1763–1825* (Montpelier, Vt.: Vermont Historical Society 1949), 15.

56 Claim of Thomas Sherwood, AO Report, 1904, 1089; Israel, Richard, and Farrington Ferguson, 1075; John Coon, 962; Israel Tompkins, 1108; see also Henry Jackson, 1267, for another sharecropping agreement; Alexander Nicholson, 1255–6.

57 Sung Bok Kim, *Landlord and Tenant in Colonial New York: Manorial Society, 1664–1775* (Chapel Hill, N.C.: The University of North Carolina Press 1978), and "The Impact of Class Relations and Warfare in the American Revolution: The New York Experience," *Journal of American History*, 69 (September 1982): 326–46; Patricia U. Bonomi, *A Factious People: Politics and Society in Colonial New York* (New York and London: Columbia University Press 1971).

58 Kim, "Impact of Class Relations and Warfare," 327; Rowland Berthoff and John M. Murrin, "Feudalism, Communalism, and the Yeoman Freeholder: The American Revolution Considered as a Social Accident," in Stephen G. Kurtz and James H. Hutson, eds., *Essays on the American Revolution* (New York: W.W. Norton 1973), 256–88.

59 Staughton Lynd, "The Tenant Rising at Livingston Manor, May 1777," *New York Historical Society Quarterly*, 48 (1964): 163–77, and "Who Should Rule At Home? Dutchess County, New York, in the American Revolution," *WMQ*, 3rd Series 19 (1961): 330–59; Alice P. Kenney, "The Albany Dutch: Loyalists and Patriots," *New York History*, 42 (1961): 331–50; "Form of an Association on Cortlandt's Manor," *Rivington's New-York Gazeteer, or the Connecticut, New Jersey, Hudson's River and Quebec Weekly Advertiser* [hereafter *RIV*], 17 February 1775, 11 May 1775.

60 Bernard Bailyn, ed., *Pamphlets of the American Revolution, 1750–1776*, vol. 1 (Cambridge, Mass.: Harvard University Press 1965), and *The Ideological Origins of the American Revolution* (Cambridge, Mass.: Harvard University Press 1967); Gordon Stewart and G.A. Rawlyk, *A People Highly Favoured of God: The Nova Scotia Yankees and the American Revolution* (Toronto: Macmillan of Canada 1972), 3.

61 Claims, B1162, vol. 29:86, NA.

62 Edward Countryman, *A People in Revolution: The American Revolution and Political Society in New York, 1760–1790* (Baltimore and London: Johns Hopkins University Press 1981), 20–1, 23.

63 Milton W. Hamilton, *Sir William Johnson: Colonial American 1715–1763* (Fort Washington, N.Y.: Kennikat Press 1976); James Thomas Flexner, *Mohawk Baronet: Sir William Johnson of New York* (New York: Harper Brothers 1959).

64 Venables, "Tryon County, 1775–1783," 71.

65 Thomas, *Sir John Johnson.*

66 Countryman, *A People in Revolution*, 21, 33; Sir William Johnson, 11 June 1771, letter and reference for Richard Mandevell, Ms. 420, Abbott Collection, quoted in Venables, "Tryon County, 1775–1783," 64, 72.

67 See Gerald Dworkin, "Paternalism," in Rolf Sartorius, ed., *Paternalism* (Minneapolis, Minn.: University of Minnesota Press 1983), 19–34; Donald Van De Veer, *Paternalistic Intervention: The Moral Bounds of Benevolence* (Princeton, N.J.: Princeton University Press 1986), 16–23; John Kleinig, *Paternalism* (Totow, N.J.: Rowman and Allanneld 1984), 4–5.

68 Jack D. Douglas, "Co-operative Paternalism versus Conflictual Paternalism," in Sartorius, *Paternalism*, 171–200; David Roberts, *Paternalism in Early Victorian England* (New Brunswick, N.J.: Rutgers University Press 1979), 4–6.

69 See, for instance, Bryan D. Palmer, *Working-Class Experience: The Rise and Reconstitution of Canadian Labour, 1800–1980* (Toronto and Vancouver: Butterworth 1983), 12–19.

70 Palmer, *Working-Class Experience*, 14; Countryman, *A People in Revolution*, 33.

CHAPTER 2

1 "Minutes and Proceedings, Tryon County Committee of Safety," in Maryly B. Penrose, ed., *Mohawk Valley in the Revolution: Committee of Safety Papers and Genealogical Compendium* (Franklin Port, N.J.: Liberty Bell Associates 1978), 129.

2 E.A. Cruikshank, "The King's Royal Regiment of New York," *OHSPR*, 27 (1931): 193–323.

3 Petition of Richard Wilkinson, HP, A776, 21,875.

4 Sir John Johnson to Governor William Tryon, 3 January 1776, quoted in Cruikshank, "The King's Royal Regiment of New York," 199.

5 Alexander Campbell petition to Haldimand, 6 October 1778, NP, A776, 21,874.

6 Peter Rose, "Some Thoughts about Refugees and the Descendants of Theseus," *International Migration Review* [hereafter *IMR*], 15 (1981): 8; Maria Pfister-Ammende, "The Problem of Uprooting," in Charles Zwingmann and Maria Pfister-Ammende, *Uprooting and After* (New York: Springer-Gerlay 1973), 8–9.

7 Ibid.

8 "Minutes of the Committee of Safety, Westminister County," 23 July 1776, in E.P. Walton ed., *Records of the Council of Safety and Governor and Council of the State of Vermont ... July, 1775 to Dec., 1777* (Montpelier, Vt.: Steam Press 1873), vol. 1:352.

9 Samuel Seabury, *Free Thoughts on the Proceedings of the Continental Congress* (New York, 1774), 62.

10 James Sullivan, ed., *Minutes of the Albany Committee of Correspondence, 1775–1778* (Albany, N.Y.: The University of the State of New York 1923), 332.

11 "Tryon County Committee of Safety," 7 November 1775, 57.

12 Walton, *Records*, 24 January 1778, vol. 1:210.

13 Ibid., February and April 1779, 291, and 297.

14 Sullivan, *Albany Committee of Correspondence*, February 1776, 336.

15 *Journals of the Provincial Congress, Provincial Convention, Committee of Safety and Council of Safety of the State of New-York 1775–1776–1777* (Albany, N.Y.: Thurlow, Weed 1842), 22 August 1775, 115.

16 "Tryon County Committee of Safety," 21 October 1776, 93.

17 Ruth M. Keesey, "Loyalism in Bergen County, New Jersey," *WMQ*, 3rd Series, 18 (January 1961), 560.

18 Maria Susan Waltman, "From Soldier to Settler," (MA thesis, Queen's University 1981), 37.

19 *General Association*, Sullivan, *Albany Committee of Correspondence*, 3; ibid., 337; AO *Report*, 1904, claim of James Parrot, 950, Daniel McGuin, 952.

20 Michael Kammen, "The American Revolution as a *Crise de Conscience*: The Case of New York," in R.M. Jellison ed., *Society, Freedom and Conscience: The Coming of the Revolution in Virginia, Massachusetts and New York* (New York: W.W. Norton 1976), 135.

21 "Tryon County Committee of Safety," 23 April 1777, 111–12.

22 Captain William Fraser to Haldimand, 21 December 1782, HP, A748, 21,821; Report by Ensign Thomas Mann, 14 August 1782, HP, A735, 21,797; Riedesel to Haldimand, 3 April 1783, HP, A736, 21,798.

23 "Report of Five Prisoners Brought to Saint Johns," 2 November 1778, HP, A690, 21,793; Powell to Haldimand, 20 June 1779, HP, A690, 21,793.

24 "Tryon County Committee of Safety," 27 October 1775, 51; "Narrative of John Peters," Germain to Carleton, Colonial Office 42 [hereafter CO 42], vol. 36:B33, on microfilm, NA; Haldimand to Nairne, 4 December 1780, HP, A750, 21,823; Pownall to Haldimand, 1 May 1779, HP, A690, 21,793.

25 "Tryon County Committee of Safety," 3 April 1777, 188–9.

26 H.H. Robertson Papers, AO, 45.

27 Larry Turner, "Peter Van Alstine, Michael Grass, and the Associated Loyalists of Upper Canada, 1783–1784" (MA thesis, Queens University 1984), 1–12.

28 Adrian C. Leiby, *The Revolutionary War in the Hackensack Valley: The Jersey Dutch and the Neutral Ground, 1775–1783* (New Brunswick, N.J.: Rutgers University Press 1980), 38; Terrence McCoristine petition, 12 March 1778, WO 28, vol. 9: B2866, on microfilm, NA.

29 Alexander McDonell to General Howe, 30 October 1775, "Letters Extracted from the Letter Book of Capt. Alexander McDonell of the Royal Highland Emigrants written from Halifax, Windsor and Cornwallis between the years 1775 and 1779." Fraser Papers, MG 23 B33, 223–5, NA; Germain to Carleton, 26 March 1777, HP, 21,698; Carleton to Butler, 18 May 1777, HP, 21,699; Leiby, *The Revolutionary War in the Hackensack Valley*, 38; Ebenezer Jessup to Burgoyne, 17 July 1778, in HP, A776, 21,874; see also E. Stuart Rae, "Jessup's Rangers as a Factor in Loyalist Settlement," *Three History Theses* (Toronto: Ontario Department of Public Records and Archives 1961); all quotations are reproduced verbatim.

30 Captain Alexander McDonell to Dr William Hagard, 19 January 1777, "Letters Extracted from the Letter Book of Capt. Alexander McDonell," 319; "Tryon County Committee of Safety," 9 February 1778, 141–2.

31 Staughton Lynd, "The Tenant Rising at Livingston Manor, May, 1777," *New York Historical Society Quarterly*, 48 (1964): 63–78.

32 *Journals of the Provincial Congress*, 20 September 1775, 153.

33 "Tryon County Committee of Safety," 23 April 1777, 111; Cruikshank, "The King's Royal Regiment of New York," 249; Richard K. MacMaster, "Parish in Arms: A Study of Father John MacKenna and the Mohawk Valley Loyalists, 1773–1778," United States Catholic Historical Society, *Historical Records and Studies*, 45 (1957): 107–25.

34 Keesey, "Loyalism in Bergen County," 569; Rae, "Jessup's Rangers," 130–1; Cruikshank, "The King's Royal Regiment of New York," 319–21.

35 Barbara Graymont, *The Iroquois and the American Revolution* (Syracuse, N.Y.: Syracuse University Press 1972), 104–28.

36 Alexander McDonell to General Howe, 30 October 1775, 224; Major

Gray to Haldimand, 10 May 1777, HP, quoted in W.L. Scott, "A UE Loyalist Family," *OHSPR*, 32 (1937): 148.

37 Cruikshank, "The King's Royal Regiment of New York," 202; Rae, "Jessup's Rangers," 30.

38 Sullivan, *Minutes of the Albany Committee of Correspondence*, Declaration of the Grand Jury and Magistrates of Tryon County, 6 April 1775, 2.

39 "Tryon County Committee of Safety," 19 May 1775, 4–6; Sullivan, *Albany Committee of Correspondence*, 22 May 1775, 33–4.

40 Freel, "Tryon County Committee of Correspondence," 60–1.

41 Ibid.

42 Printed handbill in *Public Papers of George Clinton*, vol. 7:27, quoted in E.A. Cruikshank, *The Settlement of the United Empire Loyalists on the Upper St. Lawrence and Bay of Quinte in 1784* (Toronto: Ontario Historical Society 1934), 260–1.

43 See, for example, Mary Beth Norton, *Liberty's Daughters: The Revolutionary Experience of American Women, 1750–1800* (Boston: Little, Brown 1980).

44 *A Dialogue Between a Southern Delegate and His Spouse* (New York, 1774).

45 Petition of Ann Novil, Frances Child, Hannah Tomlinson, British Headquarters Papers [hereafter BHP], NA.

46 Francis Hopkinson, "The Battle of the Kegs," quoted in Philip Young, *Revolutionary Ladies* (New York: Alfred A. Knopf 1977), 59.

47 Walter Hart Blumenthal, *Women Camp Followers of the American Revolution* (New York: Arno Press 1974), 30–2.

48 Hannah Winthrop to Mercy Warren, 11 November 1777, quoted in ibid., 27.

49 Petition of Mary Driskill, BHP, 27 November 1779, vol. 20.

50 Blumenthal, *Women Camp Followers*, 21–2; Kerber, Linda *Women of the Republic: Intellect and Ideology in Revolutionary America* (Chapel Hill, N.C.: University of North Carolina Press 1986), 56–61.

51 "The Barbara Heck Bi-Centary," *Mail and Empire*, 17 August 1934, Blanchard Papers, AO.

52 Kerber, *Women of the Republic*, 48–9; John Slegel, "Minutes of the Committee & of the First Commission for Detecting and Defeating Conspiracies in the State of New York, Dec. 11, 1777 to Sept. 23, 1778," *Collections* of the New York Historical Society, 1924, 30; Andrew Billings to Pierre Van Cortlandt, ibid., 25 August 1777, 443.

53 Justus Sherwood to Powell, 23 July 1778, HP, 21,789; Powell to Haldimand, 25 July 1778, HP, 21,789; Victor Hugo Palsits, ed., *Minutes for the Commissioners for Detecting & Defeating Conspiracies in the State of New York, Albany County Sessions, 1778–1781*, 3 vols. (Albany:

J.B. Lyon 1909), 15 September 1780, 2:522; ibid., 26 November 1778, 1:290; Alexander McDonell to Donald McLean, June 1777, "Letters Extracted from the Letter Book of Capt. Alexander McDonell," 361; St Leger to Mathews, 29 November 1780, HP, 21,793.

54 Tryon County Committee of Safety, 27 August 1777, 129; Palsits, *Minutes*, 13 August 1781, 2:762–3; ibid., 25 July 1781, 2:751–2; ibid., 3 October 1778, 1:252; "Minutes of the Committee and of the First Commission for Detecting and Defeating Conspiracies ..." Kinderhook, 27 August 1777, 367–3; see also ibid., 4 September 1778, 1:224; 20 May 1778, 1:122; 17 June 1778, 1:146; 3 August 1779, 1:398; 3 October 1778, 1:252.

55 Palsits, *Minutes*, 26 July 1780, 2:470–1; Sullivan, *Albany Committee of Correspondence*, 27 September 1776, 564; memo by F.J. French, French Papers, AO; Walton, *Records* ..., in Council, 28 May 1778, 260–1.

56 "Tryon County Committee of Safety," 27 August 1777, 129; Walton, *Records*, 12 September 1777, 166; Kerber, *Women of the Republic*, 121.

57 Walton, *Records*, 12 September 1777, 166; "Tryon County Committee of Safety," 27 August 1777, 129; Isaac Paris, *Journals of the Provincial Congress of the State of New York, 1775 to 1777*, 2:474, quoted in W.L. Scott, "A U.E. Loyalist Family," *OHSPR*, 32 (1937): 147.

58 "Tryon County Committee of Safety," 21 October 1776, 93.

59 New York State Library, MSS 2212, Orderly Book, p. lxxxii.

60 Memorial of John Munro, Munro Papers, AO.

61 Graymont, *The Iroquois in the American Revolution*, 132, 189.

62 Barbara Graymont, "Konwatsi'tsiaienni," *DCB*, 4:416–18.

63 Ernest Green, "Frey," *OHSPR*, 23 (1937): 54–5.

64 Claus to Haldimand, 3 November 1780, HP, A685, 21,774.

65 Extract translated from Mary Brant's letter to Col. Claus, Carleton Island, 12 April 1781, HP, A685, 21,774.

66 Claim of Sarah Kast McGinnis, Audit Office 12, vol. 27; Claus to Haldimand, 5 November 1778, HP, 21,744; see also H.C. Burleigh, "A Tale of Loyalist Heroism," *OHSPR*, 42 (1950): 91–9.

67 Palsits, *Minutes*, 8 September 1779, 1:411; claim of Israel, Richard, and Farrington Ferguson, AO *Report*, 1904, 1075.

68 Palsits, *Minutes*, 9 June 1781, 2:733; Isabel Parker, n.d., HP, 21,875; "Tryon County Committee of Safety," 25 August 1777, 127; Mathews, *The Mark of Honour*, 32–3.

69 Walton, *Records*, 12 September 1777, 166; Palsits, *Minutes*, 10 January 1781, 3:615; 18 July 1780, 2:461–2; 26 November 1778, 1:290; 22 February 1781, 3:635.

70 McDonald, 14 April 1776, "Letters Extracted from the Letter Book of Capt. Alexander McDonell," 263.

71 Sullivan, *Albany Committee of Correspondence*, 1 February 1777, 671–2, 23 October 1777, 855; claim of Richard Cartwright, AO *Report*, 1904, 1001–2; Janice Potter and George Rawlyk, "Richard Cartwright, Jr," *DCB*, 5:167–72.

72 Palsits, *Minutes*, 31 August 1778, 1:220.

73 Claim of Abigail Lindsey, AO *Report*, 1904, 1061.

74 Turner, "Peter Van Alstine, Michael Grass, and the Associated Loyalists," 19.

75 "Narrative of John Peters," H.H. Robertson Papers, AO, 3; Reid, "Johan Jost Herkimer," 216; claim of Garnet Dingman, AO *Report*, 1904, 1038; claim of Martin Waldec, ibid., 1121.

76 Pauline Maier, "Popular Uprising and Civil Authority in Eighteenth Century America," *WMQ*, 3rd Series 27 (1970): 3–35; Jesse Lemisch, "Jack Tar in the Streets: Merchant Seamen in the Politics of Revolutionary America," *WMQ*, 3rd Series, 25 (1968): 371–407.

77 Palsits, *Minutes*, 1:47.

78 Ibid., 19 July 1779, 388; see also 1 May 1779, 335–6.

79 Joseph S. Tiedemann, "Patriots by Default: Queen's County, New York, and the British Army, 1776–1783," *WMQ*, 3rd Series, 43 (1986): 35–63; Petition to Haldimand from inhabitants of the frontiers of the colonies of New York and Pennsylvania, 17 October 1778, HP, A776, 21,874; Graymont, *The Iroquois in the American Revolution*, 199–200.

80 Walton, *Records*, 29 January 1777, 212; "Tryon County Committee of Safety," 19 December 1776, 19; Sullivan, *Albany Committee of Correspondence*, 28 September 1776, 564.

81 Graymont, *The Iroquois in the American Revolution*, 146–7.

82 "Genealogy of Philippe Maton Wiltsee and His Descendants," 118–19, Blanchard Papers, AO.

83 Sullivan, *Albany Committee of Correspondence*, 4 October 1775, 260.

84 Helena McLeod, petition, HP, A776, 21,875; John Macdonnel, petition, HP, A776, 21,874; Mary Deforest, petition, ibid.; Rachel Brian, claim, AO *Report*, 1904, 939; Valentine Detlor, petition, HP, A776, 21,874.

85 Schedule of the Losses & Damages sustained by Margaret Hare, Widow of Capt. John Hare, Audit Office 12, vol. 28.

86 An Account of the real Loss and damages Sustained by Richard Cartwright of the City of Albany during the late unhappy disputes between Great Britain and the Colonies, Audit Office 13, 2:477.

87 Walton, *Records*, 3 June 1777, appendix A, no. 1:364.

88 Philip Empy Petition, 1 March 1780, HP, A776, 21,874.

89 Stephen L. Keller, *Uprooting and Social Change: The Role of Refugees in Development*, foreword by M.S. Randhawa (New Delhi: Manohar Book Service 1975), 40; Jon Kei Matsuoka, "Vietnamese in America: An Analysis of Adaptational Patterns (PHD thesis, University of Michigan

1985), 51; see also J. Donald Cohen, Jr, "Psychological Adaptation and Dysfunction Among Refugees," *IMR*, 15 (1981): 255–75.

90 Alexander McDonell to Major Small, 15 November 1776, 19 February 1776, "Letters Extracted from the Letter Book of Capt. Alexander McDonell," 220, 246; memorial of John Munro, John Munro Papers, AO.

91 Claim of Catherine Cryderman, widow of Valentine Cryderman, Audit Office 12, 322–3; claim of William Schermerhorn, late of Albany County, AO *Report*, 1904, 1024; William Schermerhorn to Sir John Johnson, n.d., HP, A776.

92 Rene to Joel Stone, October 1779, Stone Papers, AO; H. William Hawke, "Joel Stone of Gananoque, 1749–1833" (unpublished manuscript, Queen's University Archives); Kenneth Donovan, " 'Taking Leave of an Ungrateful Country': The Loyalist Exile of Joel Stone," *Dalhousie Review*, 64 (Spring 1984), 131–45.

93 "The Narrative of Joel Stone," in J.J. Talman, *Loyalist Narratives from Upper Canada* (Toronto: Champlain Society 1946), 315–22.

94 Stone Diary, 15, 25 February 1784; 15 October 1789; 2 March 1792.

95 Ibid.

96 Sullivan, *Albany Committee of Correspondence*, 23 May 1776, 410; ibid., 28 May 1777, 769; ibid., March 1778, 945 and 950; Palsits, *Minutes*, 30 April 1781, 696.

CHAPTER 3

1 Undated letter, HP, A 748.

2 Christopher Ward, *The War of the Revolution* (New York, 1952), vol. 1:408–9, quoted in Thomas Anburey, *With Burgoyne from Quebec: An Account of the Life at Quebec and of the Famous Battle at Saratoga*, Sydney Jackman, ed., (Toronto: Macmillan 1963), 4–5; Mary Beacock Fryer, *The King's Men: The Soldier Founders of Ontario* (Toronto and Charlottetown: Dundurn 1980), 186–7.

3 Barbara Graymont, *The Iroquois and the American Revolution* (Syracuse: Syracuse University Press 1972), 151–2; Grace Tomkinson, "Jane McCrea: A Martyr of the Revolutionary War," *Dalhousie Review*, 49 (1969–70): 399–403; Anburey, *With Burgoyne*, 156–7.

4 "Narrative of John Peters," H.H. Robertson Papers, AO, 34.

5 Mary Beth Norton, *Liberty's Daughters: The Revolutionary Experience of American Women, 1750–1800* (Boston: Little Brown 1980), 225.

6 Haldimand to Capt. Alexander Fraser, 18 June 1780, HP, 21,788.

7 Haldimand to Col. Guy Johnson, 3 July 1780, HP, 21,766; Capt. Fraser to Haldimand, 1 February 1779, HP 21,777.

8 Sir John Johnson, "Remarks on the Management of Indians in North America delivered to Mr. Knox at the Secretary of State's Office, Whitehall, the later end of February 1777," HP, 21,775; Haldimand to Col. Claus, 4 May 1780, Claus Papers, vol. 2, NA.

9 Graymont, *The Iroquois and the American Revolution*, 161.

10 Claim of John Deserontyon, CO 42, vol. 47:240, NA.

11 Ibid., 247.

12 Claus to Haldimand, 7 September 1770, Claus Papers, B114:68, NA.

13 Claim of Sarah Kast McGinnis, Audit Office 12, vol. 27; Claus to Haldimand, 5 November 1778, HP, 21,774; see also H.C. Burleigh, "A Tale of Loyalist Heroism," *OHSPR*, 42 (1950): 91–9.

14 Molly Brant to Claus, HP, B114:68; Colonel Guy Johnson to Claus, HP, B107:36, quoted in H. Pearson Gundy, "Molly Brant: Loyalist," *OHSPR*, 45 (1953), 103; Claus to Haldimand, 30 September 1779, HP, B114:76.

15 Graymont, *The Iroquois and the American Revolution*, 192–222.

16 Petitions of Samuel Perry, 1778, Timothy Buel, 1778, WO 28, vol. 9:B2866; Petition of Patrick McNiff, 30 October 1783, HP, 21,875.

17 Alexander McDonell to Mrs. McDonell, 15 January 1776, in "Letters Extracted from the Letter Book of Capt. Alexander McDonell of the Royal Highland Emigrants Written from Halifax, Windsor, and Cornwallis between the years 1775 and 1779," Fraser Papers, MG 23, B33, 240, NA; ibid., 22 February 1776, 249; ibid., McDonell to Mr. Reiley, 25 January 1777, 323.

18 Ibid., Alexander McDonell to Mrs. McDonell, 22 February 1776, 249; ibid., n.d., 273; ibid., Alexander McDonell to Pedros de Mendonzo, 11 January 1777, 316.

19 Ian C. Pemberton, "Justus Sherwood, Vermont Loyalist, 1747–1798," (PhD thesis, University of Western Ontario 1973), 55–70; Mary Beacock Fryer, *Buckskin Pimpernel: The Exploits of Justus Sherwood, Loyalist Spy* (Toronto and Charlottetown: Dundurn 1981), 78–80; H.M. Jackson, *Justus Sherwood: Soldier, Loyalist and Negotiator* (Kingston 1958), 1–5.

20 C.R. Young, "The Young's Came to East Lake," Henry Young Papers, 46–7, AO.

21 Jane B. Goddard, *Hans Waltimeyer* (Cobourg: Haynes Printing 1980), 122–6.

22 Claim of John Munro, John Munro Papers, AO; Vermont Council of Safety, 29 August 1777, 27 August 1777, 30 January 1778, in E.P. Walton, ed., *Records of the Council of Safety and Government Council of the State of Vermont July, 1775 to December, 1777* (Montpelier: Steam Press 1873), vol. 1, 150–1, 212.

23 Claim of John Munro, Munro Papers, AO; Mary Munro to John Munro, n.d., HP, 21,875.

24 Larry Turner, "Peter Van Alstine, Michael Grass and the Associated Loyalists of Upper Canada, 1783–1784" (MA thesis, Queen's University 1984), 32–3.

25 John McDonell to Mathews, 20 March 1780, HP.

26 "A Letter from Mrs. Elizabeth Bowman Spohn," in J.J. Talman, ed., *Loyalist Narratives from Upper Canada* (Toronto, The Champlain Society 1946) 315–22.

27 Mrs. Johnson to General George Washington, 16 June 1776, in Peter Force, ed., *American Archives*, 9 vols (Washington, 1837–53), 4th series, vol. 6, 930; Petition of Isabel Parker, HP, 21,875.

28 Linda Kerber, *Women of the Republic: Intellect and Ideology in Revolutionary America* (Chapel Hill: University of North Carolina Press 1986), 41, 85.

29 "Petition of Sundry Women, Wives of Tories for relief," n.d., and "The Humble Petition of Elizabeth Hiller," in Maryly B. Penrose, ed., *Mohawk Valley in the Revolution: Committee for Safety Papers and Genealogical Compendium* (Franklin Port, NJ: Liberty Bell Associates 1978) 156, 181.

30 Ibid., 156, 181.

31 V.H. Palsits, ed., *Minutes of the Commissioners for the Detecting and Defeating Conspiracies in the State of New York, Albany County Session, 1778–1781* (Boston: Gregg Press 1910), 1, 390; Hugh Hastings, ed., *The Public Papers of George Clinton* 10 vols. (New York, 1899–1914), 5:130, 320.

32 See Haldimand to Johnson 23 May 1780, HP, 21,819; Haldimand to Powell, 15 March 1780, HP, 21,734.

33 Ibid.

34 G.A. Rawlyk, "The Reverend John Stuart: Mohawk Missionary and Reluctant Loyalist," in Edmund Wright, ed., *Red, White and True Blue: The Loyalists in the Revolution* (New York AMS Press 1976), 55–72; Doris Mary O'Dell, "Launching Loyalist Children: The Stuart Family of Kingston (MA thesis, Queen's University 1984); James Carruthers, "The Little Gentlemen: The Reverend John Stuart and the Inconvenience of the Revolution," (MA thesis, Queen's University 1975).

35 John Stuart to the Society for the Propagation of the Gospel, 13 October 1781, in Talman, *Loyalist Narratives*, 341–4; Rawlyk, "The Reverend John Stuart," 65–7.

36 Stuart to the Rev. William White, 13 November 1780, Stuart Papers, AO.

37 Ibid., Stuart to White, 1781.

38 Stuart to White, 19 April 1781, Stuart Papers, AO; Haldimand to Sir John Johnson, 30 July 1781, HP, 21,819.

39 Stuart to White, 19 April 1781, Stuart Papers, AO.

40 See, for example, Jon Kei Matsuoka, "Vietnamese in America: An Analysis of Adaptational Patterns," (PhD thesis, University of Michigan

1985), 46–9; Barry N. Stein, "The Refugee Experience: Defining the Parameters of a Field of Study," *IMR*, 15 (Spring–Summer 1981) 323; Capt. John McDonell to Mathews, 12 December 1783, HP, 21,822.

41 Mary Munro to John Munro, n.d., HP, 21,873.

42 Petition of Richard Wilkinson, HP, 21,875; Powell to Haldimand, 3 August 1779, HP, 21,793; Riedesel to Haldimand, 4 January 1783, 13 January 1783, HP, 21,798.

43 The Memorial of Capt. Alexander McDonell, Capt. John Munro, Capt. Samuel Anderson ... July 1778, HP, 21,873.

44 Humble Petition of Martin Walters ..., n.d., HP, 21,875; Memorial of a Number of His Majesty's Subjects ..., 30 May 1781, HP, 21,874.

45 Sir John Johnson to Haldimand, 20 March 1780, HP, 21,818; Haldimand to Sir John Johnson, 24 February 1780, 23 May 1780, 30 July 1781, HP, 21,819.

46 John McDonell to Capt. Mathews, n.d., HP, 21,733.

47 Capt. John Munro to Haldimand, 30 November 1780, Munro Papers, AO.

48 Palsits, *Minutes of the Commissioners*, 21 September 1778, 1:237–8.

49 Vermont Council of Safety, 12 September 1777, Walton, *Records of the Council of Safety*, 166.

50 The Memorial of the Subscribers, 21 March 1782, HP, 21,875.

51 Palsits, *Minutes of the Commissioners*, 1778, 1:184; 15 September 1779, 1:414.

52 "Act for Constituting a Council of Safety," September 1777, in *Acts of the General Assembly of the State of New Jersey* (Trenton, NJ, 1777), 87; Raymond C. Werner, ed., "Diary of Grace Growden Galloway, Kept at Philadelphia ...," *Pennsylvania Magazine of History and Biography*, 57 (1934), 162, 186, quoted in Kerber, *Women of the Republic*, 51; An Act for the Removal of the Families of Persons who have joined the Enemy, 1 July 1780, Palsits, *Minutes of the Commissioners*, 794–6.

53 Palsits, *Minutes of the Commissioners*, 20 January 1781, 2:620; 14 May 1781, 2:709–10; ibid., *An Act for the Removal of the Families*, 795–6.

54 Palsits, *Minutes of the Commissioners, An Act for the Removal* ... 2: 795; 1:57.

55 Vermont Governor and Council, 28 May 1778, Walton, *Records of the Council of Safety*, 1:261.

56 Turner, "Peter Van Alstine, Michael Grass," 21.

57 Major Rogers to Mathews, 12 April 1781, HP, 21,820.

58 Henry Ruiter to Mathews, 10 May 1780, HP, 21,821.

59 Goddard, *Hans Waltimeyer*, 126.

60 Claim of Simon Schwartz, in A. Fraser, ed., *Second Report of the Bureau of Archives for the Province of Ontario* (Toronto: Kings Printer 1904) 1:1032.

61 Ernest Green, "Frey," *OHSPR*, 33 (1939), 55–6.

62 Ibid., 56–7.

63 "Richard Cartwright's, 'A Journey to Canada,' " Talman, *Loyalist Narratives*, 45–7.

64 Wallace Brown, Hereward Senior, *Victorious in Defeat: The Loyalists in Canada* (Agincourt, Ont.: Methuen 1984), 41.

65 Powell to Haldimand, 10 July 1779, HP, 21,793; Cruikshank, "The King's Royal Regiment of New York," *OHSPR* 27 (1931), 249; Nairne to Haldimand, 14 November 1779, HP, 21,787; Carleton to Haldimand, 27 June 1780, HP, 21,793.

66 Brigadier Powell to Carleton, 2 March 1778, HP, 21,789; John Nairne to Mathews, 30 November 1780, HP, 21,821; Major Carleton to Haldimand, 1 July 1780, HP, 21,793.

67 Memorial of subscribers ... 21 March 1782, HP, 21,874; Memorial of William Fraser, April 1780, HP, A776; Sherwood to Major Nairne, 23 February 1783, HP, 21,822.

68 Thomas Freeman to Riedesel, 26 November 1781, HP, 21,796.

69 Fryer, "Sarah Sherwood," 249–50; Fryer, *Buckskin Pimpernel*, 78–9.

70 "Narrative of John Peters," AO.

71 "The Memorial of Capt. John Munro," Munro Papers, AO.

CHAPTER 4

1 *The Anatomy of Exile: A Semantic and Historical Study* (London: Harrap 1972), 9.

2 Col. Barry St Leger to Capt. Mathews, 29 November 1780, HP, 21,793.

3 Taylor and Diffin to Daniel Claus, 11 November 1778, Claus Papers, vol. 25, C–1485, NA; Major A. Campbell to Mathews, 1 December 1783, HP, 21,794; St Leger to Mathews, 19 September 1781, HP, 21,794.

4 Milton M. Klein and Ronald W. Howard, eds., *The Twilight of British Rule in Revolutionary America: The New York Letter Book of General James Robertson, 1780–1783* (Cooperstown, N.Y.: The New York State Historical Association 1983), 36; Thomas Jefferson Wertenbaker, *Father Knickerbocker Rebels: New York City During the Revolution* (New York and London: Charles Scribner's Sons 1948), 103–4.

5 *Royal Gazette*, 12 April 1780, New York Public Library.

6 *New York Gazette*, 23, 9 September 1754, New York Public Library; Samuel Dunbar, *The Presence of God With His People, Their Only Safety and Happiness* (Boston, 1760), 6, quoted in Potter, *The Liberty We Seek: Loyalist Ideology in Colonial New York and Massachusetts* (Cambridge, Mass., and London: Harvard University Press 1983), 115.

7 Hilda Neatby, *Quebec: The Revolutionary Age, 1760–1791* (Toronto: McClelland and Stewart 1966), 176.

8 Ibid., 164–78.

9 Wertenbaker, *Father Knickerbocker Rebels*, 151–2; Proclamation, 20 January 1780, in Klein and Howard, *The Twilight of British Rule*, 151–2; Oscar Theodore Barck, Jr., *New York City during the War for Independence, with Special Reference to the Period of British Occupation* (New York: Columbia University Press 1931), 120–43; R. Ashton, "The Loyalist Experience: New York, 1763–1789" (PhD thesis, Northwestern University 1973), 155–60; *Royal Gazette*, 18 March, 8 April 1780.

10 Haldimand to Germain, 12 October 1778, CO 42, vol. 38:B34; Frederick Haldimand, *DCB*, 4:793–4.

11 Samuel Wright, 20 August 1783, HP, 21,875; Patrick McNiff, 30 October 1783, HP, 21,875; John Howard, December 1779, HP, 21,874; John Bliss, HP, A776, 21,875; Daniel McGinn, 3 November 1783, HP, 21,875; Hugh Munro, 21 December 1782, HP, 21,874; Valentine Detlor, HP, A776, 21,874.

12 Kerber, *Women of the Republic: Intellect and Ideology in Revolutionary America* (Chapel Hill, N.C.: University of North Carolina Press 1986), 85.

13 Memorial of Loyalists in St Johns District, June 1783, HP, 21,875; "The Petition of His Majesty's Faithful Subjects emigrated under the Conduct of Capt. Michael Grass from New York to this Place, Sept. 29, 1783," HP, 21,825; Petition to the Earl of Shelburne, 15 August 1782, in Klein and Howard, *The Twilight of British Rule*, 257; Ebenezer Jessup to Sir Guy Carleton, 9 December 1777, WO, vol. 4:B2863; Haldimand to Cuyler, 17 August 1783, HP, 21,825.

14 6 May 1779, HP, 21,874; 24 May 1784, HP, 21,875; Peter Gilchrist, December 1779, HP, 21,874; George Christie, 16 December 1778, HP, 21,874; claim of Francis Hogle, Burgoyne's Loyal Americans, AO; "The Petition of His Majesty's Faithful Subjects ...," 29 September 1783, HP, 21,825.

15 Barry St Leger to Major Lernoult, 1 May 1782, WO 28, vol. 8:B2865; see also Paul H. Smith, *Loyalists and Red Coats* (Chapel Hill, N.C.: University of North Carolina Press 1964).

16 Guy Carleton to Phillips, 3 April 1777, HP, 21,699.

17 Wertenbaker, *Father Knickerbocker Rebels*, 207; Neatby, *Quebec*, 177.

18 Haldimand to Captain Herkimer, 12 October 1780, HP, 21,788.

19 Brig. Samuel Fraser, General Order Regulating the Organization of the Provincial Corps, 8 September 1777, HP, 21,874.

20 Rogers to Mathews, 10 September 1780, HP, 21,820; Johnson to Haldimand, 27 March 1780, HP, 21,818.

21 Haldimand to Germain, 28 January 1780, HP, 21,714.

22 St Leger to Mathews, July 1781, HP, 21,794; Sherwood to Gershom

French, 25 September 1780, HP, 21,819; see also Mathews to Major Rogers, 24 April 1780, HP, 21,819.

23 John Nairne to Capt. Le Maistre, 29 March 1779, WO 28, vol. 5:B2864; Haldimand to Clinton, 5 March 1782, HP, 21,818.

24 Cure to Haldimand, 12 October 1781, HP, 21,799; St Leger to Haldimand, 30 October 1783, HP, 21,789; Johnson to Major Lernoult, 6 September 1781, WO 28, vol. 5:B2863; Major Gray to Haldimand, 26 May 1782, WO 28, vol. 5: B2863; Capt. Duncan to Gray, 12 June 1782, WO 28, vol. 5:B2863; Gray to Maj. Lernoult, 11 July 1782, WO 28, vol. 5:B2863; Maclean to Mathews, 24 November 1779, HP, 21,789; Powell to Haldimand, 15 May 1779, HP, 21,793; Gray to Lernoult, 24 June 1782, WO 28, vol. 5:B2863; Papers Relating to King's Royal Regiment of New York, Orderly Book of Capt. Samuel Anderson Garrison Orders, 3 December 1779, NA.

25 Papers relating to King's Royal Regiment of New York, 21 March 1780; Gray to Mathews, 12 November 1781, HP, 21,818; St Leger to Haldimand, 28 August 1783, HP, 21,789.

26 S.L. Keller, *Uprooting and Social Change* (New Delhi: Manohur Book Service 1975), 65; Henry P. David, "Involuntary International Migration: Adaptation of Refugees," in Eugene R. Brouy, ed., *Behaviour in New Environments: Adaptation of Migrant Populations* (Beverly Hills, Calif.: Sage Publications 1970), 85.

27 Mary Beacock Fryer, *Buckskin Pimpernel: The Exploits of Justus Sherwood, Loyalist Spy* (Toronto and Charlottetown: Dundurn 1981), 64–5; Samuel Adams to Mathews, 30 August 1780; memorial of John, Henry Ruiter, Sam Adams, Henry Young ..., December 1780, HP, 21,874.

28 Johnson to Haldimand, memorial, Albany County Loyalists, 10 February 1780, HP, 21,818.

29 Carleton to Phillips, 13 January 1777, HP, 21,699.

30 Mary Beacock Fryer and Lieutenant-Colonel William A. Smy, C.D. *Rolls of the Provincial (Loyalist) Corps, Canadian Command, American Revolutionary Period* (Toronto and Charlottetown: Dundurn Press, 1981), 22–3.

31 William Parker to Haldimand, 16 February 1782, HP, 21,874; Mathews to Sir John Johnson, 6 October 1783, HP, 21,819; Mathews to Capt. Leake, 17 December 1781, HP, 21,819; Claus to Haldimand, 9 December 1779, HP, 21,774; Haldimand to Sir John Johnson, 6 June 1780, HP, 21,819.

32 Haldimand to Germain, 23 October 1781, CO 42, vol. 41:B36; Cuyler to Mathews, 24 March 1783, HP, 21,825.

33 Haldimand to Sir John Johnson, 13 February 1780, HP, 21,819; "A Narrative of John Peters," H.H. Robertson Papers, AO; Maclean to Mathews, 9 June 1780, HP, 21,789.

34 Haldimand to Germain, 3 December 1780, CO 42, vol. 12; Mathews to Campbell, 13 July 1780, HP, 21,773.

35 [Name illegible] to Lt. Col. Roger Morris, 22 April 1779, BHP, vol. 16, M348; Norton, *Liberty's Daughters: The Revolutionary Experience of American Women, 1750–1800* (Boston: Little Brown 1980), 116–24.

36 Mary DeForest, December 1778, HP, 21,874; Helena McLeod, n.d., HP, 21,875.

37 Mary Beth Norton, "Eighteenth-Century American Women in Peace and War: The Case of the Loyalists," *WMQ*, 3rd Series, 33 (1976): 386–409.

38 Jean McDonell, 30 November 1782, HP, 21,874.

39 Phoebe Grant, December 1780, HP, 21,874.

40 Roger Stevens, December 1783, HP, 21,875.

41 Dan McAlpin, in petition of Neil Robertson, n.d., HP, 21,875.

42 See, for example, Cheris Kramarae, *Women and Men Speaking* (Rowley, Mass.: Newbury House Publishers 1981); Joyce Penfield, ed., *Women and Language in Transition* (Albany, N.Y.: State University of New York Press 1987); David Graddol and Joan Swann, *Gender Voices* (Oxford: Basil Blackwell 1989); Alette Olin Hill, *Mother Tongue, Father Time* (Bloomington and Indianapolis: Indiana University Press 1986); Bryan Palmer, *Descent into Discourse: The Reification of Language and the Writing of Social History* (Philadelphia: Temple University Press 1990), 145–86.

43 Helena McLeod, n.d., HP, 21,875; Nairne to Mathews, 5 December 1781, HP, 21,819.

44 Norton, *Liberty's Daughters*, 166–70.

45 Lucinda, *New York Gazette*, 6 July 1782, New York Public Library.

46 Mathews to Claus, 7 January 1782, Claus Papers, vol. 3:C1478.

47 Memorial of Sarah Kast McGinnis to Haldimand, 1782, HP, B216:32, quoted in H. Pearson Gundy, "Molly Brant: Loyalist," *OHSPR*, 45 (1953), 97.

48 Col. Bolton to Haldimand, 16 July 1779, Claus Papers, MG 29 (2): 29, quoted in Gundy, "Molly Brant," 102; Capt. Fraser to Haldimand, 21 March 1780, Claus Papers, MG 29(2): 177; quoted in Gundy, "Molly Brant," 104.

49 Claus to Haldimand, 16 July 1779, Claus Papers, MG 29 (2): 29; quoted in Gundy, "Molly Brant," 102.

50 Haldimand to Sir John Johnson, 29 July 1779, HP, 21,819; Fraser to Haldimand, 21 June 1780, HP, 21,787; ibid., 13 December 1780; Mathews to Fraser, 17 July 1780, HP, 21,788.

51 Haldimand to Fraser, 16 April 1780, HP, 21,787; Fraser to Haldimand, 21 June 1780, HP, 21,787; Fraser to Haldimand, 21 March 1780, HP, 21,787; Fraser to Claus, 23 February 1780; Claus Papers, MG 19.

52 Claus to Sir John Johnson, 26 June 1780, Claus Papers, vol. 25:C1485;
    Mary Brant to Claus, 5 October 1779, Claus Papers, vol. 2:1478;
    Norton, *Liberty's Daughters*, 119–20.

53 Claus to Haldimand, 5 November 1778, HP, 21,774; claim of Sarah
    McGinn, Audit Office 12, vol. 27:B1161; Haldimand to Germaine, 13
    September 1779, HP, 21,710.

54 Claus to Haldimand, 19 November 1778, HP, 21,774.

55 Petition to Haldimand, 1782, quoted in H.C. Burleigh, "A Tale of
    Loyalist Heroism," *OHSPR*, 42 (1950), 97.

56 Barry N. Stein, "The Refugee Experience: Defining the Parameters of a
    Field of Study," *IMR*, vol. 15:324.

57 Stein, "The Refugee Experience," 324, 327; Keller, *Uprooting*, 73–6.

58 Jon Kei Matsuoka, "Vietnamese In America: An Analysis of Adaptational
    Patterns," (PhD thesis, University of Michigan 1985), 49; Keller,
    Uprooting, 60; Stein, "The Refugee Experience," 324.

59 Alexander McDonell to Major Small, 27 January 1776, "Letters
    Extracted from the Letter Book of Capt. Alexander McDonell," in
    Collections of the New York Historical Society (1924), 243–4.

60 Wertenbaker, *Father Knickerbocker Rebels*, 213.

61 John Munro to Mathews, 20 July 1781, HP, 21,821; James Gray to
    Mathews, 5 April 1784, HP, 21,822; Sir John Johnson to Haldimand, 30
    October 1778, HP, 21,818; see also Gray to Foy, 15 November 1778, HP,
    21,818.

62 Fryer, *Buckskin Pimpernel*, 105; Account Book, Loyal Rangers, 1782–83,
    Loyal Block House, 12 November 1782, Sherwood Family Papers,
    Metropolitan Toronto Reference Library.

63 MacLean to Mathews, 9 June 1780, HP, 21,789; Fryer, *Buckskin
    Pimpernel*, 126; Johnson to Claus, 29 June 1778, Claus Papers, vol.
    2:C1478.

64 Ads in newspapers such as the *New York Gazette* offered luxury goods
    and entertainment; Wertenbaker, *Father Knickerbocker Rebels*, 121, 141,
    143, 199, 200.

65 Mrs B. Henshaw, "Female Education," *New York Gazette*, 26 April
    1783; Haldimand to Stuart, 3 November 1781, HP, 21,819; David to
    Johnson, 17 November 1779, RG 10, C1223, NA; Claus to Blackburn, 16
    August 1780, Claus to Haldimand, 27 September 1781, Claus Papers,
    vol. 2:C1481.

66 Haldimand to Col. Guy Johnson, 10 October 1781, HP, 21,766;
    Haldimand to Col. Guy Johnson, 3 July 1780, HP, 21,766; Capt. Fraser
    to Haldimand, 1 February 1779, HP, 21,771; Ordinance, 29 March
    1777, RG 10, vol. 14, NA; Haldimand to Germain, 25 October 1780, HP,
    21,714; Records Relating to Indian Affairs, RG 10, Records of the
    Superintendant's Office, 1755–1830, Minutes of Indian Affairs,

1755–1790, NA, 16, 26 November 1779; Extract of Col. Johnson's letter, 21 November HP, 21,774; Claus to Haldimand, 24 September 1778, HP, 21,774.

67 Major Gray to Capt. Le Maistre, 29 October 1779, WO 28, vol. 4:B2863; Mathews to Nairne, 4 April 1782, HP, 21,823; Haldimand to Germain, 15 October 1778, CO 42, vol. 38:B34; Mathews to Cuyler, 13 February 1783, HP, 21,825.

68 Cuyler to Mathews, 11 November 1782, HP, 21,825; Major Carleton to Haldimand, 2 February 1779, HP, 21,793.

69 For a discussion of English poor law and relief policies, see Karl de Schweinitz, *England's Road to Social Security: From the Statute of Labourer's in 1349 to the Beveridge Report of 1942* (Philadelphia: University of Pennsylvania Press 1943); Harold E. Raynes, *Social Security in Britain: A History* (London: Sir Isaac Pitman and Sons 1962); E.P. Thompson, *The Making of the English Working Class* (London: Penguin Books 1984).

70 Regulations as to Lodgings and Allowances for Loyalists, 6 March 1782, HP, 21,827.

71 Cruikshank, "The King's Royal Regiment of New York," *OHSPR*, 27 (1931): 288; McAlpin to Mathews, 27 March 1780, HP, 21,819; "Effective List of all the Loyalists in Canada Receiving Provisions not Charged for ...," 1 July 1779, HP, 21,826; Herkimer to Mathews, 14 September 1780, HP, 21,819.

72 Mathews to Herkimer, 12 October 1780, HP, 21,788.

73 Powell to Haldimand, 15 May 1779, HP, 21,793.

74 Sir John Johnson to Haldimand, 20 March 1780, HP, 21,818; Haldimand to Johnson, 23 March 1780, HP, 21,819; Johnson to Haldimand, 22 July 1780, HP, 21,818; Haldimand to Johnson, 27 July 1780, HP, 21,819.

75 McAlpin to Mathews, 3 January 1780, 3 February 1780, 27 March 1780, HP, 21,819.

76 Haldimand to Germain, 15 October 1778, CO 42, vol. 38:B34; Conrad Gugy to Haldimand, 8, 16 November 1778, HP, 21,824; Gugy, *DCB*, 4:316–17; Wilbur H. Siebert, "The Temporary Settlement of Loyalists at Machiche, P.Q.," *Proceedings and Transactions of the Royal Society of Canada*, 3rd Series, 7 (May 1914): 407–14.

77 "List of Loyalists and their Families lodged at Machiche at this date," 2 December 1778 HP, 21,826; Gugy to Haldimand, 8, 16 November 1778, HP, 21,824; Siebert, "The Temporary Settlement," 408–10.

78 Gugy to Haldimand, 2 October 1778, HP, 21,824;

79 McAlpin to Mathews, 27 March 1780, HP, 21,819.

80 Gugy to Haldimand, 2 October 1778, HP; ibid., petition to Mr Gugy, 12 November 1778.

81 Complaint by Colonel John Peters, 20 January 1780, HP, 21,827; see also Capt. Thomas Aubrey to Haldimand, 20 August 1779, HP, 21,787; Haldimand to Nairne, 22 January 1781, HP, 21,823; DeLancey to Mathews, 26 April, 4, 17 May 1784, HP.

82 Wertenbaker, *Father Knickerbocker Rebels*, 120; Barck, *New York City During the War for Independence*, 98–111; Haldimand to Germain, 25 October, 28 November 1780, CO 42, vol. 12, B25.

83 Haldimand to Germain, 23 October 1781, 18 November 1781, CO 42, vol. 15; Fryer, *Buckskin Pimpernel*, 126–73; Fraser to Haldimand, 8 September 1780, HP, 21,787; Captain Betton to Mathews, 16 May 1784, ibid.; Haldimand to Fraser, 7 October 1779, ibid.

84 Mathews to Nairne, 30 October 1780, HP, 21,823; Johnson to Haldimand, 21 December 1778, HP, 21,818; J. Carruthers, "The Little Gentleman: The Reverend Doctor John Stuart and the Inconvenience of Revolution" (Queen's University, unpublished paper 1975), 35–6; Maclean to Mathews, 9 March 1780, HP, 21,789.

85 HP, 21,826.

86 Haldimand to Johnson, 13 February 1780, HP, 21,819; Nairne to Mathews, 25 November 1780, HP, 21,819; Ebenezer Jessup to Guy Carleton, 9 December 1777, WO 28, vol. 4:B2863; Cuyler to Mathews, 11 November 1782, HP, 21,827; see also Ashton, "The Loyalist Experience," 160.

87 Major Ross to Sir John Johnson, 11 September 1780, HP, 21,818; Wertenbaker, *Father Knickerbocker Rebels*, 361, 160; "Account of Part of the Sufferings of Col. John Peters and Family," 27 October 1780, HP, 21,821; John Walden Meyers wrote that he was so poor that he would have to put his child "out to service" if he did not get more than 1/2 a ration for his wife and child – Meyers to Mathews, 17 April 1784, HP, 21,822; Gugy to Haldimand, 30 October 1778, HP, 21,824.

88 Sarah F. McMahon, "A Comfortable Subsistence: The Changing Composition of Diet in Rural New England, 1620–1840," *WMQ*, 3rd Series, 42 (January 1985): 26–65.

89 Claus to Haldimand, 23 March 1780, 19 January 1784, HP, 21,774; Claus to Sir John Johnson, 26 June 1780, Claus Papers, vol. 25:C1485; Gray to Le Maistre, 6 October 1779, WO 28, vol. 4:B2863; John Ross to Lernoult, 3 November 1783, WO 28, vol. 7:B2865; McDonald to Major Small, 17 December 1776, "Letters Extracted from the Letter Book of Capt. Alexander McDonell," p. 305; St. Leger to Lernoult, Jan. 20, 1781, W.O. 28, Vol. 7, B2865.

90 Mary Beacock Fryer, *John Walden Meyers: Loyalist Spy* (Toronto and Charlottetown: Dundurn Press 1983), 163; Ross to Haldimand, 25

November 1782, HP, 21,874; St Leger to Mathews, 27 November 1783, HP, 21,789; Mathews to DeCoigne, 18 December 1783, HP, 21,825.

91 Haldimand to Brigadier MacLean, 25 November 1779, Mathews to MacLean, 30 November 1779, HP, 21,789; James McDonell to Lernoult, 10 November 1782, WO 28, vol. 8:B2865; Fraser to Haldimand, 18 May 1780, 5 August, 22 September 1781, HP, 21,787; Wertenbaker, *Father Knickerbocker Rebels*, 131; Johnson to Claus, 17 August 1778, Claus Papers, vol. 2:C1478.

92 St Leger to Haldimand, 2 March 1781, HP, 21,793.

93 Haldimand to Stephen DeLancey, 20 December 1783, HP, 21,825.

94 Mathews to French, 1 December 1783, Mathews to DeCoigne, 11 December 1783, HP, 21,825; "Return of the Loyalists, Male and Female, on Carleton Island, Specifying their Age and Number of Rations Drawn out of the King's Store," HP, in Richard A. Preston, ed., *Kingston Before the War of 1812: A Collection of Documents* (Toronto: University of Toronto Press, Champlain Society 1959), 47.

95 Nairne to Lernoult, 22 July 1781, WO 28, vol. 4:B2863; McAlpin to French, 14 July 1780, HP, 21,819; St Leger to Haldimand, 2 March 1781, HP, 21,793 (emphasis mine); 7 July 1781, Regimental Orderly Book, 1780–83, Jessup Papers, AO.

96 Stephen Tuttle to Mathews, 13 August 1781, HP, 21,819; DeLancey to Mathews, 26 April 1784, HP, 21,825; "Distressed Families in Montreal in Great Need of Clothing by their Infirmity," 26 April 1782, HP, 21,827.

97 Keller, *Uprooting*, 74; Stein, "The Refugee Experience," 324; Matsuoka, "Vietnamese in America," 49.

98 Tuttle to Mathews, 11 July 1781, HP, 21,819; MacLean to Mathews, 24 November 1779, HP, 21,789; Fryer, *John Walden Meyers*, 140.

99 St Leger to Haldimand, 16 November 1782, 17 October 1783, HP, 21,789; John Peters to son, 11 August 1783, Peters Papers, AO; Claus to Haldimand, 14 June 1784, HP, 21,774.

100 Sherwood to Mathews, 26 March 1784, HP, 21,822.

101 Alexander McDonald to Mrs McDonald, 28 March 1776, "Letters Extracted from the Letter Book of Capt. Alexander McDonell," 261; Stuart to White, 8 February 1785, Stuart Papers, quoted in Doris Mary O'Dell, "Launching Loyalist Children: The Stuart Family of Early Kingston," (MA thesis, Queen's University 1984), 40.

102 See H. William Hawke, "Joel Stone of Gananoque, 1749–1833" (unpublished manuscript, Queen's University Archives); Ken Donovan, " 'Taking Leave of an Ungrateful Country': The Loyalist Exile of Joel Stone," *Dalhousie Review*, 64 (Spring 1984): 131–45.

103 The last will and testament of Commodore Moore, Bombay, India, 22 July 1780, quoted in Hawke, "Joel Stone," 23; Leah Moore to Captain William Moore, 24 January 1781, Lewis Moore to Joel Stone, 11 August 1786, Stone Papers, NA.

104 William Moore to Joel Stone, 16 June 1785, Stone Papers, AO.

105 Joel Stone to Stephen Stone, 5 September 1784, Stone Papers, NA.

106 "Narrative of Joel Stone," in J.J. Talman, *Loyalist Narratives from Upper Canada* (Toronto: Champlain Society 1946), 333; Stone Diary, 17 October 1783; Leman and Leah Stone to Joel Stone, 25 October 1782, Stone Papers, NA.

107 Leah Stone to Joel Stone, 26 September 1785, Lewis Moore to Joel Stone, 11 August 1786, Stone Papers, NA.

108 Leah Stone to Joel Stone, 26 August 1785, ibid.

109 Keller, *Uprooting*, 60, 91.

110 William Schmerhorn to Sir John Johnson, n.d., HP, 21,875; William Fairfield, 6 October 1778, HP, 21,874; John Fraser to Haldimand, 24 October 1779, HP, 21,874.

111 Alan McDonell, 21 July 1780, HP, 21,874; John Ryckman, 11 October 1782, HP, 21,874.

112 Solomon Johns, 29 March 1779, HP, 21,874.

113 William Lamson, 19 March 1982, HP, 21,874; Peter Gilchrist, n.d., HP, 21,874; Edward Jessup's certificate of loyalty and service, in Thomas McNight, 22 December 1783, HP, 21,875; Edward Foster, 24 May 1784, HP, 21,875; Hugh Munro, 6 May 1779, HP, 21,874.

114 James Robbins, December 1783, HP, 21,875.

115 John Fraser to Haldimand, 11 October 1779, HP, 21,732.

116 John Ryckman, 11 October 1782, HP, 21,874; Ranald McDonell, December 1782, HP, 21,874.

CHAPTER 5

1 Letter to Margaret, Broadalbin, New York, Mrs D.J. MacPherson, Private Paper, NA.

2 Capt. John Barnes to Haldimand, 24 September 1784, HP, in Ernest A. Cruickshank, *The Settlement of the United Empire Loyalists on the Upper St. Lawrence and the Bay of Quinte in 1784: A Documentary Record* (Toronto: Ontario Historical Society 1966), 112; Fryer, *The Kings Men, The Soldier Founder of Ontario* (Toronto and Charlottetown: Dundurn 1980), 317–21.

3 Anne Powell, Description of a Journey from Montreal to Detroit in 1789, AO; Wallace Brown and Hereward Senior, *Victorious in Defeat: The Loyalists in Canada* (Toronto: Methuen 1984) 46; R.A. Preston, ed., *Kingston Before the War of 1812: A Collection of Documents*

(Toronto: The University of Toronto Press, Champlain Society 1959), introduction.

4 Robert Mathews Diary, NA; the Orderly Book of John Hay, 1783, NA; *Kingston Gazette*, 10 December 1811, in Preston, *Kingston Before the War of 1812*, xlix; Patrick McNiff to Stephen DeLancey, March 1786, RG 4, Canada East, Civil Secretary's Correspondence, s Series, NA; John Johnson to Haldimand, 11 August 1783, HP, in Cruikshank, *The Settlement of the United Empire Loyalists*, 5; *Letters from an American Loyalist in Upper Canada* (York, Upper Canada, 1810), 91–92.

5 The *Royal Gazette* and the *New-York Gazette and the Weekly Mercury* were the two most important New York City newspapers.

6 Antivindicata, *Royal Gazette*, 23 September 1782; see also Oscar Theodore Barck, Jr, *New York City during the War for Independence, with Special Reference to the Period of British Occupation* (New York: Columbia University Press 1931), 144–54.

7 "The Humble Address and Petition of the Loyalist Inhabitants and Refugees within the British lines at New York," 11 August 1782, CO 5, vol. 106, NA.

8 S.L. Keller, *Uprooting and Social Change* (New Delhi: Manohur Book Service 1975), 43–4; *Royal Gazette*, 6 March 1782.

9 *Royal Gazette*, 6 July 1782.

10 Sherwood to Mathews, 27 April 1783, HP, Series B, vol. 178:187–90; Sherwood to Riedesel, 9 March 1783, HP, 21,798; Haldimand to Lord Sydney, 29 June 1783, HP, 21,716; Guy Carleton to Chevalier de Lavalette, Apr. 8, 1783, *Report on American Manuscripts*, IV, quoted in Barck, *New York City*, 211.

11 Haldimand to Ross, 26 April 1783, HP, 21,785; John Deserontyon, 8 January 1784, CO 42, vol. 4; Claus to Haldimand, 15 December 1783, HP, 21,774.

12 Ross to Haldimand, November 1782, HP, in Cruikshank, "The King's Royal Regiment of New York," *OHSPR*, 27 (1931): 287; Haldimand to Ross, 16 February 1783, HP, 21,785; W. Fraser to Riedesel, 26 January 1783, 21,798; Riedesel to Haldimand, 9 January 1783, HP, 21,798.

13 Joel Stone, "Narrative"; *Quebec Gazette*, 26 June 1783; *New York Packet or American Advertiser* (Fishkill), 17 April 1783, HP, 21,783; Haldimand to John Johnson, 14 June 1783, HP, in Cruikshank, *The Settlement of the United Empire Loyalists*, 121.

14 *New York Morning Post*, 7 November 1783, in Catherine S. Crary, ed., *The Price of Loyalty: Tory Writings from the Revolution* (New York: Knopf 1973), 392.

15 Patrick McNiff to Stephen DeLancey, March 1786, RG 4, Canada East, Civil Secretary's Correspondence, s Series; John Stuart to Bishop Inglis, 6 July 1788, quoted in Preston, *Kingston Before the War of 1812*, 133–8;

Sir Guy Carleton to Haldimand, 4 June 1783, HP, in Cruikshank, *The Settlement of the United Empire Loyalists*, 35; North to Haldimand, 8 August 1783, HP, 21,705; Munro to Mathews, 27 March 1783, HP, 21,818.

16 Nancy Jean Cameron to Margaret, 15 May 1785, Mrs D.J. MacPherson, Private Papers.

17 Campbell to Mathews, 26 May, 8 June 1784; Roubaud to Nepean, 12 May 1785, CO 42, vol. 16; Campbell to Mathews, 8 June, 6 August 1784, HP, 21,794.

18 George Smyth to Major Campbell, 15 June 1784, HP, B162:312, in Preston, *Kingston Before the War of 1812*, 79; Genealogy of Philippe Maton Wiltsee, Wiltse Blanchard Papers, AO; Haldimand to John Johnson, 18 July 1784, HP, in Cruikshank, *The Settlement of the Loyalists*, 137.

19 Maria Susan Waltman, "From Soldier to Settler: Patterns of Loyalist Settlement in 'Upper Canada,' 1783–1785" (MA thesis, Queen's University 1981) 106; see also chapter one.

20 John Johnson to Haldimand, 10 July 1784, HP, B168:42, quoted in Waltman, "From Soldier to Settler," 32; Return of Loyalists Arrived from New York at Sorel, 28 August 1783, HP, 21,872.

21 *Royal Gazette*, 30 November 1782, 15 January 1783, 16 April 1783, 27 May 1783.

22 Cuyler to Mathews, 13 August 1783, HP, 21,825; Forbes MacBean to Haldimand, 27 August 1783, HP, 21,798; Larry Turner, "Peter Van Alstine, Michael Grass and the Associated Loyalists of Upper Canada, 1783–1784" (MA thesis, Queen's University 1984), 66, pp. 59–62.

23 Peter Van Alstine, quoted in ibid., 21.

24 Peter Van Alstine, memorial 16 July 1783, quoted in ibid., 64–5; see also ibid., 119–22.

25 Van Alstine to Mathews, 17 May 1784, Mathews to Van Alstine, 20 May 1784, HP, in Cruikshank, *The Settlement of the United Empire Loyalists*, 100–1, 105–6; Turner, "Peter Van Alstine, Michael Grass, and the Associated Loyalists," 90, 119–22.

26 Petition of Capt. John Munro and a Number of Privates in the King's Royal Regiment of New York, 27 March 1783, HP, 21,818.

27 Carleton to Haldimand, 4 June 1783, Cruikshank, *The Settlement of the United Empire Loyalists*, 37.

28 Mathews to Stephen DeLancey, 15 April 1784, in Cruikshank, *The Settlement of the United Empire Loyalists*, 67; Campbell to Mathews, 2 April 1783, HP, 21,794; Haldimand to Sydney, 26 April 1785, HP, 21,717.

29 North to Haldimand, 24 July 1783, HP, 21,705; An Act for Appointing Commissioners ..., 27 September 1783, MG 23, KI, CO 34, NA.

30 Haldimand to Joseph Brant, winter of 1783, in Cruikshank, *The Settlement of the United Empire Loyalists*, 33.

31 Capt. John Deserontyon, September 1800, quoted in Crary, *The Price of Loyalty*, 426; see also Barbara Graymont, *The Iroquois in the American Revolution* (Syracuse: Syracuse University Press 1972), 284.

32 Haldimand to Johnson, 14 June 1784; Cruikshank, *The Settlement of the United Empire Loyalists*, 124; Haldimand to Johnson, 22 April 1784, RG 10, Series 2, vol. 15:C1224, NA.

33 Barnes to Mathews, 10 June 1784, HP, 21,798; Johnson to Mathews, 2 February 1784, Sherwood to Mathews, 13 May 1784, in Cruikshank, *The Settlement of the United Empire Loyalists*, 45, 94; Barnes to Mathews, 7, 21 June 1784, HP, 21,798; Preston, *Kingston Before the War of 1812*, introduction; Brown and Senior, *Victorious in Defeat*, 45.

34 Return of Axes Made for Loyalists, 18 June 1784, List of seeds sent by Major Holland for the use of Settlers in the Upper Country, 18 May 1784, in Cruikshank, *The Settlement of the United Empire Loyalists*, 126, 105.

35 Ibid., Johnson to Mathews, 16 July 1784, Mathews to Johnson, 19 July 1784, 136, 138.

36 Stuart to Dr White, 19 August 1786, AO, Miscellaneous MSS, White Letters; Wilson, *As She Began: An Illustrated Introduction to Loyalist Ontario* (Toronto and Charlottetown: Dundurn 1981), 64, Preston, *Kingston Before the War of 1812*, 132–3.

37 Barnes to Mathews, 5 February 1784, in Cruikshank, *The Settlement of the United Empire Loyalists*, 46–7; Johnson to Haldimand, 8 September 1783, HP, 21,775; Ross to Mathews, 7 July 1784, in Cruikshank, *The Settlement of the United Empire Loyalists*, 132–3; Richard Cartwright, Jr to John Collins and William Dummer Powell, 16 August 1787, in Preston, *Kingston Before the War of 1812*, 121–2.

38 Howard Temperley, "Frontierism, Capital and the American Loyalists in Canada," *Journal of American Studies*, 13 (1979): 5–27.

39 Haldimand to North, 6 November 1783, in Cruikshank, *The Settlement of the United Empire Loyalists*, 23–4.

40 McNiff to DeLancey, March 1786, RG 4 Canada East, Civil Secretary's Correspondence, S Series, NA; the Petition of the Inhabitants of the New Settlement, on the River St Lawrence, by their Representatives ... n.d., RG 4, A1, S Series, vol. 27.

41 Letter from the Magistrates at Cataraqui to Sir John Johnson, 22 December 1787, in Cruikshank, *The Settlement of the United Empire Loyalists*, 127–30; Sir John Johnson and a Group of Officers, petition, 11 April 1785, quoted in Gerald M. Craig, *Upper Canada: The Formative Years, 1784–1841* (Toronto: McClelland and Stewart 1972), 9;

the Petition of the Inhabitants of the New Settlements ..., RG 4, AI, S Series, vol. 27.

42 Norton, *Liberty's Daughters: The Revolutionary Experience of American Women* (Boston: Little, Brown 1980), 176–9.

43 Robert A. Gross, review of Norton, *Liberty's Daughters*, and Linda Kerber, *Women of the Republic: Intellect and Ideology in Revolutionary America* (Chapel Hill, N.C.: University of North Carolina Press 1986), in *WMQ*, 3rd Series, 39 (1982): 236.

44 Toby L. Ditz, "Ownership and Obligation: Inheritance and Patriarchal Households in Connecticut, 1750–1820," *WMQ*, 3rd Series, 47 (April 1990): 263–4.

45 See, Joan Hoff Wilson, "The Illusion of Change: Women and the American Revolution," in Alfred F. Young, ed., *The American Revolution: Explorations in the History of American Radicalism* (DeKalb: Northern Illinois University Press 1976), 383–446.

46 See, for instance, Yazawa, *From Colonies to Commonwealth: Familial Ideology and the Beginnings of the American Republic* (Baltimore and London: John Hopkins University Press 1985); R.A. Gross, review of Mary Beth Norton's *Liberty's Daughters* and Linda Kerber's *Women of the Republic*, *WMQ*, January 1982, 231–8.

47 Norton, *Liberty's Daughters*, 278, 299; Jacqueline S. Reinier, "Rearing the Republican Child: Attitudes and Practices in Post-Revolutionary Philadelphia," *WMQ*, 3rd Series, 39 (January 1982): 150–63.

48 Mary P. Ryan, *Cradle of the Middle Class: The Family in Oneida County, New York, 1790–1865* (Cambridge, England: Cambridge University Press 1981), 232; E. Anthony Rotundo, "Body and Soul: Changing Ideals of American Middle-Class Manhood 1770–1920," Journal of Social History, Summer 1983: 30; Jan Lewis, "The Republican Wife: Virtue and Seduction in the Early Republic," *WMQ*, 3rd Series, 44 (October 1987): 689–721; Daniel Blake Smith, "The Study of the Family in Early America: Trends, Problems and Prospects," *WMQ*, 3rd Series, 39 (January 1982): 3–28; Karin Calvert, "Children In American Family Portraiture, 1670 to 1810," ibid., 87–113; J.S. Reiner, "Rearing the Republican Child: Attitudes and Practices in Post-Revolutionary Philadelphia," ibid., 150–63.

49 Kerber, *Women of the Republic*, 243, 248.

50 Powell, Description of a Journey, 11, 3–4.

51 Stuart to Dr White, 2 November 1785, AO, Miscellaneous MSS, White Letters; [Richard Cartwright, Jr], *Letters from an American Loyalist in Upper Canada* (York, Upper Canada, 1810), 91–2; Catherine White, Narrative, in Coventry Papers, NA.

52 John Langhorn, 5 October 1787, in A.H. Young, "More Langhorn Letters," *OHSPR*, 29 (1933): 47–71.

53 The criminal court records are published in "Early Records of Ontario," *Queen's Quarterly*, 7 (1899–1900): 51–9, 137–52, 243–50, 324–31, 7 (1900–01): 65–72, 145–52, 223–30; 9 (1901): 130–45; the civil court records are in AO *Report*, 1917, 190–353.

54 AO *Report* 1904, 352; "Early Records of Ontario," 57–8; ibid., pp. 137–8; ibid., 138.

55 Norton, "Eighteenth-Century American Women in Peace and War: The Case of the Loyalists," *WMQ*, 3rd Series, 33 (1976): 400; Treasury Office: Miscellaneous Documents Relating to Refugees, MG 15 T 50, vol. 6, Loyalists' Temporary Allowances.

56 Edward Jessup, Plan for Loyalist Settlement, 11 September 1783, HP, 21,822; Mathews to Sherwood, 5 April 1784, in Cruikshank, *The Settlement of the United Empire Loyalists*, 70–1; Edward Jessup, Plan for Loyalist Settlement, 11 September 1783, Sherwood to Mathews, 14 April 1784, HP, 21,822; Alphabetical List of Loyalists Settled in Different Townships in the Province of Quebec, Agreeable to the Muster Rolls, Nov. 1 to 21, n.d., RG 1, Series A–IV, vol. 88, NA (the list had to be before 1791 since what is now eastern Ontario became part of the newly created colony of Upper Canada in 1791).

57 Ibid. They were Catherine Allen, widow Brown, widow Buck, widow Booth, Corpl Brooks's widow, widow Cryderman, widow Cronkwright, widow Davou, Hannah Elliot, widow Fraser, widow Franks, widow Grant, widow Mercle, Florence McCarty, Elizabeth McDonnell, widow Wright, widow Ross, Ann Ross, Mrs Huff, widow Howell, Catherine Koughnet, widow Orser, widow Ryckman, Mrs Swart, widow Simmons, Lydia Van Alstine.

58 Claim of widow Livingston, Audit Office 12, vol. 28; claim of widow Cryderman, Audit Office 12, vol. 29; the announcement of the widow Buck's marriage is in the Sherwood Family Papers, 9 November 1785, Metro Toronto Regional Research Library; other widows who remarried included Elinor Maybee, who married Joseph Hoffman, AO Claims, 1022; Rachel Macintosh, who became Mrs Brian ibid., 939; Elizabeth Cline, who married John Nicholas, ibid., 1028; Eva Macnut, who married John Pencel, ibid., 1040; Deborah Tuttle, who married Charles MacArthur, ibid., 1904.

59 Claim of Martin Middaugh, AO Report, 1904, 1257; Claim of Robert Dixon, ibid., 1255; claim of Alexander Grant, Audit Office 12, vol. 29; Craig, *Upper Canada*, 12; A.F. Hunter, "The Probated Wills of Men Prominent in the Public Affairs of Early Upper Canada," OHSPR, 31 (1936): 50–3; will of John Jones, 23 September 1802, Jones Papers, AO; will of Henry Young, Henry Young Papers, AO.

60 Petition, 24 July 1783, HP, 21,875; Jeptha Hawley in behalf of the people of Machiche, 4 April 1784, HP, 21,822; Sam Adams, agent for a

number of Royalists now residing in Quebec, October 1783, HP, 21,822; Patrick McNiff to Stephen DeLancey, March 1786, RG 4, Canada East, Civil Secretary's Correspondence, s Series.

61 John Freel, "Tryon County Committee of Correspondence," 60–1; Claim of John Freel, Audit Office 12, vol. 28.

62 Claim of Sarah Buck, widow Hogal, Audit Office 12, vol. 27; widow Obenholdt, ibid., vol. 40; Lydia Van Alstine, ibid., vol. 28.

63 Claim of Margaret Huffnail, widow Schermerhoorn, Audit Office 12, vol. 28; Catherine Cryderman, ibid., vol. 29; Elinor Maybee, ibid., vol. 28; Jane Glassford, ibid., vol. 29; Claim of Sarah Buck, ibid., vol. 53.

64 Claim of Sarah McGinnis, ibid., vol. 27.

65 Munro to Mathews, 30 July 1781, HP, 21,821; Loyalist Petition, 24 July 1783, HP, 21,875.

66 Catherine White, Coventry Papers.

67 Haldimand to John Johnson, 27 May 1783, HP, 21,775; Graymont, *The Iroquois in the American Revolution*, 285; Burleigh, "A Tale of Loyalist Heroism," OHSPR, 42 (1950): 97–9; French, "Barbara Ruckle Heck," *DCB* 5:728–9.

68 "The Youngs Come to East Lake," Young Papers, AO.

69 Joel Stone to William Moore, 26 April 1786, Stone Papers, AO; Joel Stone to Leah, 30 October 1786, Stone Papers, NA; document, 15 June 1789, Stone Papers, AO.

70 Joel Stone to Leman, 30 January 1797, Stone Papers, NA; see also H. William Hawke, "Joel Stone of Gananoque, 1749–1833" (unpublished manuscript, Queen's University Archives), 32–51; Jon Kei Matsuoka, "Vietnamese in America: An Analysis of Adaptational Patterns" (PhD thesis, University of Michigan 1985), 124.

71 Mary T. Jones to Dear Papa, 29 August 1798, Jones Papers, Queen's University Archives.

72 Sophia Sherwood to Jonathan Jones, 23 October 1810, Solomon Jones Papers, AO.

73 Hannah Cartwright to James, 25 April 1806, Cartwright Papers, Queen's University Archives.

74 John Stuart to James, 21 December 1804, Stuart Papers, AO.

75 Richard Cartwright to James, 13 September 1803, James Cartwright, Journal Commencing the 1st April, 1805 and ending 29th June of the same year, Papers, privately held by the Cartwright family in Port Hope, Ont., in G.A. Rawlyk, "The Honourable Richard Cartwright, 1759–1815" (unpublished manuscript, n.d.), 441, 456–8.

76 Egan F. Kunz, "Exile and Resettlement: Refugee Theory," *International Migration Review* 15 (Spring-Summer 1981): 42–51; G.M. Mirdal, "Stress and Distress in Migration: Problems and Resources of Turkish Women in Denmark," ibid., 18 (Winter 1984): 984–1003.

77 Matsuoka, "The Vietnamese in America," p. 45; petition of Captain John Munro and a Number of Privates of the King's Royal Regiment of New York, 27 March 1783, Munro Papers, AO.

78 Graymont, *The Iroquois in the American Revolution*, 285–6.

79 Stuart to Dr White, 2 November 1785, AO, Miscellaneous MSS, White Letters; Stuart to Bishop Inglis, 6 July 1788, in Preston, *Kingston Before the War of 1812*, 133–8; Stuart to White, 26 November 1798, Stuart Papers, AO.

80 Richard Cartwright, Jr, to Isaac Todd, 1789, Cartwright Letter Books, Cartwright Papers, Queen's University; *Letters from an American Loyalist in Upper Canada* (York, Upper Canada, 1810).

81 Elizabeth Bowman Spohn, 1861," in J.J. Talman, *Loyalist Narratives from Upper Canada* (Toronto: Champlain Society 1946), 320; "Reminiscences of Mrs. White," ibid., 353, 354; "Testimonial of Roger Bates," ibid., 31; "Reminiscences of Captain James Dittrick," ibid., 63; "The Reminiscences of the Hon. Henry Ruttan," ibid., 301.

82 William Canniff, *History of the Settlement of Upper Canada With Specific Reference to the Bay of Quinte* (Toronto: Dudley and Burns 1869), 616, 42, 49–50, 55–6, 51.

83 Ibid., 55–6, 197, 80–2.

84 Craig, *Upper Canada*, 1–66; S.F. Wise and R.C. Brown, *Canada View the United States* (Toronto: Macmillan 1967); Jane Errington, *The Lion, the Eagle and Upper Canada: A Developing Colonial Ideology* (Kingston and Montreal: McGill-Queen's University Press 1987); David Clifford Lorne Mills, *The Concept of Loyalty in Upper Canada, 1815–1850*, (Kingston and Montreal: McGill-Queen's University Press 1988); *The United Empire Loyalist Association of Ontario, Annual Transactions, March 10th, 1898* (Toronto, 1898), quoted in Carl Berger, *The Sense of Power: Studies in the Ideas of Canadian Imperialism, 1867–1914* (Toronto: University of Toronto Press 1970); Murray Barkley, "The Loyalist Tradition in New Brunswick: The Growth and Evolution of an Historical Myth, 1825–1914," *Acadiensis*, 4 (1975), 3–45; Dennis Duffy, *Gardens, Covenants, Exiles: Loyalism in the Literature of Upper Canada/Ontario* (Toronto, Buffalo, London: University of Toronto Press 1982).

85 Labaree, Leonard Labaree, "Nature of American Loyalism," *American Antiquarian Society Proceedings*, 54 (1944), 15–58; Bailyn, *The Ordeal of Thomas Hutchinson* (Cambridge, Mass: Harvard University Press 1974); Potter, *The Liberty We Seek: Loyalist Ideology in Colonial New York and Massachusetts* (Cambridge, Mass., and London: Harvard University Press 1983).

86 Esther Clark Wright, *The Loyalist of New Brunswick* (Fredericton, N.B.: privately printed 1985); Maria Susan Waltman, "From Soldier to Settler"; see also, Wallace Brown, "The View at Two Hundred Years: The

Loyalists of the American Revolution," *Proceedings of the American Antiquarian Society*, 80 (April 1970), 25–47.

87 Brown, *The King's Friends: The Composition and Motives of the American Loyalist Claimants* (Providence, R.I.: Brown University Press 1965); Eugene Fingerhut, "Uses and Abuses of the American Loyalists' Claims: A Critique of Quantative Analysis," *WMQ*, 3rd Series, 25 (April 1968), 245–58.

88 Paul H. Smith, *Loyalists and Redcoats: A Study in British Revolutionary Policy* (Chapel Hill: University of North Carolina Press 1964).

89 Ann Gorman Condon, *The Envy of the American States: The Loyalist Dream for New Brunswick* (Fredericton, N.B.: New Ireland Press 1984); Neil MacKinnon, *This Unfriendly Soil: The Loyalist Experience in Nova Scotia, 1783–1791* (Kingston and Montreal: McGill-Queen's University Press 1986).

90 William Kirby, *Canadian Idylls* (Welland, Ont., 1894).

Index